OUTSTANDING PRAISE FOR LOUANNE JOHNSON AND *DANGEROUS MINDS*:

"Remarkable . . . Johnson proves that unorthodox methods can turn a problem kid into an 'A' student."
—*Vogue*

"As long as there are teachers like LouAnne Johnson, there is hope . . . She wins more than she loses. Readers will be winners, too."
—*Grand Rapids Press*

"A heartwarming tale . . . A fast-paced book worthy of some attention. The stories are vivid enough to make the reader cheer for its heroes—the students who become good enough to dream again, thanks to someone who cares as much as Johnson."
—*San Mateo Times*

"This book should be read. Johnson is what a teacher ought to be, and these students' success stories are what's possible with care and creativity."
—*Oklahoman*

"[A] funny, alarming look at a city school from a dedicated, unconventional teacher . . . Johnson shows the importance of basic respect, constant encouragement, and unorthodox teaching strategies for a generation (another generation) of disenfranchised students."
—*Kirkus*

"Johnson exhibits the energy and idealism to motivate her students . . . A humorous account of teaching at an American high school."
—*Library Journal*

St. Martin's Paperbacks Titles
by LouAnne Johnson

MAKING WAVES
DANGEROUS MINDS

DANGEROUS MINDS

(previously published as *"My Posse Don't Do Homework"*)

LouAnne Johnson

ST. MARTIN'S PAPERBACKS

Dangerous Minds was previously published under the title *"My Posse Don't Do Homework."*

DANGEROUS MINDS

Copyright © 1992 by LouAnne Johnson.

Cover photograph property of Hollywood Pictures.

All rights reserved. No part of this book may be used or reproduced in any manner whatsoever without written permission except in the case of brief quotations embodied in critical articles or reviews. For information address St. Martin's Press, 175 Fifth Avenue, New York, N.Y. 10010.

Library of Congress Catalog Card Number: 92-3899

ISBN: 0-312-95620-7

Printed in the United States of America

St. Martin's Press hardcover edition/August 1992
St. Martin's Paperbacks edition/December 1993

10 9 8 7 6

For all the kids who hate school

ACKNOWLEDGMENTS

Many thanks to Ruth Nathan, my agent, for suggesting that I write this book; to Maureen Baron, my editor, for accepting only the "good stuff"; to Wayne Peterson, my friend and reader, for invaluable criticism and unfailing moral support; to Pete, Marcia, Marilyn, and Ben, for first allowing and later encouraging me to teach from the heart instead of the text; to Evelyn Hodak and Dr. Maryellen Boyling, my teachers, for showing me how it's done; and to my students, who have taught me that the capacity of the human heart truly is limitless.

AUTHOR'S NOTE

This book is based on actual incidents involving real people, but the names of all the people and places have been changed—and some characters are composites of two or more real people—to protect the privacy of the individuals concerned.

INTRODUCTION

Since the students are my primary focus, I chose to emphasize them instead of the clock and calendar. This book is not presented in chronological order. Each chapter is a separate "snapshot." Because I have taught many of the same students for two and sometimes three years, some students appear several times. I apologize for any confusion this may cause to the reader.

For the record, this material covers a four-year period. The first year, as an intern, I taught two sophomore English classes—one accelerated and one regular. The following year, the Academy program was launched and I taught two periods of Academy sophomore English and two periods of Non-English Proficient (NEP) students in grades nine through eleven who were grouped in one classroom. When the first group of Academy sophomores were promoted to junior status, fifty new sophomores (two classes) were enrolled in the program and I was appointed as program director. This year, we have a "full house." My first Academy class of sophomores are now seniors (thirty-three of the original fifty are still with us), the second group are now juniors, and there are fifty new sophomores. I teach and counsel all three groups, grades ten through twelve.

The Academy program is a "school within a school" and is one of several in operation across the country, funded by a U.S. Government grant that pays for reduced class sizes (maximum twenty-five students) and resource periods for teachers to provide personal instruction and counseling to Academy students. Enrollment in the three-year program is voluntary and begins at the tenth grade level. Although many Academy students have low grade-point averages and poor attendance, they must have average or above-average standardized test scores in order to qualify for the program. Students remain with the same teachers and the same classmates for three years, which allows a considerable amount of bonding to take place. It is this bonding that is the key to the success of the Academy model programs. When classes are small enough to allow individual student-teacher interaction, a minor miracle occurs: Teachers teach and students learn.

—L.A.J.

ONE

My Dog Ate It

I couldn't concentrate. Raul Chacon was standing in the middle of the parking lot outside my classroom, shivering in the freezing rain. It was a bitterly cold, dreary day in mid-January, but Raul, clad in his Parkmont gym shorts and T-shirt, stood with his eyes closed, his face turned up into the downpour. Several students and one teacher had tried to reason with him, but Raul was determined, for some unknown reason, to stand outside. I tried to ignore him, hoping he would grow tired of his game and rejoin the class, but he looked so pathetic with his sopping wet clothes clinging to his skinny arms and legs.

"Park your seats and zip your lips." I stared down the last few resisters and gave the class a final warning. "If you want to live to be old enough to get a driver's license, start writing and don't stop until I tell you to." They sat and they wrote, but I knew they'd be out of their seats, noses pressed to the windows, the moment I stepped outside.

"Raul!" I squished across the muddy grass. "What are you doing?" He didn't respond even when I stood directly in front of him. I put my hand on his shoulder.

"I'm okay, Miss J.," he said, without opening his eyes. "Don't worry. My real clothes are in my gym bag. I'm winning a bet!"

"I'll bet you that if you aren't in my room in two minutes, you're going to be very sorry. Do you understand?" I said. Raul opened his eyes and looked at me, surprised. Threats and orders weren't my style.

"Move!" I said, pointing to the door. Raul shrugged, sighed, and obediently sloshed across the yard and into the classroom, where the other students scrambled for their seats. I sent Raul to the restroom to dry off and change his clothes. When he returned, his best friend, Gusmaro Guevarra, handed him a navy blue down-filled jacket that swallowed Raul's wiry ninety-five-pound body as he sank into his chair and began writing along with the class.

After a fifteen-minute free writing period, I assigned the students a short story to read from their literature books while I collected their journals. I had intended to keep Raul after class and give him a stern lecture, but I ended up giving him a hundred dollars instead. During the silent reading period, I had read his journal entry:

Hi! Miss or Ms. or Mrs. Johnson, I know your probally thinking it was pretty stupid what I was doing but I don't care if I got wet because Julio gave me $20 to stand outside in the middle of the parking lot for 20 minutes while it was raining and I did it. He gave me the money as soon as I walked into class all soaked wet and dripping all over the floor—sorry. I stayed out there all those twenny minutes and I wasn't even cold because I knew I would get that money. No matter how fast the wind was blowing or how hard the water was falling I stayed out there until my time was done. I was thinking about the $20. And I would do it again. I would do just about anything you can think of for $20 even if everybody thinks I'm a dum ass.

After class, Raul explained that he needed money to pay the man who had sold him the blue down jacket. He had already given the man forty dollars, but he didn't have the balance and the man had demanded full payment, or else.

"Why did you buy a jacket on the street instead of a store?" I asked. Raul sighed and shook his head at my naiveté.

"You don't get no good deals in stores," he said. "You know how much this jacket would of costed in a store?" I looked at the jacket. It was expensive, all right, and it dawned on me that the jacket had probably been stolen and resold at a bargain price. I decided to save the issue of buying stolen goods for a later date and concentrate on the current crisis.

"How much money do you need?" I asked.

"A hundred dollars."

"I'll lend you the money," I said. Raul shook his head.

"No way," he said, his face breaking into a lopsided grin. "I can't take your money. You're always telling us teachers are poor."

"I'm not that poor," I insisted. "And I want to lend you this money. You can pay me back before you graduate. That will give you two and a half more years. Okay?" Raul hesitated for a few seconds.

"With interest?"

"No interest," I said.

"With interest," Raul insisted. "All loans have interest."

"Okay," I agreed. "With interest. I'll get the money at lunchtime and you can stop by my room later and pick it up. And there is one condition that goes with the loan." Raul's face closed immediately.

"There's always a string, huh?" he said.

"Yes," I said. "And this is a big string, but I wouldn't attach it if I didn't love you. You can't pay me back until your graduation day."

Raul drew in his breath and pursed his lips. He was a seventeen-year-old sophomore, which meant he'd be nineteen if he stayed in school to complete his senior year. He'd also be the first person in all the generations of his family to graduate. I knew that every day he was tempted to drop out and find a job to help support his large family. I also knew that he wanted an education.

"I'm counting on you to graduate, Raul," I said. "You know you can do it. Deal?" I held out my hand and held my breath. If Raul shook my hand, he'd kill himself to keep his word of honor. He shook my hand, then crooked his fingers and slid his hand down until it caught the ends of my fingers. With his left hand, he curled my fingers around his and placed our thumbs against each other.

"Deal."

When Raul came to pick up the money, he asked me if I wanted a signature receipt. I told him his handshake was enough for me. Solemnly, he shook my hand again, bumped thumbs with me, and accepted the money. The next morning, he was waiting for me outside my classroom when I arrived. He pulled a sheet of folded notebook paper from his back pocket, handed me the paper, and walked away without a word. I was afraid he'd changed his mind about our deal.

"Dear Miss or Ms. or Mrs. Johnson, I know you aren't married, but you used to be married, so you might not be a Miss anymore, and Ms. Polk says we should call all the ladies Ms. but that don't sound too good," Raul had written.

Last week, you told us to write in our journals about the nicest thing anybody ever did for us and I had to make something up because nobody never did nothing nice for me that I can remember before now. So I wrote you a lie because I know you like it when we write a hole bunch of stuff in our journals. I didn't want to lie, but I didn't want you to get mad at me for not writing in my journal. Anyway, what you did yesterday was the nicest thing and I think you did it because you think I am wonderful, honest, smart, and special! (That's what you always tell us anyway and I think you really believe it.) Anyway, I am going to work harder in school so I won't let you down because if you think I can make it then I can make it. I never did my own homework or tests before. Me and my posse always copy off whoever did it because we don't like to do homework and we can't be seen carrying books home. Besides, I don't got no time to do it anyway because I have to work almost every day after school. But I'm gonna try to do my own homework only don't be surprised if I flunk everything because I never did it before. Before, whenever my teachers asked me for my homework, I always told them that my dog ate it, but I don't got no dog so I won't tell you that lie because you trust me. And I don't know nobody else who would give $100 to a Mexican kid on a handshake.

It had taken months to convince Raul that he was intelligent, that he could learn as well as the next person if only he would try. He was the jokester of his posse, a group of four Hispanic boys who lived on the East Side and banded together for protection and courage during the daily bus trip to the alien Caucasian planet of Parkmont. Although they were fiercely loyal, the posse's loyalty didn't extend to academic transcripts. The other three boys worked hard to create a juvenile delinquent image to offset their B grade averages, but Raul often failed his courses because his friends counted on him for entertainment during class and encouraged him to act the fool. In spite of his low grades and lack of confidence in his intellectual abilities, Raul's intelligence was obvious in his quick grasp of abstract concepts and his verbal agility. Although his essays sometimes drowned in grammatical errors, they were invariably original and demonstrated his astute perception. The other Academy teachers shared my assessment of Raul's potential; Raul remained the only person to be convinced.

For a few weeks after our deal and Raul's vow to start doing his own work, his grades slid downhill, especially in math. Instead of copying his homework during the few minutes prior to class, he actually tried to do it at home. His math teacher, aware of Raul's "new leaf," encouraged him to continue in spite of the many errors in his work. The other teachers and I also bit our tongues and accepted the mangled papers Raul painstakingly prepared for us.

Our patience paid off. Just two months after he started doing his own work, Raul got the highest grade in the class on a math test. He was ecstatic. The staff was delighted. Raul's posse was indignant. Since grade school, he had been their pet clown, their scapegoat, their primary source of amusement. Now, by accepting our encouragement and succeeding on his own, without their support, he had become a stranger. They taunted him and tried to distract him during class, but he refused to let go of his newfound freedom. He was a fierce fighter, even though he was one of the smallest boys in class at an even five feet.

When the other boys—Gusmaro, Julio, and Victor—realized that Raul was not going to be intimidated, they gave up and halfheartedly joined him, complaining that the posse had lost its power because Raul had changed the group's focus. Instead of creating the "ruthless" (their highest compliment) street fighter image they had previously strived for, he had moved their group into the academic arena. Gusmaro followed directly in Raul's footsteps, with Julio and Victor trailing reluctantly behind, but determined to hang with the group. By the end of the first quarter, Raul had raised his grade point average from 1.5 to a respectable 2.8. For the first time in his life, his report card listed all passing grades, which inspired another burst of effort. By the time semester finals rolled around, Raul sat at the head of the class academically. He was the first one in class for the English final and the last one to leave. As I waited for him to complete his exam essay, I heard his stomach growl. I recognized the sound as one that I had heard several times during the exam, but at the time, I couldn't pinpoint its source.

"Raul, how many times have I told you that you need to eat something?" I asked. "Your brain needs fuel."

He looked up from his paper and nodded at me but didn't say anything, which was unusual for him. It occurred to me that maybe there was no breakfast at his house. I knew his family didn't have much money. In his autobiography, Raul had written that his father

9

had completed only the third grade, his mother the second; neither of them could read or write more than a legal signature in any language. The oldest of nine children, Raul would be the first Chacon to graduate from high school—if he could hold out for two more years. There was pressure from his father to get a full-time job so that he could contribute to the family's meager income. His father was a landscape gardener, and often Raul had to work for him after school, in addition to handling his own job as a restaurant bus-boy.

"What did you have for breakfast today?" I asked. "Anything?"

"Beans," Raul said in a very tired voice. "That's what we have every day. Beans for breakfast. Beans for lunch. Beans for supper. I'm sick of beans so I didn't eat no breakfast today. That's why my stomach was making so much noise during the test. I'm sorry, Miss J. I tried to make it be quiet, but it didn't work. It just kept on rumbling and squeaking and I hate that because some of the kids think that I'm farting—" I held up my hand to stop Raul's explanation.

"I'm not criticizing you," I said. "I just wanted you to know that it's important to eat breakfast so your brain will have some fuel for your morning classes."

"Yeah," Raul agreed. "I was feeling pretty stupid today, but I didn't know it was because I was hungry. I thought it was just my old stupid brain coming back."

"You aren't stupid," I argued. "But it's stupid not to eat anything at all. Can't you get a roll or an apple or something on the way to school?"

"I don't have time to get something because I usually just make the bus," Raul explained. "But don't worry, Miss J., I ain't gonna quit on you. You trusted me and I won't let you down." He glanced at the clock. "I

10

gotta go or I'll be late!'' Jamming his baseball cap onto his head, backward as usual, he grabbed his books. ''And you don't have to worry about your hundred dollars, neither,'' he said as he headed for the door.

At the end of the semester, we gave ''Academy awards'' for academic performance, good behavior, perfect attendance, and overall improvement. The awards were simple paper certificates created on one of the computers in our school lab, but the kids accepted them as though they had been sent directly from the White House. For many of them, it was the first time in their lives that they had ever received positive recognition from school. Raul received the overall improvement award. I shot two rolls of film and sent a few photos, along with a short article, to the local newspapers. Two days later, Raul's grinning face appeared on the front page of the *East Bay Reporter*, a paper targeted at the minority readership in Raul's section of the city. That morning, Raul bounced into the classroom and graciously accepted the compliments and catcalls from his classmates. That afternoon, Raul walked into the boys' locker room and was stabbed in the stomach by a boy with a homemade knife.

It made no sense. Raul had done nothing. He didn't even know the boy. But when I found out the boy's name—Alberto Mendoza—I felt as though I had been stabbed myself. Alberto had wanted to come into the Academy program, but we didn't accept him the first year because of his severely limited ability to read, write, or understand English. We had planned to invite him to join us at the start of the second year if his English had improved. Unfortunately, we didn't tell Alberto of our plan. Consumed by jealousy, he had

11

vented his frustration on Raul after he saw the photo in the paper.

Raul recovered quickly and was back in school in time for a special luncheon hosted by the elegant Hotel Le Bonne. As an incentive for academic progress, as well as to give them an opportunity to experience dining at a fine restaurant, the hotel management had "adopted" our Academy students and generously arranged to treat four students each month to a gourmet meal in the main dining salon, at tables set with fine linen, silver, and crystal.

Raul was among the first to be chosen for the luncheon. When his name was announced, he jumped out of his chair, shot his right fist into the air, and yelled, "Yes!" He didn't want to see the sample menu the hotel provided for the students to preview. He had only one question: Did they have chicken? Chicken was his favorite dish and a rare treat at home. Gusmaro, one of the more sophisticated students, had also been chosen to attend the lunch. He scanned the menu and asked if Raul wouldn't prefer filet mignon to chicken.

"What's filet mignon?" Raul demanded. "Is it big?"

"It's the best steak," Gusmaro explained. "About this big." He connected his thumbs and middle fingers and shaped an oval.

"No way," Raul said. "I ain't eating no little piece of steak when I can get a half a chicken."

For three days, the upcoming lunch was the main topic of conversation during class breaks. The kids who were going checked the menu several times each day and changed their minds each time about what they would order when the big day came. The kids who hadn't been chosen wanted to know if they were on the list to go next time and, if not, when they were scheduled. A few pretended not to care. One girl announced that she didn't care if she never got picked because she ate there all the time and was bored with it. The day before the luncheon, Raul stopped by between classes and said that he didn't think he'd be going to the lunch after all; he had something important to do and it couldn't be postponed. He refused to discuss it and I had to teach a class, so I didn't get a chance to talk to him until after school. I called him at home and pressed him for details.

"I just can't go," Raul insisted.

"Why?" I asked for the fifth time. Raul sighed.

"Okay. I'll tell you. Because I don't got a suit to wear. Gusmaro said you have to wear a suit and a tie and I don't got one. And I don't got fancy shoes, neither. So I can't go. But don't worry about it. You can take somebody else." He paused, then added, "I just wish I could of ate that chicken."

"You're going to eat that chicken," I said. "Just show up for school tomorrow." As soon as I hung up, I went to a discount clothing store and bought a dress shirt, a tie, a sports coat, socks, and a pair of leather shoes. I also bought an inexpensive door mirror and tacked it to the wall in the back of the classroom, thinking it might inspire some of my students to consider their appearance.

Attired in the new clothes, Raul was mesmerized by his reflection. He turned right and left to check his profile.

"I never wore a suit before," he said. "I look pretty handsome, don't I?"

"You look gorgeous," I assured him. "Now let's go get your chicken."

* * *

13

At the restaurant, before the entrée arrived, Raul had polished off five sourdough rolls and had drunk four glasses of ice water. He was amazed at the instantaneous refilling of his water glass and bread plate. He'd drain his glass, then check the second hand on my watch to see how long the glass remained empty before the smiling waiter reappeared. The only thing that impressed him more than the fast and gracious service was the wine list. He spent several minutes inspecting the list carefully, trying out the names of the various wines, pretending that he planned to order one. At length, he closed the wine list.

"How much does the wine cost?" he asked.

"It depends on whether you order a bottle or a glass," I said. "Aren't the prices on the list?"

"It says four or five dollars for the glass," Raul said. "But don't you have to pay extra for the wine?" I started to explain that the price was for the wine and not the glass itself, but Raul's chicken arrived and he lost interest in everything else until his plate was clean.

When the waiter rolled the dessert cart to our table, Gusmaro whistled and nudged Raul. "Too bad you pigged out, homey," Gusmaro said. "You won't have room for this."

"Watch me," Raul said. We all watched him. He ate three desserts. When he finished the last one, he put down his fork and beamed at me.

"All that brain fuel. I'll be smart tomorrow, hey, Miss J.?"

Back at school, Raul changed into his own clothes and returned the new clothes to me, carefully folded. As he handed them to me, he hesitated.

"What are you gonna do with these?" he asked.

"I'm going to keep them here in case somebody else needs to wear them."

"Maybe I should take these home and wash them, what do you think?"

"I doubt if they got dirty," I said. "You only wore them for a couple of hours."

"Well, I hope I didn't stink them up," Raul said. "I didn't get to take a shower before school this morning. My father was hogging the bathroom."

"I'm sure it's all right," I said.

"But I thought we had to take a shower every day. You know that sheet you gave us about whether we would get recommended for a job?"

"Yes." As part of our vocational preparedness, the Academy teachers had given each student a checklist showing which areas we felt were their strongest and weakest as potential employees. Quite a few kids received recommendations that they pay more attention to hygiene—hair, fingernails, general cleanliness.

"On that sheet, it said we were supposed to take a shower every day. Some of us guys have been staying home if we don't get to take a shower."

"Well, if you can't take a shower, you can't take one," I said. "That's it. But you should still come to school. I'll give you a pass to go to the restroom and wash up if you need to."

"Okay," Raul said. "Thanks for the lunch. It was the best lunch I ever had." He started out the door and stopped.

"If I stay in school and learn the computers and graduate, I know I'll get a better job," he said. "But do you think I'll get a good enough job so I can live in an apartment with two bathrooms?"

"Yes, I do," I said.

"Two bathrooms," Raul said, smiling to himself. He looked at me and the smile widened into his familiar grin. "And no beans."

15

TWO

Okie Dokie, Artichokie

When I made Raul promise to stay in school until he graduated, I didn't realize that I was also promising to stay. That hadn't been my original plan. Once I had my credential, I intended to teach high school for just a year while I was earning my master's degree. Then I would teach at the junior college level, and from there, I'd go on to earn my Ph.D. and become a college professor.

From the first day of student teaching, which turned out to be my only day as a student teacher, my plan went awry. I spent four hours observing a teacher who didn't seem to mind that only a handful of her students appeared to be on the same planet. Each time the bell rang, the kids raced out of the room, and were immediately replaced by an identical group of loud, ill-mannered, tacky dressers. It was like watching a skit from "Saturday Night Live." As I left the classroom that afternoon, I remember thinking how fortunate I was that I'd only have to teach high school for a year. It would give me an opportunity to assess firsthand the capabilities of high school students, which would help me prepare college-level assignments that would challenge but not overwhelm my future students—and I would be able to escape before I lost my mind.

One of the secretaries caught me as I was crossing the parking lot. She had a message from a nearby high school. The instructional vice-principal of Parkmont High wanted me to stop by on my way home to discuss an internship. Interns earn money and teach unsupervised; student teachers aren't paid and remain under the constant supervision of a master teacher. Since I was poor and I've always hated having people tell me what to do, I went to the interview.

"This is an unusual circumstance," Mrs. Nichols explained. "One of our teachers retired suddenly, due to a health problem, and we don't have anyone to take her place. We need someone to start tomorrow."

Tomorrow! While I secretly panicked at the thought of walking into a real live classroom and facing a horde of alien teens like the ones I had observed earlier that day, I said nothing. Mrs. Nichols lifted her glasses, which were on a chain around her neck, and nibbled at one of the stems. She looked at me without speaking for several seconds, then put the glasses on and opened a manila folder. She read for a few seconds, then studied me again.

"Excuse me," she said, "but you look too young to have done all these things." She read, obviously from my resumé, "Eight—no, nine—years in the military service, navy journalist, lieutenant in the Marine Corps, editorial assistant." She stopped reading and looked at me again, her left eyebrow raised into a question mark.

"I'm thirty-five," I said. "A little older than most beginning teachers, but not too old to learn."

"Oh, no, no!" Mrs. Nichols held up her hands. "The older the better. This group needs a firm hand. They've had three substitutes since Miss Sheppard left. They'll

17

be so happy to have a permanent teacher again."

Three substitutes in less than a week? "Is there something wrong with these kids?" I asked, visions of teenage mutant ninja students dancing in my head.

"Oh, no," she said. "It's a regular sophomore English class. English II-P. Thirty-four students. You can just pick it up where Miss Sheppard left off."

"Do you have her lesson plans?" I asked.

"No, I'm sorry, I don't."

"Then could I have a copy of the textbook they've been using?" I asked.

Mrs. Nichols cleared her throat and rearranged her necklace, three thick strands of braided silver rope. She ran one hand over her thick black hair, which was arranged in a perfect French braid. She looked at the clock on the wall behind me. "We don't seem to have any record of the text that the students are using," she said slowly. "Perhaps Mr. Parker, the English department chair, will be able to provide more information. He should be here any minute."

While we waited for Mr. Parker, Mrs. Nichols made polite chitchat and I continued to try to quell my panic. I had never created an actual lesson plan. Of course, I'd prepared and presented simulated lessons to my fellow graduate students, but that was different. I wasn't sure I was ready to pick up someone else's class in the middle of the school year. Still, Mrs. Nichols seemed satisfied that I could handle the job. Or else she was desperate. But she needed a teacher and I needed the money, so I kept my mouth shut.

Mr. Parker bustled into the room, shook my hand, and welcomed me to the staff. He was tall, thin, and obviously tired. He was also empty-handed.

"Mr. Parker," Mrs. Nichols said, "do you happen to

know which textbook Miss Sheppard's class has been using?"

"I'm sorry," Mr. Parker said. "I give my staff free rein, as long as they stay within the state framework for curriculum. I could check with the librarian tomorrow and find out which books she had signed out."

"Tomorrow Miss Johnson will be in the classroom," Mrs. Nichols pointed out, "so she can find out herself. Do you have a roster and roll sheets?"

Mr. Parker looked distinctly embarrassed. "To be absolutely honest, I don't have any information about the class. But I'll be here to answer any questions you may have on a daily basis, Miss Johnson." He shook my hand again and disappeared. Mrs. Nichols stood up and extended her hand.

"I'm sure you'll do fine, Miss Johnson," she said. "Your class is in room B-eleven, fifth period, which is right after lunch. Class begins at the twelve thirty-five bell. You can pick up your roll sheets at the attendance office in the morning and we'll get you a key as soon as possible. And I'll be here if you need anything at all. Please feel free to call me."

"Maybe I could call Miss Sheppard," I suggested. "Then I could get more information about the class." Mrs. Nichols frowned and fingered her necklace.

"Oh, no," she said. "I'm afraid that won't be possible. Miss Sheppard is too ill." For one wild moment, I wondered if one of the kids had shot Miss Sheppard, but I certainly would have heard it on the news.

Mrs. Nichols smiled reassuringly and patted my hand. "I'm sure you'll be just fine and the students will be so happy to have a permanent teacher again."

I couldn't tell whether the students were happy to see me or not, since none of them acknowledged my presence. When the bell rang to signal the start of class, a few kids stopped talking just long enough to register their annoyance at the interruption. Six very large, brown, muscular young men lounged silently against the faded bulletin board in the back of the classroom; the remainder of my students were sprawled in their seats or prowling the aisles between the desks, punching each other, throwing paper, cursing, coughing, creating a variety of unpleasant sounds with their hands and armpits. I cleared my throat and raised my voice.

"Excuse me, ladies and gentlemen. Please be seated." Everyone except the six boys in the back flopped onto a desk—some in the seats and some on the desktops—but the noise and activity levels remained constant. I stood silently, waiting, trustingly following the advice of my master teacher, Hal Gray. We didn't have time for a long conversation before class, but Hal did take a few minutes to sit down with me in the teachers' lounge and offer a few suggestions to get me through the first day.

"I'm a little nervous," I said as I watched Hal stir three full teaspoons of instant coffee into a small foam cup of hot water and drink it straight down.

"You'd be a fool if you weren't nervous," Hal reassured me as he prepared a second cup of coffee. "You're about to step into a room full of hormone-crazed teenagers and ask them to commit unnatural acts like sit down, shut up, and listen to someone too old to be taken seriously."

"They'd better take me seriously," I said.

"And what will you do when they don't—which they won't?" Hal asked.

"I don't know," I admitted, "but I'll have to do

something. I don't intend to take any lip from anybody."

"Okie dokie, artichokie," Hal said.

"Huh?"

Hal smiled a gentle, wistful smile. "My first year as a teacher, it was very important to me that my students respect me, that they appreciate my sincere efforts to educate them. One student—a girl, pretty sharp, but with a little bit of an attitude—was talking out of turn. I politely pointed out that I was speaking and asked her to be quiet. She ignored me and continued talking. The second time, I reprimanded her more forcefully. She grinned at me, gave me a thumbs-up, and said, 'Okie dokie, artichokie.'

"I was so furious," Hal continued. "I grabbed a referral sheet and wrote her up for disrespect. Sent her marching straight to the dean's office. She was suspended for three days and when she came back to class, she never called me an artichoke again. No, siree. I set her straight."

"Three days!" I said. "Don't you think that was a little harsh?"

"It most certainly was," Hal agreed. "And it didn't make anybody respect me. In fact, I lost the respect of some kids. It took me a long time to regain it."

"I'll try to remember that," I said. The warning bell rang and I leaped to my feet, my stomach fluttering.

"Here's one last word of advice," Hal said. "Never try to outshout the kids. Outshouting kids is like trying to teach a pig to sing. It makes you look foolish, it annoys the pig, and it doesn't work. Just stand there and wait for them to shut up. It may take a while, but it's worth the time."

I took Hal's advice when the kids in B-11 ignored the bell and my request for silence. I stood perfectly still and stared at them. It took about fifteen minutes, but finally the class quieted down enough for me to introduce myself.

"Could someone please tell me what happened on the last day that Miss Sheppard was here?" I asked.

Everyone except the boys in the back began talking again, shouting to be heard above the others. One girl with deep purple hair and black lipstick informed me from her seat in the front row that Miss Sheppard had been "psyched out." Miss Sheppard had thrown down her book and rushed out of the classroom in tears the previous Friday. The kids weren't surprised that she hadn't returned. They were obviously proud of their handiwork, but I didn't get any more details because their story was interrupted by a series of objects hurtling through the air: papers, notebooks, candy wrappers, and a very large dictionary. The dictionary barely missed my head and my stunned reaction prompted a moment of silence as the class judged its effect on me. The dictionaries were located on a shelf below the bulletin board in the back of the room. The biggest of the six boys stood closest to the bookshelf, gazing silently at the clock above my head, pointedly avoiding my gaze.

I spun on my heel and strode out of the classroom. Wild cheers erupted from my students as I walked the two doors down the sidewalk to Hal Gray's room. I should have known better, I told myself. This wasn't even a real school. The classrooms all opened into the open air, instead of into long, tiled corridors lined with wall lockers. I knocked on the door and motioned for Hal to step outside.

"What's the story on this English class?" I asked. Hal hesitated. "Please don't tell me you don't know," I pressed. "I get the feeling that everybody knows except me."

22

Hal rubbed his fingers across the light gray stubble on his chin. "You've got a tough job there," he said.

"I noticed that," I said. "What happened to Miss Sheppard?"

"You might say she lost it," Hal said. "Those kids drove her to the edge and then pushed her over. They've had three subs since then—every one of them quit after one day. Those kids have tasted blood. They're dangerous."

"Dangerous?" My voice squeaked. Those boys in the back were pretty big.

"Oh, not physically dangerous," Hal said quickly. "At least not any more than any other class. But you'll have to act real fast or you'll never get control."

Frustrated, I kicked the side of the building. A few pieces of pale green stucco fluttered to the sidewalk. "I'm not stupid. I know they're out of control and I have to act fast to take control," I snapped. "But nobody has told me how to do that."

"That's the problem," Hal said. "Nobody can. You'll just have to wing it." He glanced over his shoulder. Two students were skulking toward the back of his classroom. "I have to go. Somebody just woke up and realized I'm not there."

"Thanks a lot," I said. As I turned away, I felt a light tap on my shoulder. I turned back in time to catch Hal's wink.

"Good luck. You'll be fine. Just don't let anybody call you an artichoke," he cautioned.

In spite of myself, I had to smile, which relaxed me just enough to allow inspiration to strike. I walked back into B-11 and closed the door firmly behind me. I had the advantage; the kids hadn't expected to see me again. At the sound of the door slamming shut, they paused, shocked into silence. I pressed my advantage;

I closed my eyes for a few seconds. I'm sure the kids assumed I was either praying for guidance or struggling to hold back a flood of tears. I resisted the impulse to open my eyes right away and it worked. The kids were intrigued. I could hear them whispering to each other, assuring each other that I was about to crack.

As they whispered among themselves, I mentally transported myself back ten years to the first day of training at navy boot camp, where I had encountered a master of the art of intimidation, a feisty little drill instructor named Bertie Hawk. I visualized the posture and presence of Petty Officer Hawk. Barely five feet tall, Hawk had the presence of a giant. She moved quickly and surely, exuding bold confidence. Her primary weapon was her eyes: When Hawk looked at you, you knew you were being looked at, inside and out. I prepared myself to make my students feel a hundred percent visible.

I opened my eyes and marched down the center aisle between the desks, directly toward the young man who had thrown the dictionary at me. I didn't slow my pace as I neared him, but continued at full speed, as though I fully intended to walk right through him. As I approached, his cohorts edged quietly to each side and he tried to step backward, but he had made a serious error—his back was against the wall. He couldn't retreat. I stopped, abruptly, a few inches in front of him. He folded his arms across his chest in an effort to force me to move back, but I stood my ground so he had to pull his arms tight against his chest to avoid touching me.

"Excuse me, young man," I said, biting the tip off each word so hard that the letters spilled onto his skintight T-shirt. "I would appreciate it very much if you would sit down." I was so close I could feel his body heat. He began to sweat. He snorted softly, but still didn't speak. Every part of his body strained to move backward as he flattened himself against the wall. I continued to stare into his eyes, without blinking, fully prepared to spend the remainder of our fifty-minute class period in the same position, if necessary.

Go ahead, you little sucker, I thought to myself. *I'm getting paid to stand here and stare at you.* He held my gaze for about two minutes, but he couldn't handle my close presence. Skilled at defiance from a distance, he wasn't prepared for close-order combat. He cleared his throat and forced his voice down into his chest.

"Where you want me to sit?" he growled.

"Anywhere you choose—as long as it's in the front row," I replied coldly, still staring directly into his eyes. Then, suddenly, I flashed him my brightest smile and added, "Thank you very much, young man." I reached up to pat him on the shoulder and he flinched, like a dog that has been beaten frequently. I stepped aside and extended my right arm toward the front row of seats. As soon as he moved forward, I did a quick about-face and marched to the front of the room. He sauntered slowly toward a vacant seat, his friends following behind him, imitating his movements.

"I'm too young to retire and too mean to quit," I addressed the class, "so you may as well sit down and shut up. I'm here to stay. And I intend to teach this class. That's my job and I intend to do it." I paused to wait for the six boys to take their seats.

"Thank you very much, gentlemen." I smiled at them. They ignored me.

"Let me tell you a little bit about myself," I continued. "I joined the navy when I was eighteen and worked to put myself through college at night. After I finished my degree, I took a commission as an officer in the Marine Corps." The class was silent, but I knew that didn't mean they were listening. Maybe they were just waiting me out. "I learned a lot—"

"Were you a for-real Marine?" a voice interrupted. Someone was listening at least.

"Yes, I was."

"Did you learn hand-to-hand combat and all that shit?" another voice asked.

"Yes, I did," I said quietly, "but it's against the law for me to touch you."

"Marines can kill you with their bare hands," one of the boys explained to the class. "I seen it on TV."

I knew I was taking unfair advantage, but this was war. I didn't correct the child. Certainly, I had participated in close-order combat drills, but I had never tried to kill anyone except my brothers and sisters. Still, I thought it would be a good idea if my students believed my hands were registered lethal weapons.

"I chose to become a teacher because I didn't like what I read in the newspapers—students graduating from our high schools and colleges who can't read or write, kids taking drugs and killing themselves," I continued. "And the newspapers tell me you kids can't read, you hate books, you can't use your own language, and you don't care. Well, I care. And I think you do, too, or you wouldn't be here." I glanced around the room at those ancient eyes in adolescent faces. I saw the fear, the anger, the pain—the truth that the purple mohawks and gang colors were designed to camouflage.

"And please don't waste my time trying to convince me that you're bad," I said. "Bad kids don't go to school. Bad kids are in jail, in juvi hall, in reform schools, on the streets. They aren't sitting in high school."

They weren't sure whether to buy it or not; I could see it in their expressions. Still, they were sitting down and they were not talking. I was on a roll.

"I will make each one of you this guarantee. You come to class every day and do the work I give you here, and you do your homework. And if you *try*, I guarantee you will pass this course. There is nobody in this room who is stupid. You are all valuable human beings, which reminds me—I have only one rule in this classroom and that rule is not negotiable: Respect yourself and everyone else in this room. If you can't respect yourself, you can't respect other people. And if you don't have any self-respect, you have a problem. We're going to fix that problem because every person has the right to his or her personal dignity."

"That's bullshit!" one boy muttered. "That chickenshit rule don't tell us nothing." He raised his voice. "You're supposed to give us a list of rules and shit to follow. 'Respect yourself' don't tell me nothing."

"It tells you everything," I said. "What is your name?"

"Roderick J. Horne."

"All right, Roderick," I said. "Let me give you an example. Do you think it is respectful for you to get up and walk around the room while I am talking?"

"No," he replied.

"Do you think it is respectful for me to yell at you?"

"No," he said, quickly.

"Well, then, do you think it's respectful to say 'shit' in school?"

"No," he snapped, sighing at my stupidity.

"Then you tell me an example of something you could do in class and get in trouble for, that doesn't break my single rule," I said. He offered several suggestions, but his classmates loudly disqualified each exam-

27

ple. Roderick refused to give up and the others grew restless. Stacy Wilson, a pretty black girl with about four hundred tiny braids on her head, reached out and smacked Rod on the arm, hard.

"You acting like a stupid nigger, Roderick," she said jovially. "Shut your face." The class broke up.

"That reminds me of my only other rule," I said loudly.

"I knew it," said a voice from the corner. "No teachers have only one rule. They get off on rules."

I ignored the taunt. Although I had not intended to create any other rules, I felt compelled to add one more.

"My second rule isn't really a separate rule," I explained. "It is a result of breaking the first rule. I want you all to understand that there is one thing I will flunk you for on the spot." That was an outright lie; teachers don't have the power to flunk students based on a single incident. But the students didn't know that and I didn't either, at the time.

"I will not tolerate any racial, ethnic, or sexual slurs in this classroom. It is not fair to erase someone's face. In this room, everyone is entitled to equal dignity as a human being."

"Black kids can call each other niggers," Stacy protested.

"Not in this classroom they can't," I insisted.

Stacy shrugged her shoulders. "It don't matter what you say anyway," she said. "Miss Sheppard already done flunked most of us anyway before she left."

Without stopping to consider whether I was bound to follow the previous teacher's grading system, I found myself creating yet another rule for this class. Since I had little hope of getting my hands on Miss Sheppard's student files, I decided to use the lack of information to my advantage.

"From this moment," I heard myself say, "each one of you starts with a clean record. I have not opened your previous teacher's files. This is your one break for the year. If you want to pass, all you have to do is try from now on. At this point, everyone has an A. It's up to you to keep it."

"She's lyin'," one student whispered, without conviction.

"Shut up," another kid countered. "I never had an A before. Leave her be before she changes her mind."

The prospect of having A's apparently stunned them, so I decided to knock them out before they had a chance to recover. I waded into the middle of the room, smiling at their upturned faces.

"And, at this point, I like every single person in this room. You can make me dislike you if you want to, but you'll have to try very hard and it won't be worth the effort."

"Hah!" Stacy said, tossing her head. Her braids had little beads on them that clicked musically when she moved. I remembered how much I used to love stomping around the house with bells laced to my shoestrings. "What about Roderick?"

I walked over to Roderick's desk and put my arm on his shoulder. He looked uncomfortable, but secretly pleased. "Yes, I like Roderick very much. I can tell he has a good brain. I hope he uses it."

"You won't like me when you see my grades," Roderick challenged me.

"Oh, yes, I will," I assured him. "I will be sad if you get poor grades, but I will still like you—the person—just as much."

"We'll see," he said, with a weary sigh.

"I believe we will," I said, imitating his huge sigh and his woeful expression until he gave in to a half-smile.

Encouraged by their honesty, I decided to give the kids a real opportunity to express themselves. I wanted to know what had happened in that classroom, why their other teachers quit, but I didn't want the students to exaggerate and brag about how horrible they had been. Moving to the chalkboard, I picked up a piece of chalk and faced the class. "I'm sure you're familiar with the technique of brainstorming?"

A chorus of groans and hisses affirmed my assumption, but I didn't let them slow me down. I drew a vertical line down the middle of the board and wrote Effective Teacher in the center of one side.

"Tell me what you think makes an effective teacher," I said.

"Takes charge!"

"Kicks ass!"

"Interesting!"

"Young!"

"Fair!"

"Controls the class!"

"Smart!"

"Discipline!"

"Shows who's the boss!"

"No homework!"

"No pop quizzes!"

"Likes kids."

"Doesn't wear the same clothes every day!"

After a few minutes, it was quite obvious that the class was begging for discipline and they expected me to provide it. As soon as they started lagging on their responses, I moved to the other side of the board.

"Now tell me what makes an effective student," I

said. They were hot. I couldn't write fast enough. They mimicked the voices of their parents and teachers.

"Comes to class on time."

"No cuts."

"Does homework."

"Studies for tests."

"No talking during class."

"No writing notes."

"No throwing paper."

"No smoking in the bathroom."

"No cheating."

They worked hard to outdo each other and we filled the board in just a few minutes. I placed the chalk on the holder and dusted off my hands.

"Excellent!" I smiled brightly as I glanced around the room, making brief eye contact with each student. "You obviously know exactly how to be successful students, so I won't waste your time telling you how to behave or what to do. You just told me what you need to do. That's your job—to be effective students. And you told me my job. I'll do my best to do my job and I expect the same effort from you."

As I completed my speech, the bell rang, but the students didn't jump out of their seats immediately. They sat, stunned, aware that they had just set some extremely high standards for themselves. They had been had. And I was hooked.

THREE

Fire in My Heart

Hal Gray only gave me a couple of weeks to catch my breath after taking over Miss Sheppard's class before he sent me into the arena to face his seventh period accelerated English class. After I'd observed his class, the idea of teaching those students held zero appeal. Hal's class was a zoo.

"Well?" Hal locked his hands behind his head and leaned back in his squeaky swivel chair. "What do you think?"

I resisted the urge to express my honest opinion, which was that Hal was either deaf and blind or simply dumb. From my vantage point in the back of the room, it appeared that only two of the students in his class had even the faintest idea of what had transpired during the first act of *Julius Caesar*. The other students were too busy braiding their hair, reading Motorhead magazines, copying each other's math homework, or passing personal notes to concern themselves with Caesar's dilemma. Two boys, Nader and Brandon, often brought a deck of cards and played poker in the far corner, making no effort to hide the cards from view.

Hal was an intelligent, perceptive person, so I knew

there had to be a reason why he didn't reprimand the students, but the reason escaped me. At first, I thought perhaps he was so caught up in his presentation of the Shakespearean drama that he didn't notice the students' behavior, but he was far too bright, and the students were much too blatant in their indifference, for that to have been true. Maybe he graded students solely on the basis of their exam scores, I speculated. But the entire class would flunk, which would certainly call the matter to the attention of the district office, and I knew Hal had no desire to chat with the superintendent. Maybe he just didn't care. Immediately ashamed, I shook my head to clear it of such disloyal thoughts, but I wasn't fast enough. Hal sat upright in his chair and rubbed his palm over his silver-gray crewcut.

"I bet you think I let the kids get away with murder, don't you?" he asked.

"Well, I did notice that quite a few of them seem to be off track," I said, hoping to soften the truth with tact. Hal exhaled, blowing the tact off my response as easily as he flicked a speck of dust off his tattered green desk blotter. He leaned forward, crossed his arms on his desktop, and looked me straight in the eye, his expression solemn.

"This is an ACL class, Miss Johnson. Accelerated. That means headed for college. These kids are fifteen, sixteen years old—old enough to start being responsible for themselves. I give them the information. If they don't get it, screw 'em."

My jaw dropped about six inches, which obviously amused Hal. His tanned face crinkled into a broad smile and his eyes flashed like two small blue suns, with rays of wrinkles etched into his leathery skin. "Ah, don't mind me," he said, "I'm a crusty old fart and I'm going to retire next year. Say good-bye gracefully and sail out to sea. Thirty years is long enough, maybe too long. Teachers should retire before they get stale."

"I don't think you're stale," I lied.

"Oh, yes, you do," he responded. "And you're right. You're also young. You're fresh, energetic, creative. That's what we need—new teachers with new ideas. Young blood."

Suddenly, I felt guilty for being younger than Hal. "I'm not as young as most new teachers," I pointed out.

"Don't apologize," he said. "I used to be like you. I wanted to mold young minds, stretch their imaginations, introduce them to the exciting world of words. Make the English language and literature come alive for them. Right?"

"Exactly," I agreed.

"You'll get over it," he said, abruptly.

"How long do you think that will take?" I asked. "Before I get over it?" Even as I asked, I was silently thinking that if and when that unlikely day came, I would leave the classroom immediately. But I truly didn't believe such a day would come. Hal cleared his desk and stuffed his green gradebook into a worn leather shoulder bag as, once again, he read my mind.

"You don't believe it will ever happen to you. No one does," he said. "Maybe it won't. Maybe you'll be one of the lucky teachers who hangs on to the enthusiasm in spite of the system. It happens sometimes, to the ones with fire in their hearts." He motioned me out the door and snapped off the lights.

"Do you think you have fire?" Hal asked as we reached the front gate of the school.

"At least a spark," I said, modestly.

"I think so, too," he agreed. "So you might as well

take over the class tomorrow. Act two. No sense in waiting any longer.''

"Tomorrow?" I echoed, stunned.

"Tomorrow," Hal repeated. Before I could think of an argument, Hal was half a block away, his battered leather shoulder bag swaying in rhythm with his jaunty step.

That night, I read and reread Act II. At midnight, satisfied that I knew my stuff, I finally closed the cover on *Julius Caesar*. Lying in bed, I reviewed the past two years of studies in preparation for my teaching credential: curriculum development, reading and phonics, adolescent psychology, models of teaching. I had my finger on the pulse of today's youth; I knew what was happening. The kids wouldn't be off track when I was teaching, I vowed to myself. I was going to do it right.

The students' built-in radar told them something was up the second they walked into B-9. Unnaturally quiet, they took their seats and stared at me as Hal explained that I would be taking over the class and he expected them to treat me with the same courtesy and respect that they showed to him. He wrote my name on the chalkboard, gave me a thumbs-up, and left the room. My first mistake was to ask if the class had any questions. Adam Stone, a pale blond boy with a beautiful baby face, raised his hand.

"Miss Johnson?" he said, smiling sweetly.

"Yes?" I returned his smile.

"Where do you get off barging in here and trying to act like a real teacher?"

My initial impulse was to grab Adam's skinny neck and squeeze until his pimply adolescent face turned blue, but that was not recommended in any of my methods courses, so I took a deep breath and forced a calm smile as I explained that I wanted to be a teacher in order to share my love of language and literature with teenagers. It was the absolute truth, but it sounded phony, even to my ears, as I said it. It didn't matter what I said, because none of the students listened. They followed Hal's instructions to the letter. They acted exactly as they did when he was in the room—absolutely oblivious to the teacher.

The next day I went to class prepared. Muscle had worked well with my regular P class, so I planned to flex for the ACL kids. I had a worksheet with questions about the play. I had a firm attitude. I had a seating chart. And, for a few brief moments, I had the students' attention.

"Aw! Come on! A seating chart! You're kidding!" They moaned and groaned as they slumped into their assigned seats and slammed their books on their desks.

"Why do we have to have a seating chart?" one of the girls whined.

"Because I don't want you sitting in the back of the room combing your hair and scratching your armpits during class," I explained.

"Ee-uu! Gross!" the kids complained.

"Hey, it could be worse," I pointed out. "I could have said I didn't want you to pick your noses and wipe it under the desktops." In unison, everyone in class crinkled their noses and pressed themselves backward, as far away from the desks as they could.

"I don't want to sit by Ryan," Adam said.

"You don't have to marry him," I retorted. "You don't have to hold his hand or kiss him. You don't even have to like him. All you have to do is sit beside him for fifty minutes once a day. I don't think you'll die from it and if you do, I'll take full responsibility for your death."

I distributed the worksheets, which were designed to stimulate classroom discussion by bringing out the kids' own ideas about the play. "Let's look at the first question on the sheet," I said. "Which character do you like the best in this play and why?" No one answered.

"Nader, which one do you like best?" I crossed my fingers behind my back and hoped he would answer. Nader was a handsome kid and a natural leader—intelligent, congenial, and born with a built-in B.S. meter. If he decided to play school, I was in. No such luck. He shrugged his shoulders.

"I don't know."

"Brandon?"

"Uh-uh."

"Diana?"

Diana didn't answer, either, but at least she looked at me. She was a nice kid, with a strong need to be liked by everyone. After my first day of teaching the class, she had stopped to wish me good luck and advised me not to take Adam's insults personally. I asked her again, although her eyes begged me not to. Her face contorted in agony. She was clearly torn between her desire to earn a good grade and be liked by her teacher and the necessity of maintaining the respect and approval of her friends. I turned to Callie West, who was always willing to say what was on her mind.

"Come on, Callie. Which character do you like the best?"

"Caesar's wife," Callie said. As soon as she spoke, several of the boys started coughing loudly, protesting her participation.

"Why?" I asked. More coughs. Every time Callie started to speak, the boys coughed en masse. She flicked her hands near her head, as though waving away a swarm of pesky gnats.

"I don't know," she said, giving up.

"Okay," I said. "I'll write the names of the characters on the board so we can all see the choices." Tactical error. The moment I turned my back, someone coughed. Wham! Wham! Wham! Three books slammed against desktops. I spun around. Twenty blank faces. Forty hands folded quietly in their owners' laps. I turned back to the board. No one coughed this time but after a few seconds, a chair leg scraped the floor. Wham! Wham! Wham! Wham! Wham! I recalled Hal's earlier advice: When they test you, which they will, hit them fast right where it hurts—in the gradebook.

"With a regular class," he said, "there are always a few who don't care if they pass. Flunking them doesn't faze them. But in an accelerated class, most of the kids are college bound and all of them want good grades. If you have to, use that for leverage."

Calmly, I placed the chalk on the tray beneath the chalkboard and wiped the dust from my hands. I walked to the desk and opened the gradebook. Pencil poised, I glanced about the room.

"This entire worksheet is due at the end of the class period. It is worth one hundred points, which means that if you don't do it, it will have a significant effect on your grade. Any questions?"

A hostile silence descended on the classroom as the students attacked their worksheets. When the bell rang, the kids stalked to the front of the room, holding their completed worksheets gingerly between thumbs and index fingers to avoid further contamination, and flicked the papers into the basket on my desk. No one looked at me.

The following day, I read some of their answers out loud, providing constructive criticism of their responses. As I discussed their answers, they rolled their eyes to the ceiling, and when I handed back their graded worksheets, they rolled them into tight, crumpled balls. Each day, I gave them another worksheet and each day they quietly completed it, providing perfunctory answers. When I asked for volunteers to read, no one responded, so I assigned roles and they dutifully read them in barely audible voices, devoid of expression. During the class discussions, students responded only when called upon and even then they offered curt, uninspired answers. The message was clear. You can lead the class to the lesson, Teacher, but you can't make us learn.

After a week, the tension had built to an intolerable level. One afternoon, I lost it. Someone—I couldn't tell who—had been whistling softly at a very high pitch for thirty minutes without a break. Callie West grew so irritated that she stomped out of class. The remaining students shuffled their papers loudly every time I turned my back. I felt like screaming, so I did. I stopped dead and bellowed at top volume. It felt great, so I flailed my arms and shook my head wildly, letting my lips blubber loosely. It felt so good that I kept it up until I ran out of breath. When I stopped screaming and flopped into my chair, the kids were wide-eyed and dumbstruck.

"Anybody here see *Rain Man?*" I asked. A few kids nodded their heads, but nobody spoke.

"Remember that scene where Dustin Hoffman is in the airport and Tom Cruise is trying to make him get on a plane and he doesn't want to go, so he pitches a fit?"

Again the kids nodded silently.

"I know exactly how he felt," I said. No one responded, so we sat staring silently at each other until the bell rang. I ignored the bell. The kids waited for a few minutes until they realized I wasn't going to dismiss them. Nader quietly picked up his books and tiptoed gingerly past my desk, as though afraid any sudden movement or sound might trigger another tantrum. The rest of the class followed.

Wild screaming didn't appeal to me as a viable teaching technique, so I asked Hal to observe the class in action to see if he could identify my mistakes and offer some suggestions. They weren't angels when he taught, but at least they didn't hate him. With their official teacher in the back of the room, the students stopped throwing books for a day, but their lack of interest and unwillingness to participate remained the same. As soon as the bell rang and the kids disappeared, Hal moved forward and sat down in one of the student's desks in the front row. He raised his hand and said, "Miss Johnson?"

"Yes?" I smiled, playing my role. Hal didn't return my smile. Instead, his face wore the same closed expression I saw on twenty faces for an hour every afternoon.

"You don't like us, Miss Johnson. You're very clever and witty and educated and you can verbally demolish us whenever you want to because you're older than we are and you know a lot more, but that isn't fair. It isn't very nice. And it isn't teaching."

My knees buckled and I sat down hard. My chair rolled backward and crashed into the chalkboard with a jolt.

"You're right. I'm not teaching. Now what am I going to do?"

"Forget all that B.S. they taught you in college," Hal said. "You can't learn how to teach by sitting in a

40

classroom listening to lectures. You learn how to teach by teaching. You can't hide behind your desk or your authority or your education. Just trust your instincts. If you're wrong, the kids will tell you, loud and clear."

"That's a pretty tough assignment, Hal," I said.

He smiled. "About as tough as understanding Shakespeare when you're only fifteen years old."

Glumly, I gazed out the window at the rolling California hills and wondered whatever had possessed me to believe I could teach teenagers. A wad of paper sailed through the air, expertly launched, and landed in the trash can next to my desk, breaking my reverie.

"Hey!" Hal said softly. "Think about it. If teaching were easy, they wouldn't have to pay us such exorbitant salaries, would they?"

"I have a confession to make," I told the ACL English class. For the first time, genuine interest shone in the eyes of the students. Even Adam glanced at me over the top of the sunglasses that he had started wearing to class every day, claiming that the fluorescent lights made his eyes burn. I didn't believe him for a second, but I did believe Hal's theory that Adam was having trouble accepting his parents' recent divorce and the sunglasses gave him the illusion that his tender feelings were less exposed.

"I haven't been very nice to you," I continued. "I'm sorry. But you haven't been very nice to me, either. You put me on the defensive the very first day and I never got over it. Well, I'm over it now. The reason I made a seating chart was not to punish you or make you miserable. I made it because I want to help you be the most effective students you can be, so you can learn. Because I like you. If I didn't like you, I would let you sit in the back of the room and play cards instead of reading Shakespeare. See this little note?"

I held up a sheet of paper from a yellow sticky pad. BE NICE was printed in bold black letters on the paper.

"This is my reminder to be nice to you. And I'd appreciate it if you would do the same. What do you think?"

For a few seconds, I was afraid that my new, improved humanistic approach wasn't going to work any better than the old dictatorial one. I held my breath while the students looked around the room, checking each other's responses. I knew most of the kids would follow Nader's example.

"Nader?" I said.

"Miss Johnson?" he responded quickly, mimicking my questioning tone exactly. He didn't smile, but there was a sparkle in his dark eyes.

"Pretty please?" I smiled at him and gave a thumbs-up. He returned my thumbs-up and the class breathed a collective sigh of relief. It was hard work fighting the teacher and refusing to learn, especially for a group of intelligent students.

"Now, let's take a look at where we are in *Julius Caesar*," I said. "Does anybody have any questions about the first two acts?" Although my question was sincere, I didn't expect an answer. Brandon raised his hand.

"Yes?"

"Can I ask a real question, Miss Johnson?" he asked.

"That's what we're here for."

He took off his A's baseball cap and put it backward, and drew a deep breath, as though preparing for a dangerous dive. "What's going on? I can't tell the names apart and the words don't make any sense. It looks like English, but it isn't really. It's just a bunch of bullshit."

I was tempted to point out that during the days on which I observed the class, Brandon never had his book open to follow along as Mr. Gray discussed the play. Most of the time, he had been playing poker with Nader, and he had been reading *Hotrod* magazine when Mr. Gray showed a film of the first act. But I controlled myself. Brandon knew he hadn't paid attention, but maybe he didn't pay attention because he didn't understand. Or maybe he thought I was a sucker. Either way, I had promised to be nice, and nice I would be or die trying.

"Can somebody give a brief summary of what's happened so far?" I asked the class. "Just describe the plot in your own words?" No one responded.

"Come on, boys and girls," I said. "I thought we just agreed that we'd all be nice. Somebody must know what's going on. Why were the citizens celebrating at the opening of the play?"

Diana cleared her throat. "It was a celebration for the ides of March?"

"What an airhead!" Adam mumbled and sighed loudly.

"Not nice!" I pointed at Adam.

"Caesar made a bunch of enemies in the war," Nader suggested. "They're following him around, trying to kill him or something. But they all have the same name almost. Everybody's name begins with a C. Not very smart."

"Yeah," Ryan said. Several other heads nodded.

"I admit that it isn't an easy play to read, but the story is simple," I said. "Julius Caesar is a powerful politician and whenever someone has power, somebody else wants to take the power away. In this case, the people who want to take the power happen to be Caesar's closest friends. That's what makes the play so

43

dramatic. Imagine how you would feel if all your best friends had secret meetings and ganged up on you and eventually beat you up or killed you just because you were more popular than they were or because you got better grades."

"I would say it sucked," Adam whispered, glancing over the rims of his sunglasses, obviously testing our newly established truce.

"And Caesar would have said, 'Methinks this sucketh,' " I said.

We ended up reading the entire second act over again, this time with more enthusiasm. At the end of each scene, we stopped to discuss what had happened. It was an exhilarating, natural give and take between teacher and teachee. After the final bell, I sat at my desk, enjoying the sweet sound of students discussing the play. As they collected their books, they actually argued with each other about which of Shakespeare's characters was more believable. For an hour, I had been a teacher. And it was good.

FOUR

George Shouldn't of Shot His Homeboy

"**W**hat's the difference between an ACL student and a regular P student?" I asked out loud one day in the English department office where most of the staff gathered at lunch to compare notes and cholesterol counts. Although the reading scores of the ACL students were generally higher, the difference wasn't remarkable, and many of the kids in my English-P class were as bright and articulate as their ACL counterparts. Most of the P kids, however, had much lower grades than their standardized reading and math scores indicated that they should.

Charlie Myers, a bear of a man, rumored to have eaten students alive in the classroom, peered at me over the tops of his black-rimmed bifocals. "ACL students have above-average scores on their standardized exams and, as a general rule, plan to attend college. Regular students have average or below-average scores and most likely will not attend college. Unfortunately, many will also drop out before their senior year."

"But I have some real fluff heads in ACL English and some really bright kids in the regular P class," I said.

"Shouldn't they be switched around, even if their test scores don't jibe?"

Charlie sighed and glanced around the table with a rueful smile. "Isn't her youthful enthusiasm refreshing?" he asked of no one in particular. With the exception of two other teachers, the entire English staff was within five years of retirement age. The teacher sitting next to me, Bob Spencer, a twenty-nine-year veteran with a reputation for tough lessons and heartless grading, sniffed but didn't speak. Hal Gray winked at me across the table and cleared his throat.

"She's sharp, Charlie," Hal said. "You have to give her the straight skinny." He lowered his voice and pretended to whisper conspiratorially to me. "It's a simple matter of logistics. There isn't enough room in the ACL classes for every kid who might have potential, so we only expect success from as many seats as we have available. And since the parents of the local—translate 'white'—kids have the most money, their kids usually have the most potential."

"Hal!" Charlie interrupted sharply.

"But that's not fair," I said. "The minority kids who are bused in should have an equal chance. It's been proven that children meet the expectations of their teachers, however high or low."

Bob Spencer emitted a long, loud sigh. "We've all read that research," he said in a weary voice. "Years ago," he added pointedly.

"Many years," someone else agreed. The temperature in the room went down at least ten degrees, so I dropped the subject. After lunch, Hal walked with me back to the classroom.

"Don't be discouraged," he said. "They aren't as jaded as they sound. They want all of the kids to succeed, but after a while you have to face the fact that some students don't want to succeed. For whatever reason, they want to fail. It's emotionally exhausting to bust your buns trying to help some kid who refuses your help. Each time it happens, you distance yourself just a little bit more from the disappointment. You can't save a kid who doesn't want to be saved."

"Maybe you can't," I said. "But I'm not going to walk into that classroom and expect my kids to fail. I expect them to learn."

Hal opened the door to my classroom and bowed, gesturing for me to enter. "Expect away. But don't be so hard on the other teachers. They've all faced the same problems you're facing and a lot of them really care about the kids. They're just tired. Maybe you should try to have as much tolerance of other teachers as you do of your students. Every teacher has an individual style. We can't all be Jaime Escalante."

I decided not to pursue the argument, but to conduct my own experiment, instead. Both the ACL and P classes would read *Of Mice and Men* at the same time, so I could see for myself whether the two groups really were different. When I passed out the books to the ACL kids, most of them turned the books over, read the blurb on the back and then opened to the first page to see how the story began. Nader flipped through the pages and read the first and last line of each chapter. He then read the last paragraph and closed the book.

"What do you think?" Brandon asked Nader.

"At least it doesn't have a Hollywood ending," Nader replied with a shrug. Brandon and the other kids, satisfied that their literate leader approved the book, opened to the first chapter and started reading.

The P kids responded like a cat to a bath. As I passed out the books, they began complaining that it was "too boring" and "stupid" and "too thick to carry around."

"It's a very short book and how can you tell it's boring if you haven't even read it?" I argued.

"Come on, Miss J.," Roderick said. "All school books are boring."

"Trust me," I said. "This story is interesting. It has great characters." They didn't buy it. I saw the hopelessness in their faces, heard the sighs of defeat, the groans of consternation. I whipped out my notes on indirect and direct characterization and brandished them in the air as I wrote Characterization on the chalkboard. During the few seconds it took me to write that one word, three students fell asleep, four dropped their books on the floor, and two started a wrestling match in the back of the room. As I placed the chalk on the tray and dusted off my hands, inspiration suddenly struck without warning.

"I need a volunteer to come up here," I said. Everyone froze, some out of fear that they would be called forward, some out of the delicious anticipation of witnessing a fellow student's humiliation. No one moved.

"Fine," I said. "You'll have to appoint your own volunteer. I'm leaving the room for ten minutes. When I return, I want you to have written on the board everything you know about me."

"Everything?" Roderick asked, leering and wriggling his eyebrows.

"Everything," I repeated. "And don't worry about hurting my feelings. I don't want to know who said what. I just want the information on the board when I return. You're on your own." And I walked out the door.

"She's lying. She's just going around the corner and hide," one young cynic called out from the back of the room. "Somebody keep watch at the door."

The students rushed to peer out the windows and

doorway as I walked slowly to the far side of the parking lot. Making sure I stayed where they could see me, I walked up the side of a small hill and continued across the top and down the other side. Then I walked completely around the building. By the time I turned the first corner, I could hear the class come to life. Shouts and giggles spilled out of the open door and I could see one of the boys at the board, writing furiously. A girl joined him and began writing as fast as she could.

When I came back into view, they shushed each other and ran to take their seats. The chalkboard was filled with scribbled notes. They had outdone themselves. I selected each item on the board and asked them how they knew it was true. "Wears red boots," was the first example.

"We can see them!" a girl cried out, pointing at my feet, exasperated at my density.

"Well, how about this one. How do you know I'm fair?" I asked.

"Because you make everybody follow the same rules!" Stacy hollered.

We went through each item—they knew I was from Pennsylvania, that I had been in the navy, that I lived in Woodview, that I was divorced, that I spoke Spanish, and so on. After asking them how they arrived at each item, I wrote a number after the item, pointing out that they had learned it in one of four ways: 1) They could see it in my physical appearance; 2) Someone else told them about me; 3) They heard me say it to them; or 4) They saw me act it out. I explained that those were the ways we learn about a character, or anybody, for that matter. It worked. On their final exam later that year, every single student could list three different ways that we learn about a fictional character.

When my Ps began reading the book—rather, I began reading—not a single student would risk reading aloud in front of the class. The first page nearly killed them. When we reached the sentence that described the "recumbent, mottled tree limbs," several heads drooped and Stacy groaned loudly.

"Hang on!" I yelled, waking up the sleepers. "This is just the opening credits. He's establishing the feeling of the place, setting the scene. Get ready for the main characters to enter any moment." Most of the kids woke up, or at least sat up. When we read the description of the two main characters, George and Lennie, I could see in their faces that they still were not caught up in the story, so I tossed my book on my desk, hunched my shoulders and began clomping around the room, stiff-legged, without swinging my arms. I held my hands tightly against the sides of my legs.

"How does this look?" I said. "Have you ever seen anybody walk without swinging his arms? It looks weird, doesn't it?" I continued walking up and down the aisles, looking at the kids with a dumb grin pasted on my face, until all the students were looking at me. "What does this tell you about me? Why would a person walk this way?"

"Because you're stupid," someone yelled from behind my back. I spun around.

"Come on," I urged. "You can do better than that. What kind of a person am I?"

"Dumb!" someone else yelled.

"Come on," I said again. Mary Brown, a thin, timid girl, whispered something I couldn't hear.

"What did you say, Mary?" She covered her mouth with her hand and spoke into her fingers, "You look kind of scared."

"Great!" I yelled, thrilled at the indication of original

thinking. "What might he be scared of?" Mary shrugged and the rest of the class sat watching me, satisfied with Mary's answer. We continued with the story and after class, as the students rushed noisily out of the room, I sat at my desk, watching them, trying to figure out why this class of students had no response to my questions about the story while the ACL students offered endless ideas. When I asked the ACL kids what their impression would be if they saw a large man walking along without moving his arms, they guessed he would look "weird," "insecure," "scared," "scary," "dangerous," "retarded," "unnatural," "uptight," and a variety of other adjectives. When I asked them what Lennie might be afraid of, Brandon said he was probably afraid of himself. Nader said he was afraid of the whole world. Adam said he was afraid of people. Diana suggested that maybe he was afraid he would break something because he was so big and strong.

Each day, as we progressed through the story, the ACL kids read, discussed, and analyzed the story. They whipped through their worksheets, wrote paragraphs on symbols, characterization, setting, and plot and did a decent job on the quiz. The P kids finally got involved in the story and developed a feeling for the characters. When Curley attacked Lennie in the bunkroom and started hitting him in the face, several kids made punching motions and shouted, "Come on, Lennie, let him have it!" When Lennie grabbed Curley's hand and squeezed it hard enough to crush every bone, the kids cheered wildly. I wasn't surprised that they responded so energetically to the violent scenes, but they showed more compassion for the characters in the book than they did for each other. Mary Brown was particularly concerned about Curley's wife.

"Why doesn't she have a name?" Mary wanted to

know. "Everybody should have a name."

"What do you think?" I asked her. "Why would the author leave a character without a name?"

"I don't know," Mary said. "Maybe he didn't like her."

"You could be right," I said, "but can't you think of any other reasons?" Mary thought for a few minutes and shook her head, but the boy seated behind her raised his hand.

"Maybe she doesn't have a name because she doesn't have a life," Joey said. "All she does is get bossed around and nobody likes her."

"Do you like her?" I asked Joey.

"She's kind of a whore," he said, "but I feel sorry for her sometimes, just a little bit."

At the end of the book, when George faced the decision of killing Lennie or letting Curley and his men kill Lennie, some of the kids refused to continue reading.

"He's gonna kill him, isn't he?" Stacy burst out, interrupting Roderick's reading.

"Shut up," Roderick said. "You're gonna ruin the story."

"I just know he's gonna kill him," Stacy said. She shut her book and crossed her forearms on her desktop, resting her forehead against her arms. Mary Brown and a few other kids also closed their books, silently, although they listened intently as Roderick read the final scenes.

When we finished the story, Amador Carrera, who had not offered a single comment during the reading, threw his book down on his desk and spat into the air.

"Pssh!" he sputtered, disgusted.

"What's the matter?" I said.

"He didn't have to shoot his homeboy," Amador

said. Several of the other other boys and girls voiced their agreement, loudly.

"What else could he have done?" I asked. "The men would have lynched Lennie and hung him if they had caught him."

"Who says they would of caught him?" Amador argued. "He was big. He could of ran. Him and George could of ran into the woods and hid and then went up and bought their ranch. They had the money and everything. He didn't have to shoot him."

"What if Curley and the guys caught up with them?" I asked.

"Then they could of stood up together and fought it out like men," Amador said. "They had a gun."

"But Lennie was dangerous," I said. "He killed a lady because he didn't know his own strength. He might have hurt other people."

"There's plenty of dangerous people in my neighborhood and nobody shoots them in the head," Amador said. "He didn't do it on purpose anyway, so I still say it sucks. George shouldn't of shot his homeboy. That's all I'm saying." He crossed his arms across his chest and refused to discuss the matter further.

Amador's response to the story, and the others' fierce support of his point of view, helped me understand the P kids' perspective of the world a little better. In their minds, the world was a dangerous and unfriendly place and friends had to stick together. The ACL kids also objected strongly to the ending, but Nader and Callie convinced the rest of the class that it was the kindest thing George could have done for Lennie. Both groups wrote good essays comparing the book and the movie version of the story, and both agreed that the book was better, except for the scene in which Lennie broke Curley's hand. They begged me to rewind the tape and play that scene several times.

I was satisfied that, aside from their outlook on life, the two groups of kids had the same basic ability to handle academic subjects—until I gave them the test on the book. As soon as I handed out the exams in the P class, I heard several different kids make "tsk" noises, and others clapped their hands to their heads in frustration. At first, I thought they were simply being melodramatic—as they loved to be—because the ACL class had completed the test the previous day with no problems. After a few minutes, Roderick raised his hand tentatively. I went to his desk. He spoke so softly that I had to lean down and put my ear next to his lips.

"I don't know the answer to number eight," he said, pointing to the question: Why do you think John Steinbeck wrote this book?

"It's easy," I said. "You can't get it wrong. I just want to know what you think."

"But what if I don't get the right answer?" Roderick asked.

"I just told you," I said. "You can't get it wrong, if you answer it."

"But I don't know the answer," Roderick said and heaved a mighty sigh.

"All you have to do is think about it and write down what you think," I explained. "It isn't hard."

"Yes, it is!" Roderick insisted. "I don't know why he wrote that stupid book."

"Well, why do you think he wrote the stupid thing?" I said.

"I don't know!" Roderick whispered fiercely. "Forget it!" I touched his arm, but he pushed my hand away and waved his pencil in my face. "Don't worry about it," he said. "Just go away." By this time, nearly half the class had their hands in the air. After speaking to two or three of them, I realized that they all had the same problem as Roderick. They couldn't figure out what kind of answer I wanted to question number eight.

"Class, listen up," I said. "Lots of people seem to be having trouble answering number eight. It isn't hard. It's a thinking question—not a right or wrong question. If you tell me what you really think, you can't get it wrong. All I want you to do is tell me why you think John Steinbeck wrote the story." Roderick groaned and slapped his head. Amador rolled his eyes, but didn't say anything. At least half the class shook their heads.

"What's the matter?" I said.

"We don't know the answer," Stacy said. She stuck her pencil into the elaborate topknot that had recently replaced her hundreds of tiny braids.

"Look, kids," I said slowly. "I'm just asking you what you think. If you don't know why he wrote the book, just think about why he might have written it and then tell me what you think. Just don't give me some B.S. answer. Give me a real reason."

"What if we get it wrong?" Stacy asked.

"How can you get it wrong if I ask you what you think and you tell me?" I asked.

"I usually do," Stacy said.

"Me, too!" Roderick sputtered. Mary nodded her head and the rest of the kids traded looks that clearly said, "Humor her, she's a teacher and they never understand anything."

It took nearly twenty minutes for me to convince the kids that they could think of a reason why someone might write a story and that their ideas were valid. When I realized what the problem was—the students were unable or afraid to express their own ideas—I was unnerved. I resolved that my project for the next quarter would be to get the kids to form their own opinions, to share them with the other students, and to articulate their ideas in class. It seemed like a simple plan, but it took more time and effort than the rest of the curriculum combined.

Once I had set the goal for the class, I read everything I could find that might give suggestions for accomplishing the task. I found hundreds of worksheets designed to test student comprehension of literature and some that gave practice evaluating stories on the basis of conventional literary standards. But I didn't find anything that outlined steps for leading students to form their own opinions, based on their own knowledge. One journal article discussed an interesting concept called "timed responses." The general idea was for the teacher to write a controversial statement on the board and require the students to respond in writing for a five- or ten-minute time period. At the end of the time, papers were collected for grading by the teacher. It sounded straightforward enough.

IT'S OKAY TO STEAL, AS LONG AS NOBODY GETS HURT.

When the P kids entered the classroom and saw that statement on the chalkboard, they immediately began arguing about whether Miss Johnson believed it or not and whether they agreed.

"Quiet!" I said. "No talking. Get a piece of paper and write down what you think about that statement."

"You shouldn't steal, Miss Johnson," Mary Brown said. "It's bad."

"I didn't say I agreed with this statement," I explained. "I just put it on the board for you to read and think about. Now everybody get writing. Tell me what you would say if one of your friends walked up and said that to you. Your papers will be graded on content only—no points deducted for poor spelling or grammar.''

It was magic! They wrote. And they wrote. At the end of the ten-minute period, I collected the papers and read their responses aloud without revealing the names of the authors.

"I use to steel," wrote one girl,

but then I got caught and my mother beet me black and blue and grounded me for a hole entire month, so I don't do it no more. I still think it's ok to steel little stuff, but I don't do it because even if you don't get caught, it makes you feel dirty inside yourself.

A few kids nodded in agreement, but no one disagreed, which surprised me.

"If you read the Bible," I read from one paper, "then you know it's against the ten commandments to steal." I couldn't finish the essay—the kids whistled and booed me down.

"It don't matter who you steal from or what you steal," wrote another girl,

but somebody ends up getting hurt. Even if the person doesn't need the thing you stole, you end up hurting yourself because you can't have no self-respect if your a stealer. And that person who got ripped off will be really pissed cause it makes you so mad when somebody takes something from you. People work to get their stuff and you shouldn't take it. Lots of people who get stole from go out and steal from somebody else and then it goes on and on. That's a bad thing to get started.

The kids were riveted, eager to hear what their class-mates thought of their papers from the security of ano-nymity. For the first time all year, the kids were all seated, awake, and attentive when the bell rang to sig-nal the end of class.

After a few weeks of timed responses, the kids were pros. They had opinions on everything and weren't shy about expressing them. But I still had a problem with boys falling asleep in class. Girls rarely fell asleep in my class, but the boys were comatose. One minute, a boy would be sitting upright; the next minute, he'd be dead asleep, drooling on his desktop. One afternoon just before Thanksgiving, Denzel Tucker, my champion sleeper, started snoring right in the middle of an excit-ing exercise involving intransitive verbs. Denzel was a frequent napper, but an above-average student, so I didn't want to send him to the office. He had a part-time job at night and I knew he needed the money, so I understood why he was tired. But I also understood the need for him to develop enough self-discipline to stay awake in school.

When Denzel started snoring, I was sitting at my desk, rummaging through my purse in search of some Chapstick for my chapped lips. I couldn't find it, but I did find a tube of Red Raisin lipstick. As I applied a light coat, I thought of a wild but possible solution to Den-zel's problem. I applied another, thicker layer of red to my lips and tiptoed quietly to Denzel's side, motioning for the other kids to remain quiet. I puckered up and kissed Denzel soundly on the cheek. His head jerked up and he blinked repeatedly, startled to see all the kids cheering and hooting and pointing at him. He reached up to touch his face where I had kissed him, but I held his hand.

"Don't waste your time," I explained. "You can't wipe it off." I turned to face the class. "Does anyone know what indelible means?"

"It means you can't eat it, I think," one boy ventured.

"You're thinking of inedible," I said. "Inedible means you can't eat it. Indelible means you can't erase it. This is special, indelible lipstick I'm wearing. It cannot be erased. You can wash it off your face, but the lip print will remain on your face forever, like an invisible scar."

I couldn't believe it! Not one student offered an argument. They sat, staring at me, not completely convinced, but obviously not unconvinced, either, so I continued.

"If you look in the mirror, you won't be able to see the lip prints, but everyone else will be able to see them, if the light is right," I told Denzel. "I'm sorry, but I just can't resist. If you fall asleep in my class, I have to kiss you because you look like little angels when you're sleeping. And for the rest of your life, people will be able to see my lip prints on your face. They'll say, 'There's a student who fell asleep in Miss Johnson's class!' "

Don't believe it when people tell you that today's teenagers are wise beyond their years. These were street kids, punkers, cutters, the wisest of the wise guys in the school—and every single one of them wore the same look of quasi belief. Some of them suspected that I was kidding, but they weren't certain enough to contradict me.

Just to make sure they remained convinced of the lipstick scar, I asked Hal Gray to come into my class the next day, on pretext of delivering some papers to me. He quietly handed me the papers and turned to leave the room when, as rehearsed, he stopped short and stepped closer to Denzel, peering intently at Denzel's face.

"Are those lip marks?" Hal asked, feigning astonishment.

Denzel quickly raised his hand to his cheek as the remainder of the students stared, mouths agape. Hal smiled and nodded.

"She caught you sleeping, huh?" he whispered conspiratorially. He patted Denzel on the shoulder gently and walked out of the room.

That one kiss has been effective for over three years. Every time I have a new class of students, someone asks me if I really kiss kids who sleep in class. I assure them that it's true and I'm fully prepared to do it again. They squeal and giggle and maintain a daily vigil, hoping to see history repeat itself, but it's too noisy. As soon as a student begins to nod, the other kids poke each other excitedly and whisper, "Miss Johnson! Miss Johnson! He's sleeping! Kiss him!" The would-be sleeper, of course, can't catch even a wink with all that commotion taking place.

FIVE

Mrs. West, You Have a Lovely Daughter

Out of nowhere, Callie West suddenly developed "an attitude." During class, while I was talking, she would frequently look me straight in the eye and yawn loudly to indicate her lack of interest in the exercise at hand. Callie's yawns were long, dramatic affairs that sometimes lasted a full minute and, of course, they were contagious to the other students, often setting off a chain of yawns that circled the room and included my own, in spite of my efforts to resist the impulse. The reason Callie's yawns irritated me so much was that her timing was right on—she yawned in the spots where I would have yawned myself, had I been sitting in the student's seat instead of the teacher's. I couldn't argue with her; the grammar lessons were boring and the literature texts were bland, but I did my best to liven them up. I couldn't alter the curriculum, especially for an ACL class, because it would throw them off track for their next year in school.

After each yawn, Callie would smile sweetly and apologize ever so sincerely, although we both knew she was not the least bit sorry. I couldn't bring myself to send her to the office. What would I write on the referral report: Student yawns in class? Student appears to be bored? If she had had a real problem with sleeping, I could have sent her to the nurse, but this was obviously a case of Test the Teacher.

I ignored the yawns, hoping Callie would grow tired of her game, but she didn't. Instead, she added another irritating habit to her growing repertoire. Ten minutes before the end of class each day, she'd sit bolt upright and noisily gather her books and papers together on top of her desk. Her purse went on top of the pile and she peered over it, first at me, then at the clock, then at me, then at the clock, the way people's heads turn when they are viewing a tennis match. Naturally, Callie's head turning distracted the other kids, which meant that the daily lesson time was cut by ten minutes each day—a twenty percent loss that I couldn't recoup simply by talking faster.

Callie was counting on my policy of handling problems in the classroom. I had never sent a student to the office and I wasn't eager to break my tradition because of her childish antics. If a kid pulled a pistol on me, or threatened me with a switchblade, I was prepared to call for reinforcements if I didn't faint first, but I couldn't envision myself calling the principal and complaining that one of my students kept looking at the clock. Neither could I order Callie to sit still and not turn her head. I'd feel like a drill sergeant.

"Call her parents," Hal Gray suggested. "Kids suddenly cooperate when you make a short phone call home."

"But my dad would have whopped me good if a teacher had called to complain about my behavior," I said. "Every year, at the start of school, he used to call up the principal and say, 'This is Bob Johnson. I got five kids in your school. Any of them get out of line, you have my permission to tan their hides and tan them good.' "

"Well, you don't have to say she's acting terrible," Hal said. "All you have to do is call and chat with her mom or dad for a while. She'll get the message."

I couldn't picture myself calling up Callie's father or mother and just shooting the breeze for a while. They would ask me how she was doing in class and I'd have to tell the truth. Lying isn't one of my talents. Still, I had to do something about Callie. Maybe I could write a note to her parents, I mused. That way, I could say what I wanted to say without answering any questions from them.

My first inclination was to write a note gently suggesting that Mr. and Mrs. West speak to Callie about not working up to her potential, which was true. She was a bright girl who quickly grasped each new idea, but she rarely bothered to finish an assignment. She'd complete seven or eight out of ten questions, then lose interest, satisfied that she'd receive a C on the paper. But I hesitated to use the word *potential* because I remembered so clearly how disgusted and bored I was when my own parents and teachers suggested that I work up to mine when I was fifteen. I knew it wouldn't work. I considered telling the Wests outright that Callie was rude to me and disruptive in class, but then her parents would be forced to take my side or Callie's. If they took her side, I'd lose any possible leverage. If they took my side and threatened her, it might change her behavior, but her attitude would probably grow even more sour.

Finally, I decided to try a "bet you can't eat all those carrots" approach. I wrote a note telling Mr. and Mrs. West how much I enjoyed having Callie in class, that she was a bright and charming student with a delightful sense of humor. The next day, the first time Callie yawned, I handed the note to her, unsealed, and asked her to give it to her parents. Naturally, she sneaked the note open during class and read it. Her eyes opened wide and she quickly stuck the note into her purse. That was Callie's last yawn. She didn't mention the note that day, a Friday, but on Monday, she stopped by my desk after class.

"Thanks for that note, Miss Johnson," Callie said. "I couldn't believe you said all those nice things about me."

"It was my pleasure, Callie," I said. "And they're all true."

"Nobody ever sent my parents a good note about me before, you know," she confided. "My mother taped it to the refrigerator so everybody could see it. That's the place of honor at our house."

"That's wonderful," I said.

"My father doesn't believe I have a B in your class," Callie said to the notebook she was holding.

"I don't know why not," I said. "You're very smart."

"No, I'm not," Callie said as, to my surprise, a pink blush crept across her cheeks.

"You most certainly are, too," I said. "You never have any problems with the material we cover in class."

"That's just because of Nader and Diana and Ryan," Callie said. "I just listen to them. I don't really belong in this class, you know. The office made a mistake once and stuck me in an ACL class and they just keep putting me in them. I shouldn't be in here with the smart kids. I'm not going to college."

"Then why do you usually finish your assignments

before all those geniuses do?'' I asked. ''You know you always hand your papers in first.''

''Yeah,'' Callie said, ''but I never get A's on them.''

''That's because you don't finish them,'' I said. ''If you finished them, you'd get A's.''

''But I never get an A on the tests,'' Callie pointed out, still looking at her notebook. ''I always get Cs. Sometimes Bs.''

''Do you ever study?'' I countered.

''No.''

''Well, I bet if you studied, you'd get A's.''

''I don't think so,'' Callie said, looking at me out of the corner of her eye.

''I do,'' I said. I tapped my finger on her notebook until she looked me in the eye. ''I really do.''

''Do you really think I have a good sense of humor?'' Callie asked.

''Yes,'' I nodded. ''I really believe that, too. I'll tell you what. When we're doing an exercise orally in class and you get bored, just go ahead and work on your own. Finish the exercise on paper and hand it in at the end of class. I'll grade it right away. If you get an A on it, you won't have to do the homework for that night.''

''For real?'' Callie asked.

''For real,'' I answered. ''But there is one thing I want you to do for me.''

Her face fell. ''I knew it.''

''I want you to promise to study for the next test, just to see how you do.''

''Is that all?'' Callie eyed me distrustfully.

''That's all, folks,'' I said. ''Deal?'' I extended my hand to her. She looked at me for a few seconds, sighed, and shook my hand.

''Why not?'' she said with a sigh. ''It won't kill me.''

Naturally, Callie earned A's on her classroom exercises, which, incidentally, were longer than the home-work assignments she would have done. And she earned a B-plus on the next exam. By the end of the year, she had an A in English and a B average overall, although she still insisted that it was an accident and she didn't belong in the "smart class."

Encouraged by my ￢uccess with Callie, I decided to write notes to the parents of every student in both of my classes. I wrote the notes in three batches: The first students to receive them were the "bad" kids because I thought they needed the most encouragement. It was difficult, at times, to find something positive to say, but I didn't lie. I didn't tell parents that their kids were rocket scientists, but I did include a statement in each note to the effect that I was happy to have the child in my class, or pleased to have the chance to be his or her teacher for some reason—the student's wit, charming personality, delightful sense of humor, courteous be-havior, impeccable dress, ability to get along with other kids, quick grasp of subject matter, and so on. In most cases, the notes didn't address the subject of academic achievement; most of them simply praised the student as a person.

When I handed the notes, unsealed, to the kids and asked them to give them to their parents or guardians, I invariably got the same response from the students: What did I do now? I told the kids they were free to read the notes, but they had to take them home. A few of the kids crumpled up the notes and threw them on the floor on their way out of the room, which hurt my feelings a little bit and annoyed me quite a lot because it was taking much longer than I had anticipated to write fifty-six notes by hand. But the results were worth the effort. I was amazed. Of course, a few kids still held out, but most of them changed their perceptions of themselves. Jason was no longer a mouthy brat; he was a "quick-witted young man whose comments added a welcome touch of humor to class discussions." Sherri, a straight D student, held her head high, proud to be "a young lady whose tasteful clothes and gracious manner set a good example for other students." Danny, my hyperactive desk thumper, had never thought of himself before as a "bright and charming young man with boundless energy."

When the students with good study habits and high grades realized that their academically less successful counterparts had received complimentary notes to take home, several of them privately requested similar notes. I assured them that every student in class would receive a note as soon as I could turn them out. The model student notes were easy to write. I complimented them on their neat handwriting, their high-quality work, their excellent attendance, their high test scores, and the like. But I tried to remember to include a personal compliment in each note, since the kids valued those more highly than the academic kudos.

As I approached the third batch of notes—for the "middle" students who were neither especially good nor noticeably bad—I was appalled to realize that I couldn't picture some of those kids in my mind, although I thought I knew them all so well. Sometimes a trivial detail such as hair color escaped me; other times it was the entire body that disappeared, leaving me with a mental image of a young face floating above a school desk. I realized then why so many good kids are so easily lost in our school system—they have softer voices, better manners, less extreme personalities. They don't cause problems or constantly seek attention or assistance in class. They go along with the program and fade into the background, often by choice, but sometimes simply because they are overshadowed by the others. I took extra care and spent a lot of time on that final batch of notes and when I distributed them to the students, I looked into each one's face until I was satisfied that I saw the boy or girl looking back at me.

After writing all the individual notes, I actually felt the bonding between the students and me that I'd read about but hadn't experienced before. It was a wonderful feeling and it completely changed the dynamics of the classroom. When the students truly believed that I liked them just as they were, it was no longer Teacher versus Students. It became Teacher and Students versus Curriculum. Together, we hated vocabulary exercises, grammar exams, reading proficiency tests, and spelling quizzes, but we had to do them. Teaching was the best thing I had ever done in my life. Before I knew it, June raced around the corner and crashed into the classroom, spinning all my students out into the summer sun.

SIX

Thunderbolt Jones

On the last day of school, I sat in my deserted classroom, feeling abandoned and forgotten in spite of the treasures presented by my departing cherubs: a pint of slightly squashed strawberries, a bookmark, two potholders, and a bottle of Atom Bomb cologne.

"Quite a haul you got there," Hal Gray remarked when he spied my gifts. He sauntered into the room, sniffed the cologne, inspected the bookmark, and sampled the berries. "What's on the agenda for summer vacation?"

"I just signed a contract to teach summer school," I said.

"Summer school is no place for a teacher," Hal said. "Summer school kids hate everybody. It's their own fault they have to go to summer school, but they blame it on the school. And you, my dear, represent The School."

"Maybe I'll be lucky and they won't hate me," I said. Hal shook his head.

"Nope," he said. "They'll hate you. Just don't take it personally."

Hal was right, as usual. The summer school kids hated me on sight. They also hated each other. I was happier than they were when the bell sounded the end of the first hour. A few kids remained slumped sullenly in their seats, but most of the kids ran outside into the sunshine. I stood in the doorway, watching them and wondering how I was going to make it through eight weeks of summer school. Foolishly ignoring Hal's advice, I had signed up for both four-week sessions.

A crowd of students had gathered outside in front of my classroom, but I didn't pay much attention to them until the bell rang and half of the crowd dispersed, leaving a semicircle of kids facing two girls. At first, I thought the girls were playing. Then one of them grabbed the other's waist-length hair and yanked her head to the ground. I heard a sickening crunch as the girl's face met the cement sidewalk.

"Way to go! Ruthless!" a boy crowed, raising his fist, egging the girls on. I raced outside and tried to squeeze through the students to reach the girls, but the kids moved to block me and I had to force my way through, stepping on their feet and thrusting them aside. As I broke through the line, I recognized the girl whose head was on the sidewalk as Rebecca Chevez, one of my students. She was a tiny girl, barely five feet tall, with fine, delicate features.

"Rebecca!" I yelled, reaching to help her. Before I could touch her, Rebecca threw her entire body toward the other girl's legs, knocking her to the ground. In a flash, Rebecca was on her feet. She grabbed hold of the other girl's hair, and then twisted her arm behind her back as she shoved her forward into the metal wall lockers that lined the outside of the building. Rebecca smashed the girl's face into the locker, yanked her back, and smashed her again. Blood spurted from the girl's mouth and as she turned her head, I saw a flash of metal; she was wearing wire braces, which had cut her lips badly. I tried to separate the two girls, but they clung to each other. The girl with the cut lips spat wildly and spun inside Rebecca's grasp. Her long, red fingernails raked Rebecca's neck, leaving four ragged, parallel scratches that immediately drew blood.

"Help me, you idiots!" I screamed at the boys. It took six of them to separate the two girls. The crowd disappeared instantly, leaving me on the sidewalk with the girls, both of them bleeding and breathless.

"Are you all right?" I put my hand on the arm of the girl I didn't know. She pushed my hand away.

"I'm fine," she said. "Leave me alone." I was torn. Of course, I was supposed to report the fight to the administration, but it would mean that both girls would be kicked out of summer school on the first day. They had been in class for one hour. I decided to try to handle it myself and give the girls a break.

"What's the problem here?" I asked Rebecca.

"That whore pushed me!" Rebecca said. "Nobody pushes me."

"I didn't push you, *puta!*" the other girl said. "You're so stupid, you walked into my purse." Her purse, an oversize black vinyl bag, lay on the sidewalk. I could see how easy it would be for someone to bump into it accidentally.

"You two know you'll be expelled if I report this to the office," I said. They both nodded. "If you give your word that this will end right here, we'll forget it." They stood, glaring at each other.

"Is it over?" I said.

"Yes," Rebecca said, with a toss of her head.

"How about you?" I asked the girl. She nodded.

"Go wash your face and get back to class," I said,

drawing Rebecca with me into my room. "Sit down and behave yourself. I'll talk to you after class."

It took about ten minutes for the kids to settle down, but we finally started reading "Thank You, Ma'am," a story by Langston Hughes. I could see that Rebecca's mind wasn't really on the lesson, but that seemed reasonable, considering the morning's events. The other students kept sneaking sideways glances at Rebecca as we read, which gave me a chance to sneak sideways glances at them. They were an interesting group. It was a large class—forty students—and I had been too busy checking names off the roll sheet to notice that the kids had segregated themselves by ethnic groups: black, Caucasian, Hispanic. I wasn't particularly concerned. Kids from four different high schools attended the same summer school and I assumed they would feel more comfortable sitting near their friends and classmates. As long as they behaved, I didn't plan to assign seats. We finished reading and watched a film strip of the story, which was a big hit because it was made in the 1950s and the ten-year-old star of the show wore his hair in an Afro. The black kids thought his hair was hilarious and the other kids thought the black kids' reaction to his hair was hilarious, so the second hour ended on an upbeat note. Foolishly, I thought the morning's fight was forgotten.

As soon as class resumed after our five-minute bathroom break, I passed out index cards and asked the kids to list their names, addresses, and parents' or guardians' names. I also asked them to include their real phone numbers because I had been warned that many listed the number of the local pizza parlor so teachers and administrators couldn't track them down at home. When I instructed them to include their

72

phone numbers, a voice from the back of the room challenged me.

"What you need my number for, man?" asked a muscular boy with chocolate velvet skin. His hair was cut close to his head, and a lightning bolt was shaved into the left side of his skull. Three tiny gemstones glittered on his left earlobe.

"You never know," I said. "I might want to call you up and ask you to go to the movies with me."

"Shee-it!" he responded under his breath, then loudly said, "I wouldn't go to no movie with her." I checked the roll sheet for the boy's name. Troy Jones.

"Well, Mr. Jones, don't hold your breath waiting for me to call," I answered. "Just put your number on the card in case I need to call and tell your mama that you got an A-plus in this class because you're so brilliant."

"That's cold!" said the girl seated in front of Troy.

"She told you!" cried the boy sitting next to Troy. He leaned over and slapped Troy on the shoulder. Moving so fast that his arm became a blur, Troy knocked the kid off his chair onto the floor.

"That's enough!" I shouted. "May I remind you that summer school has a strict behavior code. Any infraction will result in immediate expulsion. No exceptions. Raise your hand if you understand what I just said." Reluctantly, every student raised a hand.

"Mr. Jones, I apologize for my rude remark," I said. "It wasn't very courteous." Troy ignored me. I collected the index cards and distributed the course outline and syllabus. "Any questions about what we're going to cover during the next four weeks?" I asked. Not a single student looked at me. They sat staring mutely at the papers on their desktops. "Fine," I said, trying to maintain a cheerful attitude in spite of the collective cold shoulder I was getting from the class.

According to my students at Parkmont High, I was a wonderful teacher. What was wrong with these kids?

"Let's begin by reviewing this week's exciting spelling list, boys and girls," I said in my Romper Room voice. No one noticed that I was trying to be amusing. I called on twenty-five different students to spell the words on the list and wrote their mumbled, barely audible responses on the board. A bead of perspiration formed on my spine and trickled down my back as I completed the list and stood, my back to the class, until the bell rang to signal the end of the third hour. "Don't be late," I said to the herd stampeding toward the open door. To my surprise, several students remained in their seats when the bell rang.

"Don't you want to take a break?" I asked one girl. She shrugged.

"We only get five minutes. I'm not going to walk outside, just so I can walk right back in."

I sat down at my desk and took a deep breath, wondering if I could survive one more hour locked in a twenty-by-twenty-foot room with forty hostile teenagers. Just before the bell rang to signal the end of the break, I stepped to the doorway for some fresh air. As I approached the door, I overheard one of the boys tell one of his friends, in Spanish, to "pass the word for all the homeboys to be in C wing right after school." I recognized the distinctive accent as that of Hugo Barajas and, although I am hardly what you would consider fluently bilingual, four years of high school Spanish taught me enough to understand most informal conversations.

"What's going on?" I asked Hugo. He shrugged elaborately.

"Do you want to go to the office or do you want to

tell me?" I asked. Hugo pursed his lips, considering his options.

"Come on," I said. "It's not worth it. I heard what you said, anyway. Who's going to meet in C wing?"

Hugo shrugged again, unwilling or unable to break the cultural code of silence.

"Hugo," I said. "I heard you tell that boy that everyone was going to meet in C wing after school. All I have to do is go there and see. Why don't you just tell me?" Hugo shook his head. One of the other boys, a stocky blond kid with a nasty scar across his left temple, gallantly intervened on Hugo's behalf.

"It's them two Mexican girls," he said. "The lady wrestlers. They're gonna have a rematch after school, with reinforcements." He drove his right fist into his left hand with relish. "Lots of reinforcements."

I stepped outside the classroom into the warm sunshine. Our campus was designed to take maximum advantage of the California climate; only the classrooms and offices were indoors. Everything else was outside, including the rows of student lockers lining the open-air corridors. So I could see them coming three corridors away. Rebecca was walking toward my classroom, surrounded by six Hispanic girls. A group of ten or twelve Hispanic boys walked behind them. The blond kid was right; a gang fight was clearly in the works and I was responsible. I should have reported the fight in the first place. I hurried into my room and called the office to request a campus aide to take my class for a few minutes while I talked to the summer school principal, Mr. Grady. It wasn't a very pleasant conversation. As soon as I explained the situation, Mr. Grady picked up the phone and called security.

"Get every warm body you have to C wing before the end of fourth period," he said. "There's a Latino gang fight brewing." He slammed down the phone and grabbed a pad and pencil. "Names," he said. "I need names."

I gave him Rebecca's name.

"The other girl?" Mr. Grady snapped. When I said I didn't know, he swore softly under his breath and shook his head. "How long have you been teaching?"

"This is my first year," I said.

"Well, if you don't want this to be your last year," he said, "I suggest you follow regulations from now on. We don't make them up for entertainment. If you hadn't found out about this gang thing, a lot of innocent kids could have been hurt—maybe even killed. And it would have been your fault for not reporting the first incident. You want to live with that?"

I shook my head and bit my lower lip, trying not to cry.

"Look," he said, a trifle more gently. "No damage done, this time. But when we have fights, we have to get the kids who are fighting off campus so they can cool down. Usually, that's all it takes. Understand?" I nodded.

"Good," he said. "Now go teach those kids how to read. It'll give them something to do when they're in jail."

On the way back to the classroom, I stopped in the staff lounge to wash my face and gather my wits. As I entered the classroom, the security guards were escorting Rebecca outside. She glared at me as she passed by.

"Rat!" a voice hissed from inside the room. I couldn't pin it down, so I ignored it. I braced myself for the fourth and final hour. My blouse was soaking wet from my armpits to my waist. I planned to give the kids a diagnostic grammar exam, which would take most of the period. No lecture, no talking. I looked forward to a relatively calm hour. As I passed out the exams, the class was quiet, but as soon as I gave the signal to begin, the whispers and giggles began. I couldn't pinpoint the kids who were talking, because they all kept their faces turned downward toward their exam papers, but the constant noise was distracting. After about ten minutes, it became annoying.

"Knock off the talking," I said.

"Knock off the talking," a voice from the back of the room mimicked me. This time I recognized the voice. It was Troy Jones. Who could forget a young man with an entire jewelry store on his left ear and lightning bolts shooting across his head? I walked directly to his desk.

"Do you have something to say, Mr. Jones?" I asked with exaggerated politeness. He ignored me. I leaned down and spoke close to his ear.

"Excuse me, Mr. Jones. I asked you a question."

"What," he said.

"Did you have something to say to me?" I repeated.

"No," he said, again mimicking my voice.

"Good," I said. "Because I would hate to tear up your exam and give you a zero on your first day. I'd rather keep you here for the entire four weeks so you can suffer longer."

The talking stopped, but it was an uneasy silence that ruled the classroom. At any moment, I felt, the class could career out of control. I thought I could career out of control too. Ten minutes later another pocket of whispering broke out, this time in the self-selected Caucasian seating section. Although I didn't catch any of them talking, I narrowed the disturbance down to four boys on the far left side of the room.

"Excuse me, little darlings," I said. "I forgot to mention that I have a degree in psychology. Psychologists have many interesting theories. For example, when you give a class of students an assignment, the students who make the most noise are the ones who are afraid they can't do the work. They try to create a disturbance and distract the teacher from the lesson, hoping they'll be sent to the office so they can vegetate. I don't send students to the office, so it would save a lot of time and trouble if those of you who are afraid would simply raise your hands and say, 'I'm afraid, Miss Johnson. I don't think I can do this work.' I'll be happy to help you. That's my job." As I spoke, I looked directly at the four boys. Stonefaced, they tackled their tests. I turned to face Troy Jones and raised an eyebrow at him. He glared at me briefly before returning his attention to his exam. At the end of the thirty-minute test period, I began collecting papers. As I reached for Troy's paper, he pulled it back.

"I'm not done," he muttered.

"That's okay," I said. "You get credit for doing it as classroom exercise, but it doesn't count against your grade. It's just a diagnostic exam." I reached for his test paper. He flicked my hand aside roughly.

"I said I'm not done," he repeated.

"And I said it doesn't matter. Just give me the paper." I held out my hand and stared at him. He stood up. He was wearing a tight tank top, in violation of the school dress code, and I could see the outline of his pectorals—they were in great shape. So were his biceps. He had about six inches of height and at least fifty pounds of weight on his side, so I smiled at him. I backed up a step, but I couldn't back down.

"Teachers usually win. Why don't you just give me the paper and sit down," I whispered. "That would be the smart thing to do."

"You think you're smart," he said. "You aren't so smart. You know what I could do to you if you made

78

me mad?'' He flexed his biceps and clenched his fists and hulked over me. For about two seconds, I was scared. Then my glance fell on his feet. He was wearing a pair of high-top sneakers with neon pink swirls on the sides. Kid shoes. I stepped closer and spoke directly into his chest.

"Try it," I challenged. "If you touch me, I'll sock you." He turned sideways and made a muscle.

"Go ahead. Punch me."

"I wouldn't punch you in the arm, you little twit," I sneered, as coldly as I could. "I'd punch you in the pants." Shocked by my own words, but pleased with their effect on Troy—his mouth dropped open and he stared dumbly at me—I raced on. "What would you do, run to the principal's office and tell them the teacher whacked you in the wienie? I doubt it. And even if you did, I'd swear I didn't do it. It would be your word against mine and I'm a teacher. I'd say, 'Are you kidding? I'm a professional educator. I would never hit a child in the genitals. That boy is sick. He needs psychological help.'" I paused. He still didn't move, which I considered a point in my favor. "Now make your choice. Hit me or sit your butt down in that chair and act like an intelligent man."

He sat down at his desk. I sat down at mine. I was very proud of myself. I didn't cry until after the bell rang and all the students had left the room.

SEVEN

"Let's Talk" by Yours Truly

Summer school kids don't just hate school, teachers, and each other. They hate everything —especially reading and writing—and nothing I did seemed to motivate them. These weren't ACL students; they were professional flunkers. I couldn't use grades for leverage because they didn't care. What's one more No Credit when you already have four or five or an entire year of NCs? What can you take away from a kid who has nothing? Unlike my P kids, the summer kids didn't respond to my jokes with hisses and boos; they looked right through me, the same bored expression on every face. After several days of deadlock, I desegregated the classroom. The black, white, and Hispanic sections of the room did not intermingle at all. Hoping to break their resistance by separating them from their power bases, I made a seating chart that left each student near one of his or her friends, but completely mixed up the ethnic groups.

I had expected some resistance, but what I got was total anarchy. They silently took their seats according to the chart and the silence persisted after class began. Every single student refused to speak to me. Even the "brownies" shrugged their shoulders in response to my questions. No one would read aloud, no one would dictate a spelling word, no one would even look me in the eye.

My first impulse was to quit, throw up my hands, turn in my chalk, and take a walk. Not a financially feasible idea, but I couldn't think of a single thing to do, so I did nothing. I sat down in one of the empty desks and crossed my arms. As I glanced around at the stubborn faces of my students, I realized that my face bore the same expression that theirs did—my lower lip protruded in a childish pout. Most of them sat with their arms crossed, exactly as I was sitting.

"Okay." I said. "Have it your way. We'll just sit here and enjoy the silence. You can read your books or work on your worksheets. Do whatever you want to. But if you talk, you're out of here. If you don't want to talk to me, fine. Don't talk. I'm not talking to you either. Why should I waste my breath? You guys don't want a teacher. But if you decide you want me to teach this class, just let me know. I'll be right here."

We sat in near-total silence for forty-five minutes, until the bell rang at the end of the first hour. They wrote notes, slept, painted their fingernails, read comic books. I ignored them, except when someone whispered. Then I'd move to the kid's desk and stare him down. Most of the time, I simply sat at my desk, thinking of all the different jobs I could apply for after school.

Our standoff continued into the second hour, with no sign of concession on either side. Finally, the kids realized that I wasn't going to play school without them. Troy Jones broke the silence by slamming his book shut.

"Okay," Troy said. "You can be the teacher now."

"Are the other boys and girls going to play, too?" I asked.

Plenty of sighs, a few nods, a couple of kids muttered "Yeah."

"Come on," urged Troy. "This is too boring." The rest of the kids either nodded or shrugged their status.

"All right!" I said brightly as I stood up and strode to the front of the room. "I have a great idea. Let's work in small groups on our worksheets. Three brains are better and faster than one." Resigned, the kids moved listlessly into the groups I assigned.

I was a little nervous about the outcome of our first group exercise because I had put one kid from each ethnic background into each group, although I tried to temper the shock by separating the sexes. I figured the groups would be more apt to connect if they were all male or all female. I was half right. The boys quickly arranged their desks to designate their new territories and began punching each other's shoulders, stealing pencils from members of other groups, and taking advantage of the hiatus, but the girls clamped their mouths shut and sat stiffly facing their partners, waiting for instructions.

Troy Jones was in the "leader group," which consisted of the strongest personality from each ethnic group. The champion speller in the class, a tall, chunky blond boy named Jason, took the seat between Troy and Hugo, a raven-haired Mexican boy with rapid-fire wit who could barely read or write English. When I passed out the assignment, a comprehensive grammar worksheet that required listing the eight parts of speech and identifying them in sentences, all of the groups began talking, relieved to have something impersonal to concentrate on and complain about. Troy and Hugo remained silent, watching Jason expectantly. Hugo handed Jason a pencil and pointed to the paper. Jason glanced at me, but I quickly moved across the room to help another trio.

When I circulated back to Troy's group, Jason was still holding the pencil, frowning at the page. A few words had been scribbled, but most of the exercises remained undone. The back of his shirt was sprinkled with damp spots of perspiration. Hugo and Troy sat, arms crossed, leaning back in their chairs, their legs extended and crossed at the ankles.

"How are you guys doing?" I asked, although I could clearly see that Jason was stalled. He could spell anything, but he wouldn't know an adverb if it hit him forcefully in the face. I took the paper from Jason's hand and looked it over.

"He needs a little help here, Troy," I said, pointing to a sentence where Jason had identified *she* as a verb. Troy knew most of the parts of speech, although he often confused pronouns and prepositions. Hugo knew them all cold, but he couldn't spell any of them.

"What part of speech is 'she'? " I asked Troy.

He shrugged. "I don't know."

"Yes, you do," I argued. "What is it?"

"Let the whiz kid do it. He knows," Troy said, indicating Jason.

I shook my head. "He doesn't know, do you?" I asked Jason.

Blushing, Jason mumbled, "No."

Hugo grinned. "He knows, he's just playing with you, man. He's the smartest kid in this class."

"What makes you think that?" I asked.

"He gets a hundred on all the spelling tests, don't he?" Hugo asked.

"Yes, he does," I admitted. "But he doesn't know the parts of speech."

"No," Hugo insisted.

"Yes," Jason and I said, in unison. Hugo pulled his head back and squinted at Jason from the corner of one eye.

"For real?" Hugo asked Jason. Jason nodded.

"What part of speech is *she?*" I asked the group again.

"Pronoun," said Troy. "Or preposition. One of those two."

"Pronoun," Hugo said. "Write that down, Jason." He tapped his finger against the paper. "Right here. *Aquí.*"

Troy looked at Hugo in surprise, then glanced at me.

"Is he right?" Troy asked, nodding his head in Hugo's direction.

"Yes, he is," I said. "You guys could ace this paper if you wanted to."

"Yeah," said Troy, "if we wanted to. But who says we want to."

Hugo leaned forward and whispered conspiratorially. "Get her, man. She's trying to use child psychology on us. Like if she says we can't do it, we'll do it just to show her."

"I never said you couldn't do it, Hugo," I said.

"Well, I can read between the lines, *Señorita* Teacher," Hugo said, laying on a thick Mexican accent.

I didn't stick around to argue with him. I didn't care whether they even finished the assignment. All three of them had learned that their preconceptions were wrong. Until that morning, Hugo thought all the Caucasian kids were smarter than he was, Troy thought spelling signaled intelligence, and Jason thought Hispanic kids who couldn't read English were automatically dumb.

I had my own misconceptions, which were corrected during Session I of summer school. When I walked into class on the first day, I believed I could reach kids who were experts at building walls between their feelings and their environment. On the last day of the first session, the classroom was completely empty an instant after the final bell rang. Not one student stopped to say good-bye. They were gone, with only scattered debris as evidence that they had existed—a few crumpled candy wrappers, a couple of broken pencils, and a blob of dried gum on the windowsill. But I had no time to brood. The next day, their desks were filled with forty different faces and the dance began again. New partners, same old song.

Second session was a little easier because I didn't expect the kids to be disarmed by my sincerity and natural charm. Also, I designed a seating chart during the first hour of class that effectively broke up their groups before they had a chance to consolidate. I switched my approach from defensive to offensive and they responded. They were used to tough teachers and they expected tough teachers. They didn't want me to be nice. They didn't want to learn a whole new set of responses just for a month.

Troy Jones, complete with thunderbolts and earrings, was enrolled for another session in my class, since he had failed an entire year of English. When I saw his name on my roll sheets, I was a little apprehensive, but he quietly took his seat each morning and turned in most of his work on time without comment. Apparently, my threat to punch him in the pants had made an impression. From time to time, I considered confessing to him that I had spoken in anger, without thinking, and that I would never hit him. But on second thought, I decided to let it go. If it improved his behavior and classwork, I wasn't above a large lie now and then.

For the first three weeks of second session, I read every single piece of literature out loud myself. None of the kids would volunteer to read out loud. A few kids would grudgingly agree to read upon request, but not a single student ever offered to read. On the next-to-last day of school, however, courage descended on the classroom. It might have been excitement from the field trip we took to the public library during the first hour. Or perhaps it was anticipation of the upcoming week of freedom before the regular fall session began. Whatever it was, it was powerfully present. Seven students volunteered to read aloud during the last hour of class. Or rather, they demanded the opportunity to read.

Loudest among the voices calling for a chance to read was a stocky varsity football player from Parkmont who had limited intellectual ability but an unlimited desire to learn. Each day, Hakim came to class with his notebook and freshly sharpened pencil, eager to earn the credit he needed to remain on the varsity team.

"Good morning, Miss Johnson!" he would proclaim each morning with a grin that revealed a space between his two front teeth. He attacked each exercise as though it were a defensive lineman on an opposing team, yet he never offered to read aloud or answer questions during oral grammar drills. On the day before the final exam, however, he suddenly decided he was going to read. Unfortunately, he was only one of several students who made a last-minute pitch for the spotlight. Troy's hand was raised and, to my amazement, so were hands of many nonreaders. I was thrilled and half afraid the other kids would lose their nerve while waiting. When Hakim saw the other hands raised in response to my request for a volunteer, he became incensed.

"I want to read!" he shouted.

"You may read first, Hakim," I said. "Then we'll let someone else have a turn." He began immediately, reading in spastic spurts, stopping frequently to re-pronounce an unfamiliar word or repeat a troublesome phrase. After about five minutes, I said, "Thank you, Hakim. Miguel, do you want to read next?"

Hakim pounded his fist on his desk. "I'm reading!"

"Yes, I know," I said, gently. "But you had your turn, now it's only fair to let the others read."

"I want to *read!*" Hakim shouted. I quickly stepped near to his desk.

"There is no need to shout," I said. "I can hear you. And I told you that it's time to give someone else a turn." As I turned away from his desk, Hakim jumped to his feet, overturning the desk.

"I said I want to read," he yelled, "and I'm read-ing."

"Sit down," I said calmly, "before you get yourself in trouble." I turned to face the class. "Miguel, would you begin reading where Hakim left off?"

Miguel, a slight, shy boy, shook his head. "That's okay," he said. His face was unusually pale, his eyes on Hakim. "Somebody else can read." Nobody else, how-ever, wanted to take the chance of offending Hakim. All the hands that had been waving, including Troy's, were stuffed into pockets or hidden beneath the desks.

"What happened to all my readers?" I asked, which infuriated Hakim even more. He waved his arms and raced to the center of the room where he overturned two empty desks. The students quickly moved their desks toward the back and sides of the room, away from Hakim. Since he had been in my class the previ-ous year and I knew him to be a genuinely nice young man, I wasn't frightened. I assumed that he simply had lost control of his emotions for a moment and would soon regain his composure. Unfortunately, he didn't regain control and I made the mistake of moving toward him, with my hand outstretched. As I approached, Hakim drew back his fist. He was wearing a tight T-shirt with the arms cut-off and each muscle in his brawny arm was clearly defined, the veins bulging as though he had recently completed a strenuous workout. Instinct took over.

"Go ahead and hit me," I snarled, "but make it good, because you're only going to get one hit. Then I'm going to kill you." The merciless cold of my voice made the back of my own neck prickle. It was my father's voice and my father's words, spoken so often to my teenage brothers as they strutted their stuff and challenged their old man's authority. I glared at Hakim with my father's eyes, which turned black with anger and flashed fire.

Hakim froze. I walked quickly to the phone and called the office.

"Send a large security guard to room C-nine," I said, forcing my voice to its normal pitch. "Hakim Dahraman wants to visit the principal's office." When I hung up, Hakim dropped his fist, but remained standing in the center of the room.

"I don't care who they send," he said, without conviction. "I'll knock them down."

A few minutes later, a small woman wearing security blue stepped into the doorway. She nodded to Hakim who followed her meekly out the door. As soon as Hakim was out of sight, the boys came alive, hooting and hollering.

"You was scared, wasn't you, Miss Johnson?" one of the boys asked. "I seen you shaking."

"Yes, I was scared, all right," I said. The boy, and several of his friends, grinned and giggled until I added,

"I was scared I was gonna kill that boy with my bare hands." Any inklings of further mutiny died a sudden death. Obviously, they didn't know if I was kidding. I didn't know, myself.

After school, when I stopped at the main office to check my staff mailbox, Hakim rushed up to me in the hallway. Surprised to see him on campus after our confrontation, I stopped dead. Once again, those horror stories of students with machine guns sprang to mind. I eyed Hakim warily and tried to put as much distance between us as I could.

"Miss Johnson, please let me talk to you," he pleaded.

"I'm so mad at you I could spit," I said as I pulled open the door and moved into the sanctuary of the administration building. "I don't want to talk to you."

"Please, Miss Johnson," he said, his voice breaking into near sobs. "I need to talk to you." We were standing inside the main office, a few feet down the hall from Mr. Grady's office, so I figured it was safe. I pointed to a bench along the wall. "Sit," I said.

Hakim sat down, his hands folded, gripping each other tightly between his legs. He hung his head and spoke into his chest.

"I'm sorry. I don't know why I drew up on you like that."

"I don't know, either," I said. "That was a terrible thing to do. I've always been nice to you, haven't I?"

He nodded his head. "I'm sorry," he repeated. "Will you let me come back to class and take my final tomorrow?"

"Didn't the principal expel you?" I asked. "They don't give any second chances in summer school. If you break the rules, you're out."

"Mr. Grady said if you said it was okay, he'd give me

a break," Hakim said, his eyes brimming with real tears. "Please."

"What would you do if you were me, Hakim? I'd like to know that," I said. "What would you do if a student threatened to hit you?"

He sat bolt upright, incensed. "I wouldn't let nobody act like that in my class," he answered, quickly and honestly.

"Then why did you act that way in my class?" I asked. Looking sheepish, he shook his head, but didn't answer for a moment.

"All them other kids act out in class and I never do," he said, after a long pause. "I just took my turn."

"But those other kids don't play football, Hakim. They don't have a future. They don't have anything to lose. You do. You have to think about you and what you want and the heck with the other kids. Don't let losers bring you down. You're a winner."

"That's a fact," Hakim said, breaking into a broad smile. "I am a winner. So can I stay?"

"I'm going to have to think about it for a while," I said. "And I want you to think about it, too. I want you to sit right here and think until you come up with an answer. I want to know, honestly, what you would do if you were me."

Hakim crossed his arms and frowned in concentration, visibly thinking. His mouth puckered as he clamped his lips tightly together and his forehead was drawn into a mass of lines. Even his breathing grew harder as he strained to think. It broke my heart.

"You keep thinking," I said softly. "I'll be right back." I stepped down to the principal's office and tapped on the window of his open door. Mr. Grady held up a finger to indicate that he'd be off the phone momentarily.

"What is it?" he asked as he hung up the receiver.

"Hakim," I said. "Why didn't you expel him?"

"I did," Mr. Grady said. "I sent him home."

"He's sitting out in the hall," I said. "Come take a look." We both peeked around the corner at Hakim who sat in the same position, thinking with all his might. "He's thinking of what I should do with him," I explained.

"Jesus," Mr. Grady said with a sigh. "The kid is a great ballplayer. Professional potential. But he won't be playing next season."

"Because of what happened today in my class?" I asked.

"Them's the rules," Mr. Grady said. "I don't make 'em and I don't break 'em, so don't ask me to."

I glanced at his desk. "I don't see a written referral report there from me," I said. I hadn't written one and Grady couldn't expel Hakim without one. Mr. Grady sat back in his chair and clasped his hands behind his head. For a few seconds, he regarded me in silence, then he asked, "Didn't I talk to you a few weeks ago about following the rules?"

"Yes, you did," I said. "And I didn't argue with you. You were right and I was wrong. In that case."

"And in this case?"

"I don't think you were given the correct information. I simply sent Hakim down to talk to you because he became overexcited during our literature lesson. You know how excited some kids get about great literature."

Once again, Mr. Grady sat looking at me in silence, then dropped his hands and picked up a form from the stack of papers in his Out box. He handed me the form.

"Tear this up," he said. "And write me a new one. With the correct information."

"Thanks, Mr. Grady," I said.

"Hakim was here for both sessions," Mr. Grady said. "He's leaving here with ten credits. If he even breathes wrong tomorrow, I'll rescind his credits for both sessions and he'll never play football in this district again. Make sure he understands that. Make sure you understand that, too."

We both understood. Hakim was a model student during the exam and earned a C for the course. I didn't see him for several weeks after the fall term began at Parkmont and when I finally did see him in the hallway, I thought he might choose to ignore me. He didn't. A genuine smile lit up his face and he called to me over the heads of passing students.

"Miss Johnson! Wait up!"

As he approached, I wondered if he would thank me for cutting him some slack during the summer. If so, I was prepared to explain that everyone deserves a chance to make one mistake.

"Yo! Miss Johnson," Hakim said. He grabbed my hand for a four-part handshake. "How come you gave me a C in your class last summer?"

"You earned that C, Hakim," I said. "I didn't *give* it to you."

"No." He shook his head, amazed at my endless capacity for misunderstanding. "You should of gaven me an A."

I should have given Hakim a No Credit, based on his knowledge of grammar and his lack of writing skills, but I couldn't do it. Hakim came to school every day, behaved himself, worked so hard on each assignment that sweat ran down his face and neck. He tried harder than any other kid in class and I had to give him credit for it. None of the students who earned A's worked as hard for them. I was tempted to lower their grades because they didn't care, but that didn't seem fair.

With every passing day, I realized that "fair" and "school" don't often dance the same steps.

When the final bell rang on the final day of second session, I didn't watch the kids rush out. This time, I knew better than to expect anything more than a quick backward glance, maybe a brief wave of the hand. I dumped my textbooks into boxes along with my mimeographed worksheets and short story samples. I was exhausted, and the thought of dragging ten seventy-pound boxes out to my car, driving them to Parkmont, and lugging them into my regular classroom was too much to contemplate. I felt claustrophobic, surrounded by the ghosts of all those closed, hostile faces. Leaving my door standing open, which was against Mr. Grady's rules, I walked down to the staff lounge and bought a can of soda. Every classroom I passed and peered into offered the same scene: a tired teacher packing papers into boxes, collecting broken pencils from the floor, gathering stray books from behind the trash cans and under the radiators.

When I went back to my classroom, I heard a rustle of papers inside. Great, I thought. All I need is a smack on the hand for ignoring security standards. That'll make my summer complete. I braced myself for a lecture and walked into the room, expecting to find Mr. Grady or one of the senior staff members. To my surprise, Troy Jones stood behind my desk, holding some papers in his hand. Relieved to find only a student in my room, I smiled broadly.

"Troy! Can't get enough school, huh?"

"Hullo, Miss Johnson," he said.

"You still remember my name," I said. "Good."

Troy frowned at me, unsure of the proper response to such unaccustomed cheer on my part.

"Are you taking those papers or leaving them?" I

indicated the papers he still clutched in his hand. He looked down at the papers and drew in his breath.

"I didn't turn in my last essay," he said. "The one we were supposed to write after we read *Catcher in the Rye*."

"Yes, I know," I said.

"Well, I wrote it. I just didn't give it to you because—I don't know. I just didn't. But here it is." He placed the papers in the middle of my desk and immediately reached for them, as though to pick them up again.

"Fine," I said, moving quickly to his side and scooping up the papers before he had a chance to change his mind.

"Thanks very much. I'll include this in your final grade."

"Okay," Troy said, nodding. "That's good. Well, I'll be going now. See you."

"Why don't you sit down and talk for a while." I waved my arm. "There's plenty of room."

"That's okay," Troy said, shuffling sideways toward the door. "I got some, uh, friends waiting for me." His Nike high tops squealed down the hallway as he made his escape. I picked up his essay, glad to have an excuse to postpone my packing. The assignment had been for the kids to write at least a page, telling me whatever was on their minds.

Let's Talk by Yours Truly

Obviously, I'm in summer school right now. I'm pretty smart, you know. I'm not an erudite scholar or anything but I am pretty smart. I may not have as much knowledge as top students, but I have intelligence. If you have knowledge and no intelligence at all, then you're nothing but a damn computer. For example? O.K. I'll give you an example.

You pretend you're a professor who teaches Biology II at Stanford University or something. You know everything there is to know about biology, but you don't know anything about mechanics. You're driving home when all of a sudden your front right tire blows out. You try to figure out how to replace it with the spare tire in the trunk, but you can't figure it out. You don't know which tool is for what and how to get the car up, all that crap. You don't have enough intelligence or enough common sense to replace a flat tire. Knowledge counts but common sense matters.

Hopefully you understand what I just wrote in the paragraph. I elucidated it as much as possible. Elucidated? Can you believe I actually used one of the vocabulary words? Ha! Ha! Ha! In the past I cunningly eluded various vocabulary words I couldn't use sensibly. My vocabulary no longer consists of diminutive words. I'm not saying that I go around boastfully demoralizing people with words they've never heard of in their life. All I'm doing is expanding my vocabulary and learning the most I can. But if somebody inadvertently (accidentally) puts me down then that somebody better close his or her ears and run outside 'cause I can kill with words (not vulgar words) that seize your morale. I'm just kidding. Ha! Ha! Ha! I wouldn't do it on purpose. I'm too much of a nice guy, at heart, you know, Miss Johnson, even though I don't show it. I know I don't dress like a nice guy but I like to be different. I like being myself, not what others want me to be.

Now I have come to the end of my little essay. It's not really an essay. I'd say it's more of a dialogue. You know what I mean, right? I've been

95

talking to you all this time and I still am. The only weird thing is you never said a word. Ha! Ha! Ha! Off the record and excusing my language, I think you're a pretty damn good teacher, really. I think you understand the students and me more than any other teacher I know. You're not one of those teachers that just throw us some assignment due the next day. You make classwork more interesting, fun, and just out of the ordinary. You may get pissed off sometimes but that's understandable. Some students need to be disciplined. I think that writing essays is good for improving one's writing. My style in writing hasn't always been this way. After reading *Catcher in the Rye*, I tried to express my thoughts in writing as the author did. I not only learned from the author's style in writing, but a few lessons from you who taught me quite a bit. I'm not saying this because I want an A on this essay, but to express my feelings. Just as you did when you wrote letters home to our parents and said nice things about us to raise our self-esteem (bet you didn't know anybody figured that out, huh?). That's just one of those little things some teachers don't think of doing. You're the best teacher I've had as far as teachers go.—
Troy Jones

P.S. If you want to comment on how good my essay is, then just come over and tell me at my desk. Just kidding. You'll embarrass the hell out of me. Write your comments on the back of this paper and return it to me for a grade. Ha! Ha!

I saved that essay. It's hanging on the wall over my desk at home to remind me not to judge my students by the thunderbolts in their hair.

EIGHT

If Your Only Tool Is a Hammer

"Another day. Another miracle. Amazing, isn't it?"

I looked up from the papers I was grading to see Hal Gray peeking around the doorjamb. "What's amazing?"

"Every day, I walk into a room where twenty-five or thirty teenagers are being held captive and I say, 'Okay, let's open our books to page sixty-seven.' And they all open their books. There isn't any reason for them to do it. And if they decided not to play, the entire game of education would screech to a halt. Don't you think that's amazing?"

"Yes, I do," I agreed. "And I think this is amazing, too. I can't figure it out." I held out an essay written by Danny Morton, a student in my English-P class. Danny was one of the brightest students in class, but his work was sporadic. For several consecutive days, he would hand in perfect papers on his classroom assignments and quizzes. Then, for no apparent reason, he'd turn in a worksheet or an exam with all the answers wrong.

Danny's seat was in the far corner of the classroom, where he played incessantly with a shredded rubber ball that looked like a handful of red rubber hair. He tossed it back and forth from one hand to the other whenever he wasn't working on an assignment. The first time he brought the ball to class, I took it away from him, but gave it back at the end of the class because I had to ask him every few minutes to stop drumming his fingertips on his desktop. Each time I pointed out that he was drumming, Danny would look down at his hands, genuinely surprised to discover that they were, indeed, rhythmically tapping the top of his desk. He would blush and stammer an apology and fold his hands in his lap. Within two minutes, his fingers would escape and a paradiddle would interrupt my remarks to the class. So, I agreed to allow Danny to sit in the back of the room and juggle the ball as long as he agreed not to disrupt other students and to complete all his assignments.

Hal took the paper I held out to him, Danny Morton's descriptive essay. The first paragraph was written in large, bold letters that slanted to the right. In the middle of the second paragraph, the writing suddenly switched to a small, cramped leftward slant. Several words were crossed out and rewritten. The crossed-out words were scribbled over with heavy strokes, creating big dark blotches on the page. Halfway through one sentence, Danny had stopped writing and drawn a picture of some unidentified object, followed by the rest of the sentence. The third paragraph was printed in block letters and contained a few more crossouts. Toward the end of the page, the writing returned to script style, but grew lighter and lighter, fading into a feathery sketch of a face. The content of the essay was quite good, evidence of a complex thought process, but the grammar and spelling were horrible.

"What do you make of this?" I asked Hal.

"Drugs," he said, his tone very matter-of-fact, as he handed the paper back to me.

"Drugs?" I echoed. The thought had never occurred to me, but as soon as Hal suggested it, I had to admit the probability. It would explain the hyperactivity, the erratic performance, the grotesque drawings sprinkled throughout the essay. But I didn't want to leap to a false conclusion.

"But he's such a nice kid," I protested. "Maybe he's just hyperactive or has a wild imagination. Maybe he's a creative genius."

"Maybe he takes drugs," Hal said. "Lots of nice kids take drugs."

"I don't suppose you have any advice about how to handle this, do you?" I asked. Hal shook his head.

"If the kid likes you, he might talk to you," he said. "But don't get your hopes up."

I got my hopes up, but Danny didn't come to school the next day, or the day after that. I called his home and his father assured me that Danny was in school; he drove him to the main entrance on his way to work each morning. The attendance office concurred—Danny Morton wasn't absent. But I couldn't find him. I decided to check with the guidance office and find out who Danny's other teachers were. Maybe one of them would know where he was. As I passed the detention center, euphemistically called the Adjustment Center, I saw Danny slumped in the back row, his long legs sticking out from under a too-small desk. He wore a black sweatshirt from which the sleeves had been torn off, leaving ragged shreds of cloth dangling over his shoulders. Hand-drawn ink tattoos covered both of his forearms, strange, malevolent-looking creatures with wild eyes and jagged teeth. Both of Danny's hands were clenched into fists and stuffed into the pockets of his jeans. A book lay open on the desk in front of him, but I couldn't tell whether he was reading or not. His shiny black hair effectively hid his eyes. Before I knew it, I was in the classroom, asking the teacher, a gruff old-timer, if I could speak to Danny for a minute. The teacher snorted.

"Go ahead," he said. "But I don't know why you waste your time on him. He's worthless." I opened my mouth to protest, but he interrupted me. "Just kidding. Right, kid?" He tapped a wooden ruler on Danny's desk, but Danny didn't respond.

"I don't think Danny's worthless," I said, loud enough for Danny and anyone else who might be listening to hear. "I think he's a very bright young man and a good student. But he has too much energy sometimes. Makes it hard for him to sit still and focus on school." I walked over to Danny's desk and placed my hand on his arm. He still didn't look up at me, but I felt him tremble slightly, and he didn't pull his arm away. I squatted down and peered up at him, searching for his eyes under the hair.

"Hi! Remember me?" I said. "Your favorite English teacher. You used to be in my class way back when we were both young."

Danny glanced at me just long enough for me to catch a glimpse of his black eyes, then quickly dropped his gaze. The teacher, who had followed me to Danny's side, said, "He's a short-timer. Won't be with us long, will you, kid?" He snapped the ruler against the side of Danny's desk.

"How can you say such a thing to a child?" I asked.

"I'm only kidding," the man said. He had the grace to blush. "Can't you take a joke? These kids know I'm joking."

In his defense, I have to say that I knew the teacher

believed in a concept called "tough love," but he put so much emphasis on the "tough" that the "love" was unrecognizable. I decided to concentrate on helping Danny instead of arguing with the teacher about his attitude. I figured the odds were about the same of reaching either one, but Danny was my responsibility.

"I just thought if I gave him a personal invitation, Danny might like to come to my English class today. What do you say, Danny?" I kept my hand on Danny's arm until he looked at me. He didn't speak. He nodded and I saw a smile playing at the corners of his mouth, but he wasn't about to give it up that easily.

"Can't do it!" the teacher said, shaking his head.

"What do you mean, he can't do it?" I asked. "Of course he can go to class."

"Nope," the teacher said. "He's in detention for three full days, all day long."

"What for?" I demanded.

"Farting around in Crocker's class," the teacher said. "Crocker doesn't take any crap."

"But he doesn't have the right to take a student out of my class!" I said firmly, although I had no idea whether he could or not. But I doubted whether Mr. Crocker would check to make sure that Danny was in detention all day. "I want him in B-eleven third period." I looked at Danny. "Okay, Danny?" He nodded.

"Great!" I said, extending my hand. "I'll see you later." Danny looked at my hand for a few seconds before taking it in his own and shaking it.

Third period, Danny walked quietly into the classroom a few minutes early and took his seat. Quickly, I sat down beside him before the other students arrived.

"I'm glad you're here," I said. "You might as well come to my class. It's a lot better than detention. I promise not to humiliate you and I won't embarrass you. I won't ask you to do anything you can't do, but I will ask you to think once in a while. It won't hurt you. Okay?'' He nodded his head and opened his notebook, obviously uncomfortable with so much personal attention in one day.

During the following weeks, Danny came to class and participated in oral exercises, but managed to avoid most of the written assignments. Those he did hand in were messy and poorly done, in spite of his quick and correct answers during classroom drills. The content of his essays was consistently excellent, but the grammar was awful. He was an advanced thinker caught in the body of a remedial student. I considered giving him extra work to do outside of class but I didn't want to push him for fear that he would disappear again.

I asked Hal Gray and some of the other teachers for advice, but none of their suggestions worked with Danny. His attendance remained good but his work was still very uneven. When I finally did reach him, it was purely by accident. We were working on individual projects. The students had the option of writing a three-page research report or delivering a three-minute oral presentation on a topic of their choice. Since I try to model each assignment for the students, to give them a feel for what I expect, I brought in my two parakeets, Sweetheart and Violet, for a sample oral presentation.

Sweetheart is a brilliant turquoise blue male parakeet with the ego of an eagle and a versatile repertoire of whistles and trills. When his cage door is opened, Sweetheart loves to rush out, circle the room with a flutter, and return to perch on top of the cage, exhilarated by his venture into the unknown. He is quite friendly and will hop onto an extended finger for a brief visit.

Violet's coloring and personality, on the other hand, are both pastel. She is content to stay in the cage, quietly eating birdseed. She rarely sings and never leaves the cage, even when the door is wide open. The sight of a human finger in her vicinity sends her into a frenzy of squawking and wing beating.

As I was speaking to the English-P class, I realized that this class, my "regular" students, and my other class, the "accelerated" students, were very much like my two parakeets: one class was outgoing and interested in the world while the other clung to their patterns of behavior and resisted all attempts on my part to connect with them.

"Look at these two birds," I said to my English-P students. "This one is just like you. Watch." I put my hand in the cage and tried to catch Violet. She squawked and screeched and flapped her wings and raced around the cage to avoid my finger.

"That's how you guys act when I introduce a new novel or a new vocabulary list. You squeak and squawk and flap your arms and protest, 'We can't do that! Yuck! We hate it! It's boring! It's too hard!' and I spend the entire period chasing you around the room, trying to get you to look at the assignment."

I put my hand back in the cage, this time next to Sweetheart. He immediately hopped onto my finger with a happy chirp. I brought him out of the cage and he flew into the air and circled the room twice before returning to his cage. He pranced around the top twice, chirping loudly. Then he scrambled inside, hopped to the highest perch, and gave his reflection in the mirror an admiring peck as he did a little song and dance. For good measure, he rang his bell twice.

"That's what happens in my other class," I explained. "I bring in a new assignment and I show it to them. They look at it. They say, 'That looks hard, but we can probably do it.' And then we fly."

I swear I saw the proverbial light bulb go on over Danny's head. Eyes wide open, he nodded to himself, a secret smile on his lips. The next day, he waited, fidgeting with his pencil, until the class had gone, then said, "I can't do that grammar stuff."

"Yes, I know," I nodded. "Your grammar stinks. But your writing is excellent and your vocabulary scores are the highest in the class. You have poor grammar skills, but you can fix them."

"How?" he asked. I handed him a grammar textbook and pointed out the chapters he needed to study. He asked if he could take it home and work on it in his spare time. Students ask the dumbest questions sometimes!

I would have been satisfied with Danny's good attendance, better grades, and improved attitude, but he went beyond my greatest expectations. A few weeks after he started working on his independent grammar studies, he stopped by my room after sixth period and asked if he could come in during seventh period (the accelerated class) to observe. We were reading the same book, *Of Mice and Men*, and he wanted to see the ACL students "fly." I agreed that he could observe as long as he promised not to disrupt the class. He gave me his word and moved to the back of the room to wait for the students to arrive.

Unlike the P class, where students flatly refused to read aloud and I had to drag them through each chapter, the ACL students squabbled over who would read first. They were generally quiet and polite during the reading and stopped occasionally to discuss a plot point or to comment upon a character's actions.

Danny was mesmerized. During the reading, I

passed by his desk and leaned down to whisper, "This is what English class is supposed to be. And this is where you belong." He shook his head, his eyes wide.

"I'm too dumb," he whispered softly.

"No, you aren't," I argued. "You think about it."

Danny continued to come to the seventh period class every day, in addition to his regular third period class. In both classes, he completed each assignment—and earned A's in both classes. I asked him whether he wanted to switch to the ACL class to have the grade on his record. He said he was afraid that if he switched, he'd get nervous and do poorly on his work.

I asked the sophomore student dean, Phil Horner, for permission to allow Danny to take both classes and earn extra credit. When I mentioned Danny's name, Dr. Horner insisted that I must have the wrong name. Danny Morton was not an ACL student, he was a cutter, a punk rocker, a problem, and a loser. He pulled up Danny's record on the computer and showed me his dismal attendance record.

"Morton cuts more classes than he attends," Dr. Horner said. "He's scheduled for six periods and he only goes to two of them. This can't be the same kid you're talking about."

"I'm not mistaken," I insisted. "Please give him a chance."

"He's already had more chances than I can count," Dr. Horner said.

"Then one more chance won't hurt, will it?" I insisted. "What have you got to lose?"

"To be honest, I just don't want you to be disappointed," Dr. Horner said. "I appreciate your enthusiasm and idealism, but I don't want you to burn out your first semester."

"I promise not to burn out if you approve the credits

for the work Danny's doing," I said. Dr. Horner sighed.

"Now I see why your kids do their homework," he said. "You don't give up, do you?" He signed the authorization and handed it back to me. "Get Mr. Parker's autograph on this as English department chair, you're in business. Good luck."

Danny didn't disappoint me. He earned A's in both English courses and, in the meantime, began attending his other classes. At the end of the school year, Danny shook my hand and walked out of my life. I did see him again, two years later, but I barely recognized him. His hair was cut, his clothes were clean. He looked calm and happy. I was a wreck. It was Thanksgiving vacation and I was in the midst of my third flu attack since September. I had polished off two boxes of Kleenex, three rolls of toilet tissue, and a quart of Nyquil before I felt well enough to attend the district championship football game. Eight Academy students were on the team and I had promised to cheer them on. My sore throat provided the perfect excuse for silently viewing the game, since I couldn't have cheered if I had tried. I was too exhausted, emotionally and physically, to do anything more strenuous than sit in the bleachers and soak up the sun, standing every now and then to clap and smile.

At halftime, several of my students spotted me as they paraded past the bleachers in search of romance or trouble. Four girls screeched, "Miss Johnson!" and rushed over to hug me repeatedly, pausing between hugs to fluff up their hair and scan the stands for admiring glances. They huddled around me until the players returned for the second half, then wiggled back to their seats in the "cool" section directly behind the cheerleaders. A few minutes after they left, someone came up behind me and covered my eyes. I had no idea who it was, but assumed it was one of the girls.

"Guess who?" said a male voice. It sounded vaguely familiar, but I couldn't place it immediately.

"No, I won't marry you, so stop begging," I said.

"You're a trip," Danny Morton said as he dropped onto the bleacher bench beside me. "How have you been?"

"Danny! I had no idea you had such a handsome face hiding behind all that hair," I said.

"I know," Danny said, puffing out his chest. "And how about these clothes, huh? I ditched all those T-shirts with the skulls and skeletons on them. My mom almost had a heart attack."

"I bet she did," I said. "You really do look wonderful." He did. His eyes were bright and shining, his complexion had color. He looked so different from the grimy, shaggy kid who had sat in the back of my classroom, drumming his desktop and tossing his rubber ball compulsively from hand to hand.

"How are you doing in school?"

"Great!" Danny said. "I'm going to graduate with my class. I'm even going to college. I'm not sure what I want to be, but they have a good music program at Hillside Junior College." He watched the game for a few seconds, then turned back to me. "So, how about you? You don't look like you feel too good."

"I'm a little tired," I admitted.

"Tired like sleepy or tired the other kind?" He always was a perceptive kid.

"Tired like the other kind," I said. He seemed genuinely interested, so I told him about some of the problems I'd recently faced. "I don't know how much longer I can put up with the bureaucratic system. I love

107

the kids, but I can't stand to see so many of them get lost in the shuffle."

"You can't quit," Danny said, his face suddenly serious. He wrapped his fingers around my forearm and squeezed. "You were the only teacher I ever had who really cared about me. If it hadn't been for you, I'd still be taking drugs and messing up my life, and I bet there are a lot more kids like me that you helped. Please don't give up on us." Having said his piece, he concentrated on watching the game until the last quarter. He stood up and tucked in his shirttail.

"I have to go meet my girlfriend," he said with a proud grin. "She's really nice. You'd like her." He clomped down the bleachers and stopped at the bottom step to look up at me.

"Remember those quotations you have hanging on the wall all over your room, Miss Johnson?" he hollered. I nodded. "I read them all at least a hundred times," he said. "My favorite one says—If your only tool is a hammer, you tend to see every problem as a nail. Maybe you should try a screwdriver this year. Whaddya say, Miss J.?" He winked, gave me a thumbs-up, and swaggered across the cinder track toward the parking lot.

That's the trouble with kids. You teach them something and they turn around and use it on you.

NINE

You Ain't No Real Teacher

Long before I met him, I knew his name. When someone said "Attiba Mack" in the staff room one day, every single teacher in the room stopped talking and traded grim, pained looks.

"Who's Attiba Mack?" I asked Hal Gray.

"Big trouble in a small package," Hal said. "Lucky for you, he's a sophomore and it's almost June, so you won't have him this year. And if you teach sophomores against next year, you're safe."

"If he's that bad, won't he flunk?" I asked.

"No." Hal shook his head. "Nobody ever flunks him because nobody wants him back again for another year. He's been through every freshman and sophomore English teacher on this staff, except for you." I mentally totaled the English department staff.

"That's eleven teachers!" I said. "How could a sophomore have had eleven teachers in less than two years?"

"It isn't easy," Hal said, "but, then, Attiba apparently enjoys a challenge."

Shortly after our conversation, Mr. Parker, the English department chair, called in sick on a Tuesday morning. The substitute teacher assigned to Mr. Parker's room ran screaming to the office because a group of students had moved to the back of the room and burned their textbooks right in front of her face. Naturally, the book burning was the hot topic of conversation in the English department staff room.

"That woman has no business teaching school," someone grumbled.

"Let's call the district and protest," Charlie Myers suggested. "I don't want her taking over my classroom." Everyone had something to say, none of it nice, and they all started talking at once. Then Mr. Parker said, "Attiba Mack's in that class," and conversation ceased. In the silence that followed, the room itself seemed to hold its breath. After a few seconds there was a collective sigh of despair. Several teachers shook their heads and a couple left the room. I nudged Hal Gray.

"If this Attiba Mack kid is so bad, why don't they kick him out of school?"

"They would if they could ever catch him doing anything."

"If he burned a book, somebody had to see him."

"I'm sure somebody did," Hal said, "but nobody's going to accuse him. He has a lot of friends, very large friends, in this school. He's quick, too. When a group of kids gets busted and Attiba's in the group, he always points the finger at somebody else, but nobody ever points at him. That book burning, for example. He might have held the book, but you can bet that somebody else struck the match. He's a sharp little critter."

"He can't be that smart," I insisted.

"He just might be," Hal said, "although you'd never guess it from his grades. Straight D-minus average. One of the teachers tried to get him tested for special ed classes last year and he went berserk. His father came to school and he went berserk, too, so they dropped the whole idea. It's hard to describe what it's like trying to teach with Attiba in the classroom, but I can tell you that he's personally responsible for the early retirement of at least three teachers from this school."

"He must be quite a kid," I said. "I'm almost sorry I didn't get the chance to meet him." Hall rapped his knuckles softly on top of my head.

"Better knock on wood," he said.

Hal didn't knock hard enough. A few weeks later, Mr. Parker had to attend an English conference and the principal assigned staff members to substitute because so many of them had complained about Mr. Parker's last sub. I was assigned to first period and my heart sank when I saw Attiba Mack's name on the roll sheet. Hal had told me Attiba was a little package of trouble, but his reputation was so grand that I expected a much larger person than the five-foot, ninety-pound boy who responded with a thin "yo" to his name during roll call. And he was so quiet during the first ten minutes that I thought he must have arranged for someone else to sit in the class and pretend to be him.

Mr. Parker's lesson plan called for students to work in groups of three to complete a five-page worksheet covering the parts of speech, definitions of Greek and Roman roots and prefixes, rules of capitalization, and a series of short essay questions on literary techniques such as foreshadowing and symbolism. The students had one class period to complete the worksheets. When I told the kids we were going to work in groups, they cheered and clapped, except for Attiba. He crossed his arms, closed his eyes and removed himself from the planet. The other students took their places as designated, arranging their desks around Attiba's, which was smack in the center of the room. After I explained the exercise and the other kids were working, I quietly approached Attiba's desk.

"Excuse me, Attiba," I said. "You need to join your group." He didn't respond. I reached out and touched him lightly on the forearm with my index finger. In a flash, Attiba was on his feet, screeching at the top of his lungs.

"Don't you touch me!" he yelled. "You ain't allowed to touch me. I know my rights. You keep your hands off me." Surprised, I backed up a couple of steps and held my hands in the air.

"All right," I said. "I won't touch you. I used to hate it when my teachers touched me, way back when I was young. In fact, I bit my English teacher once. Bit him right in the leg." Attiba glared at me, his eyes narrowed. The other kids whooped and hollered with delight as I continued, hoping to get Attiba on my side.

"Mr. Johnson, that was his name," I said. "Gotta watch out for those Johnson teachers. Anyway, one day, he was telling the class a story and he reached out and pinched my cheek really hard. It hurt and it scared me and I yelled, but he just laughed. All the kids laughed at me, too. I was so mad I wanted to kill him, so when he left the room to get something, I ran up and hid under his desk. When he came back into the room and walked to his desk, I crawled out and barked real loud and bit him on the ankle. He was very angry, but he didn't do anything. And he never touched me again, either."

Everyone laughed except Attiba, who continued to stare at me, stone-faced. I winked at him and put a worksheet on his desk.

"I promise not to touch you, Attiba," I said, "because I wouldn't want you to bite me on the leg, but you need to join your group and complete this review worksheet. It's pretty long and it's practice for the final exam, so it will count quite heavily on your semester grade."

"I ain't working in no group with no morons," Attiba said. He stayed on his feet, but folded his arms across his chest. "I don't do group."

"I don't blame you," I said. "If I were you, I wouldn't do group, either." He stared at me, clearly surprised that I didn't banish him from the room or insist that he participate. I reassigned his two partners to work with other groups, then ignored him to move on and check the other groups. I didn't get far away before Attiba jumped out of his seat and grabbed a girl's pencil.

"That's my pencil!" the girl protested.

"Fuck you," Attiba muttered and returned to his seat and started writing. The girl shrugged and accepted a pencil from the girl next to her. A few minutes later, Attiba kicked a kid on the shin on his way to the pencil sharpener.

"Watch it!" the kid yelled. "I'll kick your ass." He was a big kid and looked as if he could easily do the job.

"Fuck you," Attiba said, not intimidated in the least. He made a point of not looking at me as he sat back down and attacked his worksheet. He gripped his pencil so hard and pressed with so much force that his writing was audible. For about twenty minutes, the classroom was calm, until Attiba's pencil lead broke again.

"Shit!" Attiba yelled. "This pencil sucks." He stomped across the room and threw the pencil out of the open window, then promptly grabbed another boy's pen. This boy was even bigger than the first one. He stood up.

"Gimme that pen," the boy said.

"Fuck you," Attiba said. The boy stood his ground, but it was clear he had no intention of tackling Attiba. I gave the boy one of my pens and motioned for him to sit down. Then I sat down on the edge of the desk next to Attiba's. Since he had pulled out his heavy artillery, I pulled out mine. My grandpa always used to say, "When some son of a gun pulls a twenty-two on you, pull a double-barreled shotgun on him. That'll set him back a step or two."

"Attiba, there will be no fucking in this classroom as long as I am the teacher. And if you fully intend to F all these people, you are going to get one heck of a reputation. Not to mention AIDS. I hope you carry a condominium with you for protection, at least." A few kids chuckled, but most of them were working on their assignment. Undoubtedly, they were used to Attiba's antics and were no longer amused by them. Attiba was definitely not amused by me. He picked up his worksheets and moved to the farthest corner of the room, where he hunkered over his desk and scribbled furiously.

A few minutes before the bell rang, I collected the worksheets. The kids protested that they hadn't had time to finish because of all the interruptions. Attiba was the only one who didn't complain. In fact, he claimed to have finished the assignment, but he had refused to turn in his worksheets so I had no idea whether he had or not.

"I'll tell Mr. Parker you worked hard, but needed more time," I told the students. "You're a good class and I enjoyed working with you today. And, Mr. Mack," I smiled at Attiba, "it has been a distinct pleasure being your teacher. I look forward to the next opportunity to share a learning experience with you."

Attiba raced past my desk and threw his worksheets at me.

"You ain't no real teacher!" he yelled as he ran out the door. Curious, I flipped through his worksheets. They were all complete and, as far as I could see, every answer was correct. Clearly, lack of intelligence was not his problem, but I thought he might benefit from some counseling, so I sent a referral to the nurse's office, suggesting that the school psychologist talk to Attiba. Two days later, my referral was returned with a note saying, "Parent denies request for counseling."

"The kid has a problem," I told the nurse. "Maybe it's his family. Shouldn't we help him?"

"I'd love to," she said, "but if the parents don't want the students tested or counseled, we can't do it."

"How about social agencies?" I asked.

"We can suggest to the student that he make contact, but we can't take action unless there is suspected child abuse or something on that order. And you can't accuse the student or the parents of drug abuse or anything like that unless you have specific evidence, because they can sue the school district if you're wrong."

"So what can we do to help this kid?"

"There's really nothing official you can do at this point," the nurse said. "I'm sorry."

I called two social service agencies located on the East Side, near Attiba's neighborhood, and they said they would follow up, but I don't know whether they did. He was an intriguing kid. I checked his cumulative folder in the guidance office and was surprised to find that, in spite of his above-average scores on all the standardized tests, he had been placed in remedial reading and low-level classes his first year at Parkmont. No wonder the kid was angry. I could only imagine how frustrating it must have been for him to be placed in classes that provided no mental challenge at all and then, when he demonstrated his frustration by acting out during classes, he was unofficially labeled as mentally retarded and treated accordingly.

It took me a few days to catch up with him because he never seemed to be where his class schedule indicated he should be. When he saw me coming down the hallway, he spun on his toes and started in the opposite direction.

"Attiba!" I called. "Please wait a minute." He stopped dead, but didn't turn around. "I'd like to ask you something."

"I didn't do nothing," he said as I neared his side.

"I didn't say you did," I said. "I thought you might like to join the Academy program next year. It's a new program for kids who want to do better in school."

"I ain't dumb."

"I didn't say you were. And this program isn't for dumb kids. It's for kids exactly like you who have good test scores, so we know they're smart, but they don't have good grades. We want to help those kids get back on track."

"Ain't nothing wrong with my grades," Attiba insisted. "I'm passing my classes."

"But you're getting all Ds," I said, "and you don't have enough credits to be a junior next year. But I know you're smart. I know it and you know it, too." I thought if only we could channel his energy and intelligence into something positive he might change. Attiba didn't say anything and I couldn't tell if he was listening, but he was still there, so I kept talking.

"You'd have three or four classes with the same kids every day, and Academy kids stay with the program for three years, so you'll really get to know the other kids and the teachers, and we'll help you decide what kind of career you want. If you want to go to college, we'll help you do everything you need to get there. If you want to work, we'll show you how to write a resumé and how to make a good impression on a job interview. We'll assign you a mentor from a local business to be your professional friend and help you learn about how big companies operate. And, if you're on track at the end of your junior year and have a good record, we'll even get you a real good job working in an office during the summer. It's a great program. Why don't you think about it and let me know.'' For a minute, Attiba stood absolutely still, but I could almost hear the wheels whirring in his head and, from his expression, I knew that a small part of him wanted to trust me. But the big part won the war.

"I don't need no help from nobody," Attiba said. The warning bell rang for the next class and he took off running. He managed to avoid seeing me for the rest of the school year. During the summer, I sent him a written invitation to attend the assembly for Academy applicants, but he didn't respond. It took me a long time to accept the fact that I can't help a child who doesn't want to be helped. I still struggle with that concept every single day that I teach. I understand that some children choose to fail, but I can't help feeling that it's me as a teacher and the school system as a social institution that are, in reality, failing our children and their future.

TEN

Junior Advani

When Hal Gray saw my class rosters for the first Academy class, his eyebrows shot up.

"This is quite a lineup of all-stars," he said. His tone was not encouraging.

"They seemed like good kids at the interviews," I said.

"They may be good kids," Hal said, "but they certainly aren't good students." He tapped his index finger against the page. "I see Junior Advani's on your list."

"He struck me as an extremely intelligent boy," I said.

"Oh, yes, Junior's intelligent," Hal agreed. "But he won't last three years."

"Why not?" I said, immediately defensive. The other three Academy teachers had voted against Junior, but I convinced them to give him a chance. There was something about him that interested me. It didn't take long for my interest to turn to confusion and, finally, to fear.

Larger than anyone else in the class, Junior had coal black hair that would have been beautiful, but he shaved one half of his head to display his four earrings and wore the other side long and intentionally tangled. During class, he often took out a comb and rearranged his long hair into one of a number of untidy, unattractive hairstyles. Once, I asked him to stop combing his hair because the class was reading a story and he was distracting other kids. He threw his comb on the floor, picked up his desk, slammed it into the back of the student's chair in front of him, and slumped down into his seat where he silently sulked for the rest of the class period.

I should have sent Junior to the office, but I felt sorry for him. He was back home for the first time in three years, he had written in his journal, because his parents had sent him away to boarding school when he was ten. Each year for three years, he had lived at a different school, with occasional visits from his parents. An only child, Junior insisted that his parents simply didn't want to bother with him because it interfered with their self-indulgent life-style.

"I know they don't love me," Junior had written,

because if they did, they would have let me come back home when I begged them to. I'll never forgive them for deserting me like that just when I really needed them. What little kid wants to go live at a school and never see his parents? They think they still live in India where the kids have to bow down and kiss the ground or something when their father walks in the room. When I grow up and get married, I'm going to have a lot of kids and be really nice to them and tell them I love them and spend time with them. I won't neglect and reject them like my parents did to me.

I stopped Junior after class and told him I wouldn't tolerate his disruptive behavior again. He had had his chance.

"I'm really sorry, Miss Johnson," Junior said, hanging his head. "I'm really tired today because my father kicked me out of the house real late last night and I didn't have anywhere to go so I slept in the car."

"Don't you have any friends you could call?" I asked. Junior shook his head.

"All of the kids' parents hate me," he said. "Just because I wear Metallica T-shirts and wear my hair like this, they think I'm a Satanist. I'm not that stupid." When he said that, I remembered that one of the other kids had called Junior a devil worshiper during an argument about who was going to sit where. I had dismissed the student's remark as too ridiculous to consider.

"Are you a Satanist?" I asked. Junior puffed out his chest and stood taller, so that he loomed over me. He narrowed his eyes.

"If I was a Satanist, I'd kill you, wouldn't I?" he snarled. I glanced at the door, which was closed. Junior was between me and the door. He saw my glance and started laughing.

"Scared you, didn't I?" he said, his black eyes dancing with genuine amusement. "I was only playing. I do that sometimes when I'm bored. People are so gullible."

Stunned, I dismissed Junior and added his name to the agenda for the Academy staff meeting that afternoon. Two of the other teachers, Jean Warner and Bud Bartkus, had the same impression that I had—Junior was an extremely bright, often likable kid who obviously had emotional problems. Surprisingly, Don Woodford, the Academy math teacher, disagreed.

"That kid is bad news," Don said. "He's a bully and I don't trust him."

"What did he do?" I asked.

"Nothing," Don said. "That's the trouble. If I could catch him doing something, I'd write a referral on him, but I never catch him."

"Then how do you know he's a bully?"

"I've seen him interact with the other kids. They're afraid of him, even the toughest kids. And after you've been teaching for twenty-five years, you have a sense of what's going on, even if you don't always see it happening. He's trouble. I think we should drop him."

"I'll take Don's word on this one," Bud Bartkus said. Bud, our computer applications teacher and Academy director, made all final decisions on disciplinary issues. I asked if we could arrange a parent conference before dropping Junior from our program. Bud objected, but Jean's vote split the staff fifty-fifty, and I volunteered to call Mr. and Mrs. Advani and arrange a meeting for the next day. When they arrived, I could tell by the other teachers' faces that they were as surprised as I was. We knew the Advanis lived in one of the exclusive neighborhoods near the school, so we knew the family wasn't poor. But none of us expected them to arrive in a Jaguar, wearing a small fortune in diamond rings and hand-tailored silk suits.

"Why would somebody who can afford that car send his kid to public high school?" Bud asked.

"Think about it," Don said softly as the Advanis entered the classroom. Mr. Advani was a handsome giant of a man; his wife's beautiful head barely reached his shoulder. She stood slightly behind him during our introductions and let him do the talking for them both.

"We are very pleased that you have taken such an interest in our son," Mr. Advani began. "Many times, the teachers do not have time for personal interaction. That is why we are so pleased that Junior is a part of your fine program." Bud glanced around the room at the rest of us, obviously hoping that someone else would volunteer to speak for the staff. We all became intensely interested in our shoes.

"Personal attention is part of our program," Bud began. "It allows us to identify our students' problems and work with them to correct those problems." Mr. Advani nodded encouragingly. Mrs. Advani smiled. Bud drew a deep breath.

"Mr. and Mrs. Advani," he said, "I'll be completely honest with you. We have been having some serious problems with Junior. Although he is a very bright young man, he is extremely disruptive during class and defiant to his teachers." Mrs. Advani stopped smiling, but Mr. Advani continued to nod.

"Yes," Mr. Advani agreed, "Junior is sometimes defiant. When he acts in an unacceptable manner, I do not allow him to remain in our home. A son who dishonors his family does not have the right to remain in their home. Do you not agree?"

"Excuse me, Mr. Advani," I said. "Forgive me if I seem to be too blunt, but I think we need to be completely honest if we are going to help Junior."

Mr. Advani nodded more deeply. "Please go ahead."

"Junior told me you kicked him out of the house last week and he had to sleep in the car."

"That is correct," Mr. Advani said. "My son did not lie to you. One thing I know, he is not untruthful. But he threatened to harm his mother. I could not allow that in our home."

"He threatened to hit his mother?" I echoed, surprised. Junior had said his father kicked him out of the house because he was watching TV when he was supposed to be doing his homework.

"No, he did not threaten to hit her," Mr. Advani said. Mrs. Advani put her hand on his arm, but he ignored her. "He took a knife from the kitchen and said he would kill her." I wasn't the only one who gasped. Mr. Advani hastened to add, "Of course, he was not serious. He meant only to scare her. But he now understands that he cannot behave in such a manner."

"Oh." One of them was a liar, but I didn't know whether it was the father or the son. Before the meeting, I would have believed Junior. Now that I had met him, I began to lean toward Senior.

"Junior said you sent him away to boarding school when he was ten years old," I said. "He seems to think that you were trying to get rid of him because you don't love him." Mr. Advani stopped nodding.

"That is ridiculous," he said. "Of course we love our son. But even at ten years, he was as large as his mother and he refused to obey her. We sent him away to school where he would have time to think about his good fortune. Now, he understands and he is a good son."

"Why did he switch schools every year?" I asked.

"We thought that perhaps a change of environment would benefit our son, so we enrolled him in a different school each year until he was thirteen years old. At that time, he returned to our family home."

I turned to Bud and shrugged to indicate that I had done my part. For once, I was glad Bud was the supervisor of our program. He looked at Don, then at Jean. Neither of them volunteered to add anything.

"Well," Bud said, "I'm sure you understand that we will do our best to work with Junior. But we cannot retain him in our program if he refuses to cooperate with his teachers. He signed the same contract that all our students sign, agreeing to put forth a sincere effort to succeed.''

"I assure you that Junior will put forth a most sincere effort," Mr. Advani said, with one last nod. "He has told me that he will do so, and I have told you that he is a truthful boy. Thank you very much for your time." As soon as the Advanis were out of earshot, Bud whistled.

"Whee! How'd you like to have him for a father?"

"How'd you like to have Junior for a son?" Don retorted. "I like the man. And I believe him, except for one thing. I don't think they changed schools out of choice. I think the kid got kicked out of every private school that would take him and when the word got out on him, they closed their doors. So he's back in public school."

"I think you're right," Bud said. "Let's get rid of the kid fast."

"Maybe we could help him," I suggested. I still wasn't completely sure that Junior was the liar in the family.

"He's such a bright kid," Jean added. "We might be able to get through to him." Bud snapped his briefcase open and pulled out a yellow pad. He wrote furiously for a minute.

"I'm going on record right now," he said. "I think the kid is dangerous. If you want to keep him, go ahead, but I won't be responsible for him. What do you say, Don?"

"You know what I think," Don said. "He's trouble."

"I'd like to give him one more chance," I said. "But if you all agree to drop him now, I'll go along with you."

"It couldn't hurt to give him one chance," Jean added.

"All right, he's yours," Bud said, with a sigh. He and Don exchanged looks of long-suffering exasperation as Jean and I exchanged smiles.

I stopped smiling two days later when the sophomore student dean, Phil Horner, called and asked me to stop by his office just as soon as I could. Junior Advani was in the detention center, awaiting suspension for threatening a group of freshmen. Dr. Horner had been on his way to the gym to see the track coach when he rounded the corner of the building and saw Junior standing on the steps behind the gym, pointing his finger at a group of kids who stood, transfixed, staring at him.

"He was chanting some goobledygook," Dr. Horner said. "Then he held out both hands, palms facing forward, and screamed, 'You will all burn in Hell. Satan is here. He sees you and he wants you. You will die. Die! Die!' It was pretty spooky, I have to admit."

"Maybe he was only playing," I said. "My friends and I used to do what we called street theater when we got bored. One of us would pretend to be blind or lame and we'd make a scene in public, or we'd stage a crazy fight, then run like mad, laughing at the shocked expressions of the unknowing bystanders."

Dr. Horner sighed. "That's what he said. That he was just playing. Maybe he was, but it didn't look like playing to me. And those kids were scared."

Junior was put on suspension for three days, but was back after missing only one day. Students on suspension are prohibited from setting foot on campus, so when he walked into my classroom, I called the office to report him. Junior's suspension had been terminated, after a visit from his father to the school. Mr. Advani insisted that Junior had been playacting, that he was sorry, and he would not do it again. Junior also told his father that other students were involved in the chanting, although none of them had been suspended. Junior felt that he was being discriminated against because he was Indian. In that case, Mr. Advani was prepared to file a lawsuit against the school. Presto! Junior was back in school.

Bud and Don insisted upon dropping Junior from the Academy. Jean and I agreed. Whether he was kidding or not, the kid was obviously troubled. He needed help. We sent a referral to the nurse's office, but Junior met with her and convinced her that he was a normal teenage boy with a wild imagination. We sent a referral to the school psychologist, but she had already met with him the previous year, after another teacher had referred him. She thought he could benefit from counseling, but the parents had refused to discuss the idea. We had no choice, at that point, other than to release Junior from our program. He was such a negative influence that we had to get rid of him to save the rest of the kids. We sent him to the guidance office and he was enrolled in regular classes at Parkmont.

For about a week, things were much calmer. Then I got a notice in my mailbox saying that one of our kids, Jenny Reynolds, a baby-faced blonde, had been suspended for carrying a weapon. There was a possibility that she would be expelled. I called Jenny's house to find out what happened. She had never been in trouble for fighting and it seemed unlikely that she would bring a weapon to school.

"I took a knife to school," Jenny said, "because Junior Advani said he was going to kill me."

"You should have told Mr. Simms or Dr. Horner or me—or somebody," I said. "We would have helped you."

"I did tell Mr. Simms," Jenny said. "He put a restraining order on Junior so he couldn't come near me. So Junior got some man to come on campus and follow me around one day. Every time I turned around, there he was, staring at me. He was creepy looking. I tried to ignore him, but he followed me the whole day."

"Why didn't you tell Mr. Simms about the man?" I asked.

"It didn't help the last time I talked to him," Jenny said. "And Junior went around and told everybody I was a fink. So I just took a knife to school and I told Junior if he tried to hurt me, I'd cut him."

"What did Junior say?"

"He went to the office and told Mr. Simms that I was carrying a knife, so they searched my backpack and suspended me."

It had to be true, it was too incredible to be fiction. But I didn't understand why Junior had threatened Jenny in the first place. Initially, she didn't want to talk about it, but when I told her I thought I could help her stay in school, she finally admitted that she and some of her friends had been hanging out with Junior and his gang of devil worshipers.

"Are you telling me that they really are devil worshipers?" I felt nauseated.

"Not like the guys in the movies who kill animals and stuff," Jenny said. "They just say chants and draw pentagrams on the desks and walls and stuff. They aren't really dangerous, but they're weird. I just didn't want to hang around with them anymore and they got mad."

After all the facts were discovered, Jenny was allowed to return to school. Nothing was done about Junior because there was no proof that he had said or done any of the things Jenny claimed he had. Because she had been carrying a knife, her word was automatically suspect. I called Junior's mother to see if she would be receptive to the idea of arranging psychological counseling for Junior. She agreed to talk to him. The following night, Mrs. Advani called me at 11:00 P.M.

"Miss Johnson?" she whispered.

"Yes?"

"Junior does not want to see a counselor. I'm sorry." She caught her breath sharply. "Please do not tell him that I called you." I could tell she was crying.

"Mrs. Advani, are you all right?"

"I am a little disturbed at this moment," she said. "Junior just came into my bedroom a few minutes ago. His eyes were very wild. 'Do you know what happens to people who make me angry?' he said. 'They get hurt.' Then he left my bedroom."

"Did you tell your husband?" I asked.

"Junior denies that he said it and his father believes him. His father always believes him. He says I must leave the matter in his hands. I must go now. Thank you for your concern, Miss Johnson. I will remember you always. Good-bye."

That was my last conversation with Mrs. Advani. Junior is still in school and every time I see him on campus, he smiles at me and says, "Hello, Miss Johnson. How's my favorite teacher?" It makes my blood run cold. He's a scary kid. I don't know whether he's scary because of his parents or whether his parents are scary because of him, but something is definitely wrong. I couldn't imagine locking my own child out of the house in the winter, but I couldn't imagine having a child who threatened me with a butcher knife, either. Sometimes, I wonder if I'll pick up the newspaper one day and learn that Junior hacked up his parents with an ax. I can only pray that I'm wrong.

The Junior Advanis and Attiba Macks break my heart, but for every student who slips through the cracks, a dozen—or two dozen—step over the cracks and walk out of high school with a diploma in one hand and a dream in the other. It's these kids—the ones you don't read about in the newspapers because good news doesn't sell—who keep me coming back every year to my lopsided wooden desk, my crumbling bulletin boards, my outdated textbooks, and my own handful of dreams.

ELEVEN

What If This Year Ain't No Different?

The fifty sophomores who volunteered for the first year of the Academy program were evenly split into three groups—black, white, and Hispanic. I was surprised, and a little embarrassed, to realize that I had not expected to see as many pale faces in a drop-out prevention program, although Parkmont High is located in an all-white, high-income community. I was even more surprised to find that only half of the Academy class rode buses from the poverty-stricken East Side; the other half came from Buffy and Jody land where a quarter of a million dollars is considered a reasonable price for a three-bedroom house and a Mercedes convertible is the standard birthday gift for the sweet sixteen.

The common denominator in our program wasn't money or ethnic origin—it was failure. Some of the kids had failed one or two classes during their freshman year, others had failed every single class. And, although a few were documented truants and had been assigned probation officers, in most cases there was no obvious explanation for the failures. Their scores on standardized reading and math tests ranged from average to excellent. If there was nothing wrong with their brains, and nothing wrong with the instruction provided, then there was clearly something missing. The Academy was an attempt to provide the missing link. For many of the kids, the Academy was the last resort. If they couldn't make it with us, they probably wouldn't make it at all; they'd end up in an alternative high school, at juvenile court, or on the street.

The Academy kids had signed contracts agreeing to attend every class, do their homework, stay out of fights and away from drugs for the next three years. In return, they would be placed in smaller classes, they'd be assigned mentors from local businesses, and they'd receive more personal attention from the four Academy teachers who taught the core classes—English, history, math, and computer applications. A federal grant provided funds to reduce class sizes and establish a computer lab. Computers were the key to the program. With three years of computer training, including data entry, spreadsheets, and word processing, our kids would be a step ahead of their contemporaries when it came to getting jobs or completing college assignments if—and this was the big if—we could keep them in school long enough to graduate.

On the first day of every school year, I hand out index cards and ask the kids to provide their full names, addresses, and phone numbers. I also ask them to list their hobbies, out of school activities, and their future career goals, so I can get an idea of their personalities. Usually, kids fill the fronts of the cards with information, but with very few exceptions, the Academy kids gave me nothing but the bare essentials—name, address, and phone.

"Come on," I gently prodded one boy who looked

relatively friendly. "You must have some hobbies, don't you?"

"Naw," he mumbled.

"Well, what do you do when you're not in school?"

"Nuthin'."

"Don't you listen to music or play baseball or ride your bike or skateboard or build model cars or anything?"

"Naw." He shook his head.

His response was typical. The kids insisted that they did nothing, went nowhere, had no interests outside of school. I knew they were holding back, but I didn't push them. They had to trust me before they'd let me know them. It was clear that they honestly believed any and all information sought by a school staff member would be used against them. I thought maybe they'd be more comfortable writing about themselves, instead of talking about themselves, so I distributed their personal journals and explained that I didn't want any names printed in the journals. They were to be anonymous. Each journal had a letter or number code printed inside the front cover. I was the only person who knew the codes, so if the journals were lost or stolen, no one would know who owned the book. I wanted them to have some place safe to express their ideas.

"Who paid for these?" one boy yelled out as I distributed the journals.

"Why?" I countered.

"I'm just interested," he insisted.

"Why?" I repeated.

"Leroy don't take care of nothing the school pays for," said a thin girl with half blond–half brunette hair. Her eyes were outlined in thick black eyeliner and her lips were painted white. "Tell him you paid for it out of your own pocket."

"Shut up, flat ass!" the boy yelled.

At that point, I explained my single rule of SelfRe-spect—no sexual, ethnic, or racial slurs in or outside of the classroom.

"That's only one chickenshit little rule," Leroy inter-rupted. "You was sposed to give us a list of rules and shit. And a sheet telling how you do grades and shit. That's what you're sposed to do on the first day. Don't you know that?"

"Shit isn't an appropriate word to use in school," I responded. "Don't you know that?"

"Sure, I know that," Leroy replied.

"Well, I know I'm supposed to give you pages of rules and stuff," I said.

"So, why don't you?" he asked.

"Why should I?"

"So we'll know what we're supposed to do."

"Don't you know what you're supposed to do?" I asked.

"Maybe," Leroy said with a sigh, his patience wear-ing thin.

"Then do it," I said. "No sense in wasting paper. Save a tree. All right?"

"Okay," Leroy said, with a shrug. "You're the teacher."

"Yes, I am," I said. "And here's your first assign-ment. In your journals, I'd like you to write your auto-biographies." As expected, a chorus of moans and groans followed.

"This class is supposed to be different," said Nikki, the blond girl with the black eyeliner and white lips. "I must of written a million autobiographies in English class."

"There are two differences in this assignment," I explained. "First, I don't want you to tell me when and where you were born and where you went to school. I want you to tell me why you are the person you are—

what makes you different from everybody else. And second, don't worry about spelling and punctuation. This semester, I'm grading your work on content only. I'll mark the spelling and grammar, but I won't take off points for it.''

No one argued with me, although I could see from their faces that they either didn't believe me or didn't believe it was a good idea.

"Any questions?" I asked.

A small, thin boy with red hair raised his hand.

"Yes, Phillip?"

"How are you going to grade it if you don't take off for spelling and verbs and stuff?"

"I'm going to grade it on how much effort you put into it," I explained. "If you really try to improve your writing, I'll know it. Nobody else will. And I don't care what everybody else does. I expect each one of you to improve your own writing. I'm not going to compare your work with your neighbor's work. This is between you and me."

"For real?" Phillip asked, with a tentative smile.

"For real," I assured him.

"Cool," Phillip said.

"Yeah, that's a hell of a cool idea 'cause I can't spell anything," said Nikki. "I would of had an A in English last year if I could of spelled." I didn't point out that I doubted whether she could have earned an A, since she was absent four out of every five days last year, according to the records in the attendance office.

As the kids wrote in their journals, I walked around the room, constantly pacing up and down the aisles. It was the only way to keep them in their seats and on track. A number of kids gripped their pencils as though they might try to escape, and they pressed the points onto the paper so hard that they nearly tore it. I noticed that Phillip was writing with a pencil so dull that the thick point made his writing nearly illegible, but he refused my offer of a sharper pencil.

"I hate them when they're pointy," he explained, moving his pencil out of reach, as though he expected me to grab it from him. "This feels better."

At the end of the first period, two boys still had not turned in their journals, Durrell Lewis and Santiago Gonzales. I held them both after class. Durrell refused to look at me, but softly said that he'd like to do it at home because he couldn't write in class. I said okay because he seemed so painfully shy that I didn't want to intimidate him the first day. He had chosen a seat in the back, near a group of other black boys, but rarely spoke to them or anyone else.

Santiago claimed that he simply couldn't write the essay. His accent was so thick I could barely understand him.

"Why can't you write an essay?" I asked, distracted by his hair. The front was cut short, but the back was long and wavy and hung more than halfway to his waist. It was so black that it shimmered in the fluorescent light and his teeth were so white they seemed illuminated from within his body.

"I cannot write in English," Santiago explained. "Is too hard."

"All you have to do is try your best," I explained. "I won't take off points for spelling or grammar. But you will never learn if you don't try."

"I can't," he insisted.

"Then write it in Spanish and then change it into English," I said.

"This is also too hard," he insisted.

"I can't give you a grade for nothing," I explained. "You have to write something."

"Okay," Santiago said, without conviction. "I will try."

He didn't turn in the journal that day or the next, and he didn't do the next writing assignment, either. It took me several days to learn that Santiago's "I will try" meant he had no intention of doing the assignment, although he was too polite and too smart to blatantly refuse a teacher's request. When I finally realized that Santiago's "trying" produced no work, I took advantage of his good manners, his obvious respect for school, and his pride. After each assignment, I would ask him whether he intended to complete the task.

"Of course," he would say with a brilliant flash of white teeth.

"Then shake my hand and give me your word as a gentleman that I'll have the assignment tomorrow," I'd say.

"You can trust me, Miss Johnson," Santiago would say each time, as he took a step backward, away from my outstretched hand. Once he shook hands, we both knew I had him.

"I do trust you," I pushed. "But I want to shake on it just to be sure."

After we finally shook on it, Santiago turned in his autobiography—three weeks late. It consisted of one long sentence:

I come to U.S. ago three year from ranch in mexico where I work very hard in field because my
famile want me to have the educacion here so I
can have good job and make the money but I
don't speek the inglish good and school is very
hard sometime peeple laughs at me so I sit in the
back of the room and hoping the teacher don't

136

ask me nothing but I try to be very good student so I can lern averyting.

Santiago's journal prompted a huge sigh, as I realized how hard it would be to teach him and how far he had to go. His journal made me sad. But some of the other kids' journals made me cry. I read all fifty autobiographies in the evening after the first day of school and I didn't sleep well that night. One boy, Lance, wrote his entire autobiography in third person:

One day, a beautiful baby boy was born to a happy young couple in East Parkview. The baby was so happy and his parents loved him very much. They had a wonderful life. The baby was the happiest baby in the world. Then one day, his life ended. His father, a twenty-five-year-old man, dropped dead of a heart attack. His handsome father was dead and his mother never got over it. She started drinking and taking drugs and abandoned her little son who had to go live with his grandmother. Sometimes the mother would say to the boy, "I hate you. You look so much like your father. Every time I look at you, I see his face and I can't stand it. I wish you were dead." The boy wishes he was dead, too, sometimes, but his grandmother loves him and tells him that God will be angry if he kills himself, so he is trying to live with this. But he will never ever love anyone like he loved his father.

I'd read five or six journals that described uneventful childhoods, then another one would stab me straight in the heart. Eddie Villaflores, a handsome young man with large, sad eyes, wrote about his childhood in Nicaragua. On the first page, Eddie described in detail the beautiful countryside where he lived with his parents, grandparents, and two sisters. Eddie's handwriting changed on the second page. His flowing script became cramped and inconsistent. His father had been killed in an auto accident and his mother was persuaded by relatives that Eddie, the only male child, would be safer and would have more opportunity for education and prosperity in the United States. At first his mother resisted, but family pressure and political unrest convinced her. Eddie wrote:

> I knew my mother was going to send me away when she kissed me and told me she would always love me. When I got to America, a man and lady took me home with them and adopted me and told me they would be my new family. They were my uncle and aunt, but I didn't know them. I never saw my sisters or mother again since then and I miss her very much, but I don't know what happened to her or if she is even alive. At first, it was very hard in school because I did not speak English, but I worked very hard because I do not want my family to be ashamed of me in case I ever see them again. Sometimes I feel very sad and I miss my family and my country and I don't feel like doing my homework, but I know I have to get an education so I can earn enough money to go and look for my mother one day.

Nikki Anderson took two pages to list all the reasons why she hated her life. Her mother had gotten pregnant with Nikki when she was sixteen, but stayed in school to graduate and did not marry Nikki's father. Later, Nikki's mother got married, but her husband refused to have a "bastard" child in his house, so Nikki was shipped off to live with her grandmother. Her father also married, but Nikki's mother wouldn't let a strange woman raise her daughter. "If he would just try to get to know me, my stepfather would like me because I'm not a bad person," Nikki wrote,

but he won't even try. So, I get tired of being good because nobody cares anyway and then I get in trouble in school. Last time I got in trouble in school, they couldn't reach my mom so they called my father. He drove seventy miles to come here and help me and when he got here, I was standing outside the office with a bunch of kids and I was so proud because my daddy was coming to see me. Then he went up to some other girl and hugged her. He didn't even know who I was.

I was emotionally exhausted by the time I reached the last two notebooks in the stack. Raul Chacon, who was a new student in my class at that time, had written two paragraphs:

What makes me different than the other kids is that I may be a little guy but I can fight real good. I don't care how big is the other guy because I fight like a tiger. I don't let nobody mess with me or my posse—Gusmaro, Julio, Victor, and me. We go everywhere together and if you hit one of us you better hit us all because we stick together. Homeys have to stick together in the East Bay.

Something else that makes me different is that I'm already 16, but I want to graduate in school because nobody in my family didn't never graduate. My father went to the third grade and my mother went to the second grade. They don't know nothing. They can't even read, not even in Spanish. My father he tells me I should quit school and work for him but I don't want to. I think I can graduate maybe except I messed up pretty bad last year and sometimes I have to stay home to take care of busasness or earn some money for food and then my teachers get mad and the school calls my house and yells at me. But I'm going to try and I think maybe this year will be better, what do you think, Miss or Mrs. Johnson?

The last journal was Leroy Wyman's. "I already know about me," he wrote.

What I want to know is about you. What makes you so different? I'm sitting in the same old desk in the same old school. It don't look no different to me. It looks just the same as last year—ugly and boring. I thought this Acadamy program was sposed to be different. I know I only been here one day, but what if this year ain't different? What if I don't cut no classes no more and do my homework and all that shit. You said we could write anything we want in these journels. Did you mean that? We'll see. So, what if I do all that shit and I still get NC's? That's my question.

In every journal, I wrote a personal response. The only one I had trouble with was Leroy's. He had asked the same question I had been asking myself, and I didn't have an answer. I believed, at the time, that unconditional love and acceptance might make the difference, and it eventually did, but I could hardly tell a child who didn't know me that I loved him.

TWELVE

One Hug or Two?

"**N**ever touch a student" was one of the first rules I'd learned as a high school teacher. It's a good rule and a sensible one, too, because it prevents legal complications, personal confrontations, and inappropriate familiarity between students and staff. But it was a rule I couldn't follow, and breaking it was one of the best things I ever did as a teacher.

Detrick Davis had spent the entire period in English class throwing paper wads, poking Tony Young in the ribs, and spitting staples into Holly Baker's hair. I gave Detrick one of my warning cards that read:

> Your present behavior is unacceptable.
> I know you can be more polite.
> Please do so and return this card to me—
> in person—after class.

Usually, when I dropped a card on a kid, he quieted down immediately, but Detrick did the opposite. He drummed his desktop and whistled under his breath until about ten minutes before the bell rang, when he slumped down into his seat and sat with his chin on his chest, looking lost and forlorn. When the bell rang, he picked up his backpack and wrapped his arms around it, peering at me over the top of the bag. His eyes, which were a strikingly clear green, usually shone with good-natured mischief, but that day the glimmer was gone, along with his usual devilish grin.

"What's your problem today, Mr. Davis?" I asked after the other students had gone. I sat down sideways in the desk in front of Detrick's so I could face him. He shrugged his shoulders but didn't speak.

"Can't you talk to me?" I asked. "I promise not to call all my friends and tell them your secrets." Detrick didn't respond.

"Okay, then write me a note in your journal," I said.

"I already did," Detrick said.

"Did you put it in my basket?" I asked. "I didn't see it." Detrick shook his head.

"It's in my backpack," he said. I held out my hand and waited quietly until he unzipped his pack and handed me the notebook. I started to open it, but Detrick quickly reached out and shut it.

"Don't read it while I'm here," he said.

"Okay, I'll read it tonight," I said, "and you'd better get to your next class before the tardy bell rings. You don't need any more detention demerits."

Detrick looked much younger than his fifteen years. He was barely five feet tall and his face was as round and smooth as a baby's. Without thinking, I put my arm around his shoulder and pulled him close to me. Suddenly, he was in my arms, hugging me fiercely. His entire body trembled as he struggled to hold back his tears. He clung to me for a few seconds, then pulled back, slapped at his eyes with the back of his hand, and ran out of the room. As soon as he left, I opened his journal and read:

Dear Miss Johnson, I lied to you when I wrote my autobiography on the first day of school. Well, I didn't lie all the way, but most of it was lying. I do have two sisters, but they don't live with me and my dad and neither does my mom. Last year, my mom went on a vacation to San Diego and she never came back. I didn't know what happened to her. Then, one day, she came back and took all her clothes and my two sisters and left again. After that, I didn't do too good in school. I thought if she didn't care about me, then I didn't care about me, either. But I know my dad cares about me, so I came in this program and I try to get good grades, but every time I get good grades I do something stupid to mess it up. Last year I was in accelerated classes and I got good grades for the first semester, but I flunked almost every class second semester so I'm real behind on my credits and my GPA stinks. My dad is tired of yelling at me and you probably are, too, except you hardly ever yell, but I know you get tired of trying to help me. Maybe I should just quit the Academy and give up. What do you think?

"I think you should sign up to be my student clerk during your free sixth period class," I told Detrick on the phone that night. "You'll earn two-point-five credits if you do a good job. And you won't have to act like a turkey just so you can stay after school and talk to me. Ask your dad if it's okay and let me know tomorrow."

Every day, when Detrick finished his tasks, I gave

him a hug and told him I loved him. The effect was amazing. Although he was still far from being a model student, he calmed down enough to maintain passing grades in every subject. One day, after I hugged him, Detrick whispered, "Do you think *she* loves me, too?"

"I'm sure she does," I assured him, hoping I was right.

"Then why did she leave me?"

"This is only my theory," I explained, "but I'm pretty sure that she probably thought you'd be happier with your father, since you're a young man. And maybe she thought your father would be happier if he had you because you're such a wonderful kid." Detrick nodded thoughtfully.

"She never visits me," he said.

"You told me she was supporting herself and two teenage girls," I reminded him. "She probably doesn't have a lot of money to spare. Why don't you go visit her?" Detrick looked at me.

"Do you think she'd want me?"

"I'd want you," I said. He didn't say anything else, but two weeks later, he rushed into my classroom waving a letter in the air.

"She invited me for summer vacation!" he said, grinning. "My dad made a deal. I get a part-time job to pay for the plane ticket, I pass all my classes, and I sign up for summer school in San Diego to make up some of my credits."

To ensure Detrick's continued success in school, Mr. Davis bought a slightly used Toyota Celica, painted it metallic blue, polished it to a high gloss, and parked it in his driveway. When Detrick came home from vacation, Mr. Davis handed him the car keys and told him he could keep the keys as long as he paid the insurance and kept his grades up.

* * *

Detrick's best friend, Bryan Richmond, also required daily hugs, but they only affected his behavior; his grades remained spotty in spite of his obvious intelligence and high test scores. Bryan was the last person I would have picked as a candidate for hugging, since he took great pains to keep as much distance as possible between himself and the other students. If no seat was available in the back row when he arrived at class, Bryan would mill around the classroom, waiting for a chance to move somebody else's books and claim their desk in the back. He criticized every lesson plan and pronounced them all "boring, boring, boring."

It wasn't until several weeks into the semester that I realized Bryan intentionally bumped into me frequently. He'd ask to see my gradebook, or hang around my desk with the ever-present question askers, although he rarely asked a question. When I noticed that he often brushed against my arm with his shoulder, I asked the other Academy teachers if they had noticed the same behavior.

"Now that you mention it, yes," Jean Warner said with a nod. "He comes up every day before class and asks to borrow a pencil or asks what we're going to be doing. I'm constantly bumping him with my elbow and apologizing. I thought it was me, but maybe it is him."

We agreed to hug Bryan whenever he made himself available. He couldn't handle a two-armed hug; one was enough for him, but he smiled in spite of himself each time I put my arm around his shoulder and gave him a squeeze. His behavior in class improved dramatically, and his grades in English and history classes shot up, but his grades in all his other classes continued to go up and down. Whenever we tried to discuss his grades, Bryan would close up and shut us out. He was absent one day and I decided to call him at home to see if he'd be more open if he wasn't talking face to face.

Unfortunately, Bryan's stepfather, Mr. Burton, answered the phone and I forgot he was The Enemy. How could I have forgotten Bryan's frequent journal stories entitled, "My Life with the Stepdick"? Mr. Burton asked why I was calling and I said I had missed Bryan in school that day and just wanted to check to see if he was all right.

"What do you mean you missed him in school today?" Mr. Burton thundered. "He went to school. I dropped him off myself. Thank you for letting me know, I'll take care of it." I hung up as soon as I could, before I made things any worse. It wasn't soon enough. The next day, Bryan stalked into my room and took his seat in the back row. He didn't say a word until the bell rang, then he approached my desk.

"Thanks a lot," he said. "Now I'm grounded for the rest of my life for cutting and it's your fault."

"I'm not the one who cut," I reminded him.

"Yeah, but you're the one who said, 'I'll call you before I call your parents. You're old enough to be responsible for yourselves.' Aren't you always saying that?" He was right. I had broken my promise not to call any parents until I had tried to work out a solution with the student involved.

"I asked for you," I said, "but you weren't home."

"You didn't have to tell on me," Bryan said. He picked up a paper clip from my desk and straightened it into a long, thin wire which he then used to stab holes in a piece of notebook paper. "It doesn't matter anyway. He'd ground me for something else if you didn't tell on me."

"What do you do to get yourself grounded so much?" I said. Bryan sighed.

"Everything. Grades usually."

"But you're smart. Why do you get such bad grades?"

"Why not?" he said. "Maybe they'll kick me out of school and I can go to Montana."

"Why Montana?"

"That's where my father lives. My sister ran away once and went to see him, but they brought her back and put her in a school for juvenile delinquents. She hates the stepdick, too. He's a real asshole. I'm not kidding."

"Why don't you go live with your father?"

"My mother won't let me. She says I have to stay here and graduate from high school."

"Are you sure you don't get bad grades just to make your mother and your stepfather mad?" Bryan's face twisted into a grimace.

"Oh, sure, that's exactly why I do it," he said. "You sure figured me out, didn't you?"

"If you really want to hurt your stepfather, don't flunk school. Eat a lot, especially steak. Grow real fast so he has to buy you new clothes. Flunking only hurts you."

"See you later," Bryan said, unimpressed with my words of wisdom. For a couple of weeks, he avoided me as much as possible. I felt guilty for having him grounded, though it was his own fault. Still, I had promised not to tell on the kids until I gave them a chance to correct their misbehavior. One night, after dinner, I called Bryan.

"What are you doing?" I asked.

"Sitting in my room," Bryan said. "I'm supposed to be reading. He can make me hold my book, but he can't make me read."

"Ask your parents if you can go to the library with your teacher," I said.

"What for?" he said, immediately wary.

"I thought you were grounded and you were a prisoner after school every day."

"Yeah," Bryan said.

"So, ask your parents if you can go to the library with your English teacher. At least you'll get out of the house, won't you?"

He dropped the phone and was gone for a few minutes, then returned and said, "They said okay."

I put on my glasses and pulled my hair back into a knot so I'd look very teacherish. When I arrived, both Bryan's parents were waiting in the living room to meet me. Mrs. Burton gripped my hand tightly and frowned.

"This is certainly a surprise," she said. "It's the first time anybody at that school ever showed an interest in either of my children." Mr. Burton was a large, disheveled man with wire rim glasses and balding blond hair. He shook my hand and introduced himself, but didn't offer any conversation. I was more relieved than Bryan when we got outside. We drove to the library and I asked Bryan to put my library books in the book drop.

"I thought you said we were going to the library," he said.

"We're at the library, aren't we?" I said.

"Yeah."

"Well, I wouldn't want you to lie to your parents. Now put the books in the book drop and hurry up. We've got places to go and things to do."

Bryan stuffed the books into the book drop and climbed back into the car, but didn't say a word until I pulled into the parking lot of Pizza Heaven, one of the local hangouts for teens.

"What are we doing here?" he said.

"Do you know how to shoot pool?" I asked. He nodded and frowned, looking very much like his mother.

"Well, here's the deal," I explained. "We play straight eight ball. Call your shots. No slop. Best of three games. If you win, I give you an A on your final report card and you don't have to do a single assignment."

"And if you win?"

"If I win, you have to try to get an A in my class. Just try. Deal?"

Bryan looked at my glasses.

"Are those real?" he asked.

"Of course they are," I said.

"It's a deal." We shook hands and went inside. My sister Sue is a pool shark and taught me how to handle a stick, although I usually need at least one game to warm up. Bryan immediately bummed a cigarette from a kid playing video games and leaned against the wall, trying to look worldly and sophisticated, which is hard to do when you're five feet tall and about as big around as a pool cue. I ignored the cigarette and racked the balls.

"You can break," I said. Bryan made a lucky shot and dropped one stripe and one solid on the break, but he played with a complete lack of control. He won the first game and smiled at me, a cigarette dangling from the corner of his mouth.

"Bet still on?" he asked.

"Damn straight," I said as I racked the balls again. Bryan lost the second game and blamed it on overconfidence. He still had four balls left on the table when I sank the eight on the third game.

He kept his word. The next morning, I gave his class a vocabulary worksheet that required the students to write a sentence using each of twenty words. In the past, Bryan had always been the first one to turn in his paper, but he never bothered to look up the words he didn't know. He wrote short sentences for the words he remembered and left the rest blank. This time, Bryan not only wrote a sentence for each word, he wrote creative, grammatical sentences—and still managed to complete the assignment before the rest of the class. I was so pleased that I called his stepfather and told him what an excellent job Bryan had done in class. Two days later, Bryan aced a quiz on the same words. I called his parents again and reported his A-plus. Bryan called me that night, just before bedtime.

"I'm ungrounded," he said. "The stepdick was so excited about my good grades that he let me out on parole for the weekend. He's walking around grinning like an idiot. He's so stupid."

"Adults are like that sometimes," I said. "We can't help it."

In addition to Bryan and Detrick, I tried to call at least two or three kids per week, just to let them know I was thinking about them. After they got over the initial wariness, they started to respond and most of my discipline problems disappeared. If I called a kid and explained, for example, that talking during my instruction was impolite and I'd appreciate it if he or she would try not to be rude, there was no reason for the student to create a power play out of the situation because nobody else knew what I had asked. Most of the kids got a kick out of receiving a phone call from a teacher and they liked to say casually, "Oh, yes, I was talking to Miss Johnson on the phone last night . . ."

Leroy Wyman was on my list, but I hadn't had a reason or an opportunity to call him and he grew impatient. He interrupted class one day to find out whether I had, indeed, been calling his classmates.

"You been calling kids at home?" he asked.

"Yes," I said.

"What for?"

"Just to talk to them, see how they're doing," I said.

"Ha!" Leroy said. "You calling them to scare them and you know it. If they don't act right, you probably ask to talk to their mother on the spot."

"No, I don't," I insisted.

"You say you just calling to talk, but you really calling to scare people. You can't fool me with that psychology."

I called Leroy that night. The moment he heard my voice, he broke out in loud laughter.

"Ha! Ha!" he chortled. "I psyched you. I knew you was gonna call me."

"You were right," I said.

"So what's on the agenda?" he asked. "Usually people got something to say when they call you."

"I just wanted to tell you how much I enjoy having you in my class. You have a bright, inquiring mind and you're always open to discussing new ideas and concepts. That's a rare and wonderful trait and I'm very proud of you."

Leroy didn't respond for a few seconds.

"You sure you don't want to tell that to my mother?"

THIRTEEN

My Spanish Babies

It was a miracle. I'd been speaking for twenty minutes and thirty-six teenagers still sat quietly, nodding and smiling, listening attentively. This is going to be a piece of cake, I thought—an entire class of students who have good manners and self-discipline. And I had the same kids for two consecutive hours, one for reading, one for grammar.

At first, I'd been hesitant to accept the job, because Chet Norton, the principal, had asked me on a Friday to take over starting the following Monday.

"This isn't another class that drove their teacher to the edge of insanity, is it?" I asked him.

"Oh, no," Chet assured me. "Nothing like that. This is a new program called NEP, Non-English Proficient, for kids who don't speak English very well. These kids are from all over the world—the Philippines, Tonga, Japan, Central America, Mexico. Most of the kids speak Spanish. You do speak Spanish, don't you?"

"Yes, I had four years of high school Spanish and a year of college Spanish," I admitted, "but absolutely no experience or training in teaching people to read."

"Doesn't matter," Chet explained. "They have to

learn to speak English before they can read it. In the meantime, you can learn how to teach reading. And, since you'll have the same kids for two hours straight, you can really immerse them in English."

I immersed them in English, all right. Speaking slowly and using simple vocabulary, I introduced myself and outlined the course objectives. From time to time I paused and asked if everyone understood what I was saying. Nods and smiles. I ended my introductory speech and asked everyone to take out a pencil and a sheet of paper. No one moved. I repeated the instruction.

"Everyone take out a pencil," I said, as I held up a pencil, "and a piece of paper." I picked up a piece of paper off my desk and waved it in the air.

Again, the kids nodded and smiled at me. They had the most beautiful faces—smooth and golden brown. Some of them held up pencils, others held paper, but it was clear that very few of them had even the faintest idea of what I was talking about.

"Does anybody in here speak English at all?" I asked. More smiles and nods. "Great! Excuse me, class. I am going to jump out the window right now and break both my legs." A few kids giggled.

"Aha!" I said, trying to pick them out of the crowd. "Some of you speak English, don't you? You can't fool me." Suddenly the nodding stopped; they all shook their heads and shrugged their shoulders elaborately and rolled their eyes to indicate that they did not *entiendo* anything I was saying.

"Fine," I said, turning back to face the chalkboard. "If you don't do your homework, I'm going to throw you out the window on your heads." I spun around in time to catch the gigglers—four boys in the back row and five girls seated in the front.

"If you can understand what I'm saying, then you don't belong in this class. You should be in a higher level English class so you can learn more. This class will be boring for you." The girls shook their heads. The boys stared silently at me. "Why don't you want to move up?" I asked. "You could go to an LEP class—Limited English—where the teacher speaks Spanish. But you'd be with other kids who speak a little English." Again, the girls shook their heads and one of them started to cry. The boys still gave me the cold stare. I decided to let them stay until I found out how well they could read.

After I reviewed the students' records, I knew that the kids who could speak some English would become bored and restless before long because the rest of the class was so far behind them in every respect. Not only were most of them unable to read, speak, or write English, many of them couldn't read or write in their native languages. Nearly half of them had never been to school before, anywhere, in their lives. They had worked picking fruit, mowing lawns, washing dishes, cleaning houses, since they were old enough to walk and talk, to help support their families.

When the bell rang to signal the ten-minute break between first and second periods, half of the NEP kids got up and headed outside. The others sat there, looking confused. They had no concept of school. They had to learn about bells and bathroom passes and homework before they could begin to tackle reading and writing. Each new thing was more wonderful than the last. My NEP kids came to class smiling each morning. There was always a crowd waiting outside the door, no matter how early I arrived, anxious to begin another day of learning. When they saw me drive up, two or three would run to my car and offer to carry my books, my purse, my briefcase, my lunch bag. Each morning they asked me how I was and told me they were "very fine." They proudly showed me their homework, painstakingly printed, and asked for a precious few minutes of personal time before class started. They came prepared with pencils and notebooks, and they took copious notes because they wanted to learn everything. It was such a contrast to my American kids who never brought pencils, forgot their books, refused to take notes, and insisted that school was absolutely unnecessary and boring, boring, boring.

Of all the NEP kids, Francisco Garcia was the most eager to learn. Each day, he'd bring a list of new English words for me to define. After he jotted down the definitions, he'd create sentences using the words and ask me if they were correct. Although he spoke little English, he could read and write quite well. Most of the students wrote sentences such as "I ride the bus to school." Francisco would grab a piece of chalk and scribble, "If I had make such a ridiculous remark, I would not deny that I have say it." Then he'd turn to me to find out whether his sentence was *bueno* or needed a little fine-tuning.

Francisco's vocabulary lists contained words that were much more difficult than those I had intended to use, so I offered to let the class create their own lists of words they wanted to learn. Every Monday, we'd brainstorm a new list of ten words for the week. The first week, the kids chose: flirt, birthday, bring, vacation, excuse, sorry, permission, question, sentence, and hurry. The second week, Francisco raised his hand to offer the first word.

"What is buttwipe mean?" he asked in a voice so innocent that I knew he wasn't setting me up. Had I been thinking clearly, I'd have told him to ask me after class and moved quickly to another word. But it was Monday morning and he caught me off guard.

"Who told you that word?" I asked. From the tone of my voice, Francisco guessed that it wasn't a good choice for the vocabulary list. He shook his head and waved his hand, indicating that I should forget it. I was willing, but the other kids weren't. "Buttwipe," they whispered to each other, frowning, trying to figure out what it meant. Obviously, if I didn't tell them what it meant, they'd keep asking until someone did. I wrote the word *slang* on the chalkboard. In Spanish, I explained that there were many words in any language that were very informal and not proper to use in school. I also explained that there are words that are not nice and should never be used in polite society. Rather than explain what buttwipe meant, I defined both parts of the word and let it go at that. All the kids immediately grasped the idea of wipe when I ran a cloth across a desktop, but when I pointed to my rear end and said that *butt* was a slang word for the human posterior, one of the girls in the front row shook her head vehemently and waved her hand in the air.

"*But* means *pero*, Miss Johnson," she said, "not that other thing." She blushed and pointed to my rear. I wrote the word *but* on the board beside the word *butt* and explained the difference. We left it at that, with a reminder that they should use only good words so they would not sound like uneducated or bad people. Satisfied, the class offered a list of ten good words to learn and the rest of first period sailed by. Second period was always more fun than first. Instead of learning words and tackling grammar drills, we read stories and practiced dialogues. Since none of the curriculum materials in the school library was suitable for NEP kids, I wrote nearly everything we used in class. It took a lot of time at night, but it was worth it when the kids actually began speaking and reading English. Each day, I would write a one-page story and illustrate it with stick figures. The characters in the stories had the same names as the kids in class, which caused delighted giggles. At the end of each story were four or five basic questions to answer: How old is Maria? Where does Juan live? What time does the bus leave for school?

After we finished our daily story, we got to the good stuff—the daily dialogue. I made up dialogue charts to hang on the wall, based on actual student conversations that I'd overheard in the hallways and classrooms. To their conversations, I'd add American idioms and speech patterns, to help them learn the rhythms of the language. Each conversation chart had a distinctive title and two parts for the kids to read aloud. "Sharing," for example, featured two sisters who took turns using the bathroom mirror to wash their faces, comb their hair, and brush their teeth before hurrying off to school.

The conversation on the day of the "buttwipe" episode was entitled, "Hungry Harry." It was about two brothers who are about to eat breakfast. They greet each other, then the first brother, Jimmy, says, "Harry, hurry up. It's time to eat breakfast." Harry responds, "Good. I'm starving. I'm so hungry I could eat a horse." I wanted to discuss the way we exaggerate ideas—Harry was not actually starving and nobody eats a horse. Unfortunately, we never made it to the explanation of idioms because Armando Barajas read the line: "I'm so hungry I could eat a hore."

As usual, when the kids were reading the dialogue charts, I stood beside the chart, facing the room, pointing out each word with my ruler. When Armando said,

"I could eat a hore," I pointed to the word and said, automatically, "Horse."

"No, *Maestra*," Francisco interrupted. "That is not horse. Horse is spelled h-o-r-s-e." I looked at the chart. Francisco was right. There was no *s* and I was in another mess because the kids were all looking at each other, saying, "What is hore?" I could feel a deep blush spreading across my cheeks and I burst into hysterical laughter, tears streaming down my face. I raced to my desk, grabbed a felt-tipped marking pen, and inserted the missing *s*, hoping that the kids would move along to the next line. But they insisted upon knowing why my face was so red. What was so funny? What was a *hore?* I debated lying to them, but I couldn't. I tried to convince them to forget the whole thing, but they wouldn't. Finally, I showed them how I had made the error, using the chalkboard to demonstrate. Francisco grabbed a dictionary and flipped through the pages.

"*Maestra,*" he said, with a shake of his head. "There is no word *hore* in here." Happy to have an excuse to change the subject, I quickly wrote the correct spelling of *whore* on the board. Then I wrote the word *whole* and launched into a detailed discussion of silent letters in words such as whole, light, thought, and so on.

Fortunately, the bell rang before I had time to embarrass myself further that day. As soon as the kids left, I rushed to erase the board before anyone else saw it. I could just imagine the principal passing by and looking in the window to see *whore* written on the chalkboard. As I was erasing the board, Karlene Wilson, who taught the LEP English class next door, stopped by to say hello. When she saw the words on the board, her eyes opened wide.

"Pretty racy words for NEP kids, don't you think?" Karlene asked. I explained the fiasco I'd made of both the vocabulary and conversation exercises. She laughed and patted my arm.

"It happens to us all," she said with a sweet smile. I couldn't imagine Karlene ever doing such a thing. She looked like the quintessential English teacher—tall, slim, pretty, with dark curly hair drawn back into a loose bun that left a few feminine tendrils to frame her face. Her taste in clothes ran to lacy white blouses and cameo pins. She didn't look as if she'd ever said a dirty word in her life.

"Thanks for trying to make me feel better," I said, "but I can't picture you doing anything so stupid."

"Well I have. One time, one of my students came to school wearing blue jeans and a leather belt with a giant silver buckle," Karlene said. "As I passed by his desk, I stopped short, amazed at the size of the buckle. Without thinking, I said, 'My goodness, Jose! That's so big!' Of course, the other students couldn't see the buckle, they could only see me staring at Jose's lap. I didn't even try to explain. I just kept right on going with my lesson."

It made me feel a little better to know that other teachers made similar mistakes, but for weeks I felt slightly apprehensive each time I introduced a new conversation chart, until we had gone over the chart once and read each line. It was amazing how quickly the kids learned. Within a matter of weeks, they were speaking and reading quite well, although writing was an entirely different matter. Only one or two of them could write script. The first time I wrote something on the board, most of them wrinkled their brows and shook their heads. They couldn't read it; even the students who spoke English were baffled. They said they couldn't read my writing, so I erased it and wrote it more carefully, forming each letter distinctly. Still, they shook their heads and shrugged their shoulders.

"No, Miss Johnson," Francisco informed me. "It looks very fine. But they don't know those kind of writing. You would like for me to show you?" I nodded. He came to the board, took a piece of chalk and printed the words underneath the ones I had written. "This writing is good."

Appalled that fourteen- and fifteen-year-old students could not write script, I hunted through the library until I found a workbook that taught cursive writing. I made copies for the class and instructed them to keep them in the bookcase in our room. Each day, more booklets were missing. I was surprised, since the NEP kids usually followed my instructions completely. When I asked where the booklets were, no one knew. Finally, one of the girls drew me aside and whispered that many of the youngsters had taken the booklets home because their parents wanted to learn how to write, too. They were afraid I'd be angry with them for "stealing" the booklets.

The girl, Leonora Aguirre, spoke English very well, but I recognized her accent as Filipino. When I was in the navy, I'd spent three years working at the radio-TV station at Clark Air Base and during that time I'd learned to speak a little Tagalog, the national language of the Philippines. I had also learned to recognize the distinctive accent that Filipinos give to the English language.

"*Pilipina ka ba?*" I asked Leonora.

"O-o." Her face broke into a broad grin that revealed a large set of bright white teeth.

"What are you doing in this NEP class?" I asked.

"I don't know," she said, with a shrug. "They tell me to come here, so I come here." After class, I took Leonora to the guidance office.

"Why was this student placed in my NEP class?" I asked the freshman counselor, Mr. Rankin. He checked his files, looked at Leonora and then at me.

"She doesn't speak English," he said.

"Yes, she does," I said. "Say something, Leonora." I smiled at her and nodded.

"What you want I should say?" she asked in a voice so low I could barely hear it. It sounded like, "Wat chu wahnt ee chood sigh?"

Mr. Rankin held out one hand, palm up. "What did I tell you?"

"That was English!" I insisted.

"It was not," he said.

"Yes, it was. She has an accent, but that doesn't mean she doesn't speak English. Trust me, she speaks English and she needs to be in a regular English class."

"Okay," Mr. Rankin said. "If you're willing to sign the class change form, I'll do it. In this case, I have to have a teacher recommendation." I signed the permit and he changed her schedule immediately, placing her in a more appropriate class.

Encouraged by my success in changing Leonora's class, I asked about the nine Hispanic students who also spoke English. Not so easy to change their classes, I learned. According to state regulations, they had to pass the Nelson Reading Exam at grade level in order to leave the NEP program. I asked for permission to administer the test to my entire class, since I knew the nine kids would intentionally flunk the test if they knew good grades would result in their removal from my class. I had already sent a few of them to see the counselor about upgrading their English classes. Each time, they returned with a note telling me that they spoke no English at all. I assumed, at first, that the counselors hadn't understood them. Later, I learned that the counselors spoke Spanish, but the kids refused to speak English because they didn't want to leave their friends or their beloved teacher. Flattering as that was, I wanted them to get the best possible education, so I told them the class was taking the exam to see if I was a good teacher. The better their grades, the better my "report card" would be.

The Nelson Reading Test consists of a one-page vocabulary exam and three pages of questions based on short paragraphs. The words on the exam are not words that a non-native American would know—*mock, stall,* and so on. Most of the NEP kids tested at zero grade level, meaning that they registered below first-grade reading level. But the nine who spoke English tested at grade two or three. Not high enough to move them out, I was told, in spite of my argument that an arbitrary list of vocabulary words did not prove a valid reading level for non-native English speakers. I went to the head of the guidance office. She said she understood my position, but could not move the kids because it was against school policy. She handed me a document that outlined the complicated procedure needed to upgrade students from NEP to LEP or regular classes.

Parents were my next approach. I sent notes home to the parents of the youngsters I wanted to move, urging them to call the office and protest the placement of their children. It didn't work. The Latin culture demands utmost respect for all professionals—doctors, lawyers, and school administrators. Such professionals should not be challenged, since they are the best ones to judge how to perform their jobs. None of the parents called.

At the next staff meeting, I brought up the issue of NEP placement. After a brief discussion, Justin Carter, one of the senior department heads and the unofficial but unchallenged leader of the teaching staff, explained the prevailing opinion: It's unrealistic to expect all of "these kids" to graduate. If they learn even a little bit of English during their time at Parkmont, isn't that enough? Around the room, heads nodded in support of Carter's statement. Clearly, they were satisfied with his assessment and shared his attitude. Stunned, I sat silently running the faces of the kids through my mind, wondering whether there was a potential doctor or teacher or writer in the group. Meanwhile the staff discussion quickly moved on to a new topic—whether there would be money in the budget to carpet the staff lunchroom this year.

At last, I understood: It didn't matter what I taught in my NEP classes, because I wasn't really expected to teach. My job was to babysit. My job was to keep the NEP kids from making life difficult for the other teachers. If they had two Japanese students, or five Mexicans, or one Tongan, or two Nicaraguans in their classrooms, they'd have to deal with them. They'd have to learn to communicate while the kids learned English. It was easier to lump them all together in one place where they couldn't clog the system.

For the rest of the semester, I sent the nine Spanish kids to the library each day, where, with the help of a classroom aide, they took turns reading aloud from ninth-grade literature books. At the end of the year, I hand-scheduled their classes for the next year, putting them all into higher level English classes. The guidance counselors, grateful for my help at the busiest time of the year, didn't bother to check the schedules I wrote. It was a small victory, but at least I knew that nine of the Hispanic students had a shot at learning more than "a little English."

FOURTEEN

No Problema

"You must of forgot to give us the assignment," Leroy suggested, "or else we would of remembered it. Right?" He looked around the room for support from the other kids who still hadn't done their homework, even after I allowed a day's grace. The negligent students nodded their heads and put on their best innocent expressions.

"Nice try, Leroy," I said, "but there are three worksheets in the homework basket." I held up the completed papers on which I had pasted colorful little Garfield or Snoopy stickers that read "You deserve a pat on the brain" or "Born to eat knowledge."

"Who wants some stupid sticker," Leroy muttered. "That's for babies." Nevertheless, he accepted the sticker that Terrence Hill offered him a few minutes later. Leroy stuck it to the front of his notebook. The rest of the class pretended to be too cool to care, as well, but the next time I gave a homework assignment, half of them did it. Again, I put stickers on the papers and, again, most of the kids pretended not to notice, but Detrick Davis stuck his sticker in the middle of his forehead and danced around his desk. Each time I gave an assignment after that, more of the class did the work, until about seventy percent of the kids routinely did their homework.

I was pleased to see so many students completing their assignments, but I was not pleased with the quality of their work. Those who were getting stickers and extra credit were doing average work. I wanted everyone to do at least average work, but I knew if I insisted on legible handwriting, complete answers, and no copying, I'd lose most of the kids who had recently converted. So, I started putting stickers and extra credit points only on the papers that exceeded the minimum standards for passing. LaTisha was the first to protest.

"How come I never get stickers no more?" she asked. "I did my homework." She pointed at Leroy, whose paper boasted two stickers and five extra credit points. "How come he got stickers?"

"I'm so glad you asked," I said. "Leroy's paper has neat handwriting, complete answers that show me he knows the material, and no questions left blank. That's an excellent paper."

"That's right!" Leroy held his paper over his head and waved it. "This is an excellent paper. For a dollar, I'll let you look at it."

After a few weeks, everyone was earning stickers, so I stopped putting stickers and extra points on any but the very best papers. When the kids complained about the lack of stickers, I told them they were all getting so good that a paper had to be really outstanding to earn extra credit. By that time, all those who had handed in their assignments were doing average or above average work. It was time to go after the holdouts. Gusmaro Guevarra, one of the brightest kids in the class, refused to do any homework at all.

"I can't be doing homework, Miss J.," Gusmaro explained. "My posse don't do homework. It ain't cool. And besides, don't I always pass my tests?"

"No problem," I said, "nobody has to do homework in this class." I interrupted the kids' cheering. "I want you to be happy, so I even have a little gift for the people who didn't want to do their homework. I made this especially for you, just because I love you so much." Lots of frowns appeared. The kids who hadn't done their homework were rightfully suspicious; those who had were indignant.

"Hey! That ain't fair!" Leroy yelled. "You shouldn't give presents to people who don't do their work."

"Well, even though you did your homework, if you want one of my gifts, you're welcome to have one," I assured Leroy. "But you might want to wait and see what it is."

To each student who had not done the homework assignment from the previous night, I gave a two-page worksheet that covered the material in depth.

"Now, this isn't homework," I explained as I distributed the worksheets. "I know some of you are very busy at night and don't have time to mess around with homework. So you can stay after class today or tomorrow and finish this worksheet if you don't have time to do it at home tonight. And if you can't stay after class, feel free to come in after school to do it. You can call your parents and tell them that I will personally drive you home after you've finished your work."

Everyone but Gusmaro Guevarra turned in the homework the next day. I did hold him after class to finish the worksheet and I did drive him home. He carried it off until we reached his street, then the sweat started to form on his upper lip.

"You could drop me off at the corner here," Gusmaro said. "It'll be easier for you to get back on the freeway."

"That's okay," I said. "I'm not in a hurry and I'm looking forward to meeting your parents." It was cruel and unusual punishment, but I didn't care. I wanted the boy to graduate. By the time I had parked the car, Mrs. Guevarra was standing in the open doorway of the house. She did not look pleased. As we started up the dirt path to the front door, Gusmaro turned to me with a big smile.

"I forgot to tell you," he said. "My mother don't speak English. She won't understand you."

"She *doesn't* speak English," I corrected him, returning his grin. "*Y no te preocupes. Yo hablo español muy bien y puedo hablar con su mama con facilidad.*" Suddenly, Gusmaro looked sick to his stomach. He stood, staring at his shoes, as I shook hands with his mother. In Spanish, I told her how much I enjoyed having such an intelligent and well-behaved boy in my class, and that they should be proud of themselves for having done such a good job raising him. I apologized for keeping him after school, but I had wanted to go over his assignments with him and make sure he was ready for the semester's final exam. I gave her my home phone number and told her to call me if she had any questions at all about Gusmaro's progress in school. Gusmaro stood staring, openmouthed, as his mother graciously invited me in for refreshments. I graciously declined; Gusmaro had had enough for one day. I shook his hand and winked.

"*Sueñas con los angelitos, mi amigo,*" I said and turned to leave. Gusmaro didn't find his voice until I had reached my car.

"Thank you, Miss Johnson," he called softly.

"*No problema,*" I said. As I drove off, the two of

them walked into the house together, a proud mother and son. It made me feel delicious and kind of omnipotent to be able to create such a good feeling so easily.

When the other students found out that I wasn't kidding about driving them home after school, they were convinced. Homework was a given; everybody did it. As additional motivation, I promised them that if they did all their assignments in class and really tried to learn the material, I would not fail them, even if they flunked their tests. What I wanted them to understand was that if they did all their homework and classroom assignments, they would pass their tests because they would know the answers. They accepted my promise, but many of them became obsessed with making sure there were no missing assignments on their gradesheets. Every day, I spent ten minutes at the start of class, reassuring kids that their A's and Bs hadn't mysteriously changed into Ds and Fs overnight.

"Let me see it myself," Bryan Richmond demanded at least three times a week. He wanted to make sure that his A hadn't disappeared. Every time I opened my gradebook to show him, several other students would jump out of their seats and race to my desk, jostling each other to peek over my shoulder, straining to catch a glimpse of their grades. Obviously, they needed some tangible proof of their progress, so I made a giant wall chart with everybody's name on it. I listed every assignment and checked each one off when it was completed. The kids could see their progress toward the end of the quarter and, for most of them, that was all they needed. There were still a few holdouts who took personal vacation days during class when we did grammar exercises or literature worksheets, then flunked the quizzes.

Those youngsters obviously preferred threats, so I complied.

"Don't worry about flunking any tests in this class," I assured them. "If you flunk a test, I'll give you ten or fifteen worksheets to make up the grade. You can do the worksheets with me, after school, so you won't fall behind the other kids."

Just in case goal-setting or threats didn't motivate all of them, I added a little blatant bribery. I announced that, at the end of the semester, all students who had passed my class and completed a hundred percent of their classwork would be eligible for a special prize drawing. Prizes included a Walkman radio, a 35mm camera, and several silly items such as bubble gum in a tube. I figured a hundred and fifty dollar investment in fifty kids was a bargain if it motivated them to succeed in school. It did. Every single student passed English class and several earned A's.

"Every good grade should be balanced by a bad grade," Bud Bartkus said. We had just received the first semester grade reports for the Academy students. Almost half had failed Bud's computer applications class. A few had failed math and history. None had failed English. I was delighted; Bud was disgusted. He drew a circle around my grades on the computer printout that showed the kids' transcripts.

"You can't have that many good grades," Bud insisted.

"Why can't an entire class of students decide to succeed?" I asked.

"Because an A doesn't mean anything if too many kids get one," Bud said. "It diminishes the value."

"But what if everybody decides to pass and does it?" I said.

"Simple," Bud said with a satisfied smile. "Then the class is too easy."

"Too easy!" I sputtered. "Those kids worked their butts off. They passed because I told them exactly what I expected them to do. I gave them challenging assignments, but I made them believe they could do it. And I also made it very difficult and unappealing to fail."

"We know you're Wonder Woman," Bud said. "But you can't have an entire class of above-average kids. Especially Academy kids."

"Why?" I countered. "Because they have problems? Or because they're minority kids?" I could feel my face begin to flush with anger; Bud's face was growing paler.

"Take it easy, you two," Don Woodford interrupted. "Teachers don't have to justify their grades to anybody except the principal—if he asks." I tried to be quiet, but I couldn't.

"I object to having somebody who has never set foot in my classroom criticizing my grading policy and accusing me of making the work too easy," I said. "I spent a lot of time and energy motivating those kids to succeed and they did. But I'm not surprised so many kids flunked Bud's class. I don't think he even likes most of the kids in our program."

"If you are implying that I am racially biased, you are wrong," Bud said. "As a matter of fact, I volunteered to teach at Bay Point for three years." Bay Point, which had been closed, was a dilapidated high school in the poorest section of the city, where there was zero white population.

"Well, that was real white of you to go help those poor little nigra and beaner heathen," I said.

"Enough!" Don slapped his hand flat on his desktop. "Stop it right now. You are both acting like kids. Worse than kids. You're old enough to know better. We need to pull together and work as a team or this program isn't going to work, and the students are the ones who will suffer." Don was right. Bud and I both shut up, but I knew he wasn't any closer to compromise than I was.

Don opened his grade book and ran his finger down the list of names. "I have ten Ds and four No Credits," he said. "That's almost one-third of the class. I think I'm going to try some nonpenalty methods to connect with these kids. It's worth a try." Jean Warner nodded.

"I've been doing some similar things in my class and they've worked," Jean said, "but I think the primary factor is that these kids believe that we like them. It's very important to them to be liked."

"It's okay to like your students," Bud said, looking directly at me, "as long as you don't give them grades just because you like them."

"Oh, shut up!" I shouted. Don put his hand on my arm to silence me. I stood up and walked outside the room to get some air and regain my composure. After I returned, we managed to get through the rest of the meeting agenda without any dissension. When we finally adjourned and began to gather our books and papers, I was relieved that a truce, however temporary, had been called. I hoped it would last a few days, at least. It didn't. As I reached for the doorknob, Bud cleared his throat and said my name. I turned around.

"I hope you didn't take any of my remarks personally," he said with an insincere smile. "I certainly didn't intend to criticize you or your grading policy." I returned Bud's fake smile, held up my right hand in a fist and rotated my thumb in a circle, a gesture I had seen old salts use many times during my years in the U.S. Navy.

"Sit on this and spin, Bud," I said, then walked out

and slammed the door. I didn't stay mad. My behavior had been tacky, but it was off my chest and I forgot it—until the next morning when I walked into the admin office to pick up my mail and the vice-principal's secretary, Joyce Lewis, called me aside and whispered that Bud Bartkus had just left her boss's office. I had been the subject of his conversation.

"What did he say?" I asked. Surely, Bud wouldn't have run to Steve Simms to tattle on me.

"He was really yelling. He told Mr. Simms that you have no discipline in your classroom at all and that you give A's to all the kids you like," Joyce whispered. "And he said you should be investigated for kissing students—"

"I kissed one kid who was sleeping in summer school!" I protested. "If I had anything to hide, I wouldn't have told anyone, would I?"

"Of course not," Joyce said. "I just thought you should know."

"Thanks," I said. "I appreciate it." I turned to leave, but she touched my arm.

"He went into Dr. Horner's office, too. And the principal's."

I started toward Chet Norton's office. Again, Joyce touched my arm to stop me. "You can't say anything to them. They'll know I told you. I could get fired for revealing confidential information."

"What am I supposed to do?" I asked.

"Forget about it," Joyce said. "I don't think they'll take him seriously. They know you're a good teacher. I just thought you should know is all."

"She's right. Forget about it," Hal Gray said, when I asked for his advice. Although he had been in the midst of grading a stack of essays when I stomped into the lounge, Hal put his pencil down and lit a cigarette.

"Chet didn't get to be principal by being stupid. And you won't get tenure by being stupid," Hal said. He leaned back in his chair and crossed his legs. "Why do you care so much what Bud says about you? Is he important?"

"No," I said. "But he doesn't have any right to go around talking about how I teach when he has never even observed my class."

"Conversation would be extremely boring if we only talked about things we knew for certain," Hal said. "But that isn't the point here."

"What is the point?" I snapped.

He tapped his cigarette against the sole of his shoe and caught the ashes in his hand. He blew the ashes into the air and looked at me. "Now, correct me if I'm wrong. But I believe you have a poster hanging in your classroom—one that you lettered yourself—that reads 'He who angers you enslaves you.'" He gazed at me for a few seconds. "Funny, but you didn't strike me as the slave type."

"I'm not," I said.

"So you say," Hal said. He sat there smiling at me until I smiled back, in spite of myself. "Now go teach those little children. Go ahead and give them A's if you want to."

"I don't *give* grades to kids!" I nearly screamed. "What's the matter with you?"

"I know you don't give them grades," Hal said. "But so what if you did? It would be just as fair as any other grading policy, wouldn't it?"

"No," I said. "They should reach at least a minimum standard to earn a grade."

"Minimum standard of what?" Hal asked. "Commas? Spelling? Vocabulary? Should a kid know four ways to use a comma and the correct spelling of four hundred words? Should he know what defenestration means? What if he doesn't know that word, but he knows a thousand other ones? What is the standard? I'm not talking about the District's objectives. I'm talking about your standards. What is it you expect those kids to know when they leave your class?"

I thought for a few minutes, but couldn't articulate my ideas. I shrugged. "I don't know. I guess maybe I'm not really teaching them anything, when I think about it. I worry about that a lot."

"Of course you do," Hal said. "All teachers wonder whether they're really teaching anything. I used to wonder it myself, hundreds of years ago when I was your age. But then I learned something important. You aren't teaching English. And Bud isn't teaching computers and Don isn't teaching math." He smashed his cigarette butt into the ashtray and stared at me in mock amazement.

"What are you teaching, you may ask?" he said. "I'll tell you. You're teaching kids how to analyze information, relate it to other information they know, put it together and take it apart, and give it back to you in the form that you request it. It doesn't matter what the class is, we all teach the same things. We just use different terms. You use commas and adjectives, biology teachers use chromosomes and chlorophyll, math teachers use imaginary numbers and triangles. And you're also teaching an optional agenda—you're teaching your kids to believe in themselves. So don't worry about whether you're teaching grammar. You're teaching those kids. Trust me, you're teaching them."

That night, I thought about what Hal had said. Talking to Hal always helped me see things from a different perspective. He was right, I decided. Grades were just grades. Preparing my students to be self-confident critical thinkers was the important thing. I arrived at Parkmont the next morning prepared to sit down with Bud Bartkus and work out a compromise on our discipline and grading policies so we could present a consistent program for the kids. As I entered the administration building to pick up my mail and roll sheets, Joyce Lewis motioned to me.

"Your friend was here again," she whispered.

"My friend?"

"Mr. Bartkus," Joyce said. "This time he had a computer printout of your grades. He stopped Mr. Norton right out here, right in front of all the secretaries, and showed him the printout. He said you had too many A's and Bs and you just give grades away so the kids will like you and their parents will think you're a good teacher."

"What?" I shrieked. I felt my eyes fill with tears, which made me furious. I hate to cry in public. Everyone in the office turned around to stare at me, including one of my students, a nosy, talkative boy named Peter Haddix, but I was too shocked and angry to care about my privacy. I grabbed a tissue off Joyce's desk and slapped at the traitorous tears running down my cheeks.

"What's he trying to do?" I yelled. "Make me quit? Get me fired? Drive me crazy?"

"No, that's your students' job," Chet Norton's voice answered from behind me. "Would you mind stepping into my office for a minute?" Blushing and sniffling, I followed Chet into his office and sat in the chair he indicated. He pretended not to notice my red nose and teary eyes.

"I have observed your classes in person," Chet said. "So have Mr. Simms, Dr. Horner, and Miss Nichols.

New teachers are overobserved, if anything. I know you have discipline and I know you don't give away grades. I also know that you're letting your disagreements with Bud Bartkus get out of control. Your constant bickering sets a poor example for your students."

He was right, but my pride was injured.

"But he's running around telling everybody I give away grades and let my kids do whatever they want in class," I protested. "It isn't true."

"So what?" Chet asked. "That isn't the issue here, and we all know it. You're a threat to Bud's idea of how the world should turn. He's a little bit of a chauvinist."

"A little bit!" I sputtered.

"Yes," Chet said. "And he gets carried away sometimes. But that's his problem. Don't make it yours."

I sighed. "What am I supposed to do when he runs around bad-mouthing me all over the school?"

"Nothing," Chet said.

"Do you believe it's possible for an entire class of students to decide to succeed and then do it?" I asked. Chet nodded.

"Yes, I do," he said. "I used to teach English and I believe it's possible, because I've done it myself. Why don't you worry about those kids and forget about Bud? You're doing a fine job. Just keep on doing what you're doing unless you hear otherwise from me."

"But he's writing referrals for students who turn their heads in his class or forget their books. It's ridiculous."

"Yes, it is," Chet agreed, "and I'll have a little chat with him about that this afternoon. I'll tell him I want him to ease up on the referrals. And I want you to ease up on him."

I felt better after talking to Chet, but I was still so mad that my teeth hurt from clenching them and my stomach ached with unspent anger. Bud had declared war and I was determined to fight for the kids, if not for myself. It was clear: The better I treated the kids, the worse he would treat them to balance me out. I seriously considered getting into my car and driving home, but my non-English-speaking class was waiting for me, so I collected my attendance sheets and shuffled off to Buffalo.

Normally, the two hours spent with my lovable, obedient "Spanish babies" was the highlight of my day, but their kid radar must have picked up my emotional signals because they were absolutely terrible. Juan smacked Octavio in the face for stealing his pencil; Maria and Eneida lined up six bottles of nail polish on a desk in the back row and started painting their fingernails while my back was turned; Sergio sneaked out of the room and followed a girl down the hallway until one of the campus security aides brought him back. At one point, every single student was doing something other than what I asked them to do. I lost it. I threw the chalk on the floor, picked up my gradebook, and stomped to the door. For the first time all morning, the class was silent, but it was too late.

"Fine!" I said. "If you don't want to learn, I don't want to teach you. Teach yourselves. You are wasting my time." I walked out the door. Juan was right behind me and the rest of the kids rushed to the windows to watch.

"*Maestra,*" Juan pleaded. "We're sorry. You come back." I shook my head.

"No," I said. "I'm tired of trying to teach people who don't want to learn. Go back to your seat and start working. Now." I pointed at the kids in the window. "All of you! Sit down!" They scrambled to take their seats, but I didn't go back into the room. Instead, I went to the restroom and splashed my face with cold water. It was only ten minutes before the final bell and there was an aide in the classroom, so I knew the NEP kids would be okay. I wasn't so sure about myself. I dried my face and stared at the mirror for a few minutes. I looked old and tired and hopeless. I felt old and tired and hopeless. But the Academy kids were waiting.

The classroom was quiet. Normally, I would have been suspicious. My third period class never took their seats without several minutes of pleas and threats, but I was too distracted and disgusted to question my good fortune. I passed out a worksheet on matching pronouns with their antecedents. Another miracle. Nobody complained. A few minutes later, I heard a soft rapping at the door. I opened the door and found four chubby faces with big, brown, tear-filled eyes. Maria, Eneida, Carolina, and Isabel looked at each other and back at me. Isabel handed me an envelope.

"Please," she said, at a loss for any other English words. I opened the envelope and withdrew a typed letter, written first in Spanish, followed by its English translation:

"Dear Miss Johnson, We are very sorry. We were rude and impolite. Please come back to be our teacher. We will work very hard and we will be polite. We love you." At the bottom of page were thirty signatures—every NEP student had signed the letter. Three crooked red hearts decorated the bottom of the page.

"Mrs. Gomez typed this for us, but we wrote it ourselves," Isabel explained in Spanish. "We don't want you to stop being our teacher."

They were serious! They thought I could, and would, just walk out of the classroom and refuse to be their teacher because they didn't behave for one day. I felt like the wicked witch of the West. "Oh, honey," I said, hugging Isabel, "Of course I'll come back. I love you kids, too." Isabel burst into tears and the other girls did, too, which made me cry. We all hugged each other again and went back to our respective classes.

As I walked back into the room, holding the letter, drying my eyes for the second time that morning, I noticed several kids exchanging pointed looks with Peter, but they didn't say anything. I asked if something was wrong, but they assured me that everything was fine. Something *was* up, but I couldn't figure it out and, after class, they raced out of the room before I had a chance to corner anybody individually. The fourth period Academy kids arrived and were as strangely quiet as third period had been, but I didn't question their unusually good behavior. I was too exhausted to face whatever it was that was driving them to the un-known land of cooperation and obedience. I figured it would be a one-day visit at best.

The phone rang just as the last kid scurried out of the room after seventh period. It was Chet. Would I mind stopping by his office on my way home, he wondered. I'd be happy to, I lied. The admin office was deserted by the time I arrived, but Chet was in his office, waiting for me.

"I thought you might like to see this," Chet said, indicating a piece of paper on his desk. "Some of your Academy kids' handiwork." I closed my eyes and prayed for strength, because I had none left. I didn't want to see another picture of a naked person with enlarged genitals and a hilarious but obscene caption. The kids had been passing them around school and the teachers had been ripping them up, although I believe a few teachers copied them first. Chet handed me the paper. It was a petition, signed by forty-five students, demanding that I be retained as their English teacher.

If I were fired, the petition declared, the students would all quit the Academy immediately.

"It's flattering," I said, "but do they know something I don't know? Are you planning to fire me?"

"It wasn't on my agenda," Chet said.

"Then where did they get that idea?" I asked. "Who gave you this?"

"Peter Haddix."

I started laughing. Good old nosy Peter. No wonder the kids had stared at him when I came back into the room carrying the letter from the earlier NEP class. Peter had been in the office when I was screaming and hollering about quitting or getting fired. Naturally, he told the other kids what he overheard. They were on their best behavior, hoping it would make me look good and I wouldn't get fired. Then someone knocked on the door and gave me a letter that made me cry. Academy kids don't cry happy tears, so they concluded that the letter must have carried bad news—my pink slip. During lunch period, they drew up the petition, signed it, and delivered it to Mr. Norton. I was so proud of them. Even if they didn't always have a firm grip on grammar, they were learning the important stuff. Time after time I had told them that if they truly believed something was wrong or unfair, they shouldn't just give up or moan and groan, but should protest in writing, in an articulate way. That's exactly what they did. Suddenly, I didn't feel so tired or old. I felt young and energetic and eager to see my students the next day.

FIFTEEN

Play It Again, William

"**A**re you sure this is English?" Leroy Wyman frowned at his copy of *The Taming of the Shrew*. "I see some words I know, but they don't make no sense. Look at this." Pointing to a paragraph on the first page, he read aloud: "This were a bed but cold to sleep so soundly." He looked at me. "That don't make no sense, and I know every single word in that sentence. How come we have to read stuff that don't make no sense? And the grammar ain't too good, neither. Even stupid people know you don't say 'This were' something." Leroy tossed his book down on his desk, put his hands in the air, palms up, and looked around the room for support. The other kids nodded agreement. Satisfied that he had discredited Shakespeare's style, Leroy sat back in his seat, crossed his arms, and finished him off.

"I got better grammar than Shakespeare," Leroy said, "and I got a D last year, so he would of got an F."

"I'd give him an F," said a girl seated beside Leroy.

"Me, too!" several others agreed. Stacy Wilson's voice rose above the rest.

"You said this was a good story, Miss Johnson,"

Stacy said, "but it doesn't look good. It looks hard."

"It *is* hard," I said. "Even people in college think Shakespeare is hard to read." Most of the kids stopped grumbling and stared at me, dismayed that I expected them to read something a college student would find difficult.

"I think you kids can handle this," I assured them. "And if you can't, we won't finish it. We'll read the first two acts and take a vote. If nobody wants to finish the story, we'll stop right there and forget it."

"I already know what I'm voting," Leroy said. "N,O, in capital letters."

From the expressions on the faces of the others, I knew they fully intended to vote with Leroy. I was confident that they'd change their minds once they began reading, but after I distributed the books I began to wonder if Charlie Myers had been right. Earlier, when I was on my way out of the library, with the books on a cart, Charlie, who was coming in, held the door for me. As I rolled the cart past him, he glanced at it and shook his head.

"I wouldn't try to teach those kids Shakespeare," he said. "You're just asking for trouble."

"There's nothing wrong with their brains," I said, immediately defensive.

"I didn't say there was," Charlie said, "but I still think you'd be better off with something they can relate to. Asking them to read Shakespeare is like asking them to build a house without a hammer. They may have the raw materials, and they may even have the will, but they simply don't have the tools."

"I have the tools," I said, "and I'll help them."

"Or end up doing all the work for them," Charlie said, his voice rich with condescension. Seeing that I had no intention of backing down, Charlie stepped back. "Have it your way," he said as he waved me through the doorway.

"I usually do," I said, mimicking his arrogant tone. His attitude only increased my determination to tackle the reading project. I wasn't worried. Following the advice of some journal articles written by experienced teachers, I had first introduced the idea of reading Shakespeare to the students several weeks previously.

"You kids are sharp," I'd say, after someone correctly answered a question in class. "You'll be ready to read Shakespeare pretty soon, just like the big kids." Or after a spelling quiz that everyone passed, I'd whistle and shake my head and whisper, "Shakespeare would be a piece of cake for this crowd."

The first time I mentioned Shakespeare's name, every single kid in the class groaned. I grinned at them.

"Oh, goody," I said. "I love to make you miserable. That's my job. Teachers lie awake all nights in their beds, thinking of ways to bore their students to tears. The more bored the better. If you drop dead from boredom, I get a special award. Bet you didn't know that, did you?" They rolled their eyes and sighed, but nobody spoke. I think they hoped if they ignored me, the idea would go away. It didn't. By the time we finally got around to reading *The Taming of the Shrew*, the kids were tired of hearing about it.

"Let's just read the dude and get it over with," Leroy Wyman said one afternoon. "I'm tired of hearing about it."

"What a wonderful idea, Leroy!" I said, opening the storage cupboard door with a flourish. "I just happen to have twenty-five copies of Shakespeare's delightful comedy *The Taming of the Shrew* right here in our very own classroom."

"Way to go, Leroy!" Detrick Davis shot a paper wad at Leroy's head.

Because he had suggested reading the play, although his suggestion had been unintentional, Leroy obviously felt responsible for complaining the loudest as we started Act I, but his voice was one of many. None of the kids thought it was funny for a bunch of rich guys to pick a drunken bum up out of the street, dress him up in fancy clothes, then wake him up and tell him he was a very wealthy person who had been ill for several years.

"That isn't funny," Stacy protested. "It's mean."

"Yeah," Detrick said. "I'd kick their ass when I found out."

"You said this was a comedy, Miss J.," Leroy chimed in, "but it ain't funny."

I tried to explain, but nobody bought it and, when we reached the scene in which the page, a young man, is called upon to masquerade as an older man's wife as part of a practical joke, the kids really lost it. Several times, I had reminded the kids that all parts were played by men in Shakespeare's theater, and each time, they had hooted and hollered and flipped their wrists.

"I wouldn't wear no dress," Leroy insisted. "Not even for a joke."

"Me, neither," Raul said and the rest of the boys nodded their agreement. I saw it coming, but there was no way to avoid it.

When the older man, Sly, wakes up and finds his "wife" (the page) waiting by his bed, he immediately asks her to undress and join him in bed.

"Sly's a faggot!" Leroy yelled.

"He is not," Stacy argued. "He thinks the boy is his wife."

184

"Then he's stupid," Leroy insisted. "If some boy came hanging around me, dressed up like he was a woman, I'd still know he wasn't no woman."

"Sly's been drinking," Stacy pointed out. "He got so drunk he passed out right on the sidewalk, so he probably has such a bad hangover he can't see straight. If you—"

"Shut up," Leroy interrupted. "Stop running your mouth and read your part, so we can find out what happens."

Stacy read the next paragraph, but as soon as she finished reading, she looked up at me expectantly. So did the others. They couldn't translate the language into modern English, so I had called for a pause after each character's speech and asked the student who was reading the part to explain what he or she had just said. In every case, the student responded with a shrug and a headshake, unwilling or unable to make the connection, counting on me to explain the dialogue. Up until that point, I had provided the translation, but remembering Charlie Myers's prediction that I'd end up doing all the work, I stood my ground, determined to make the kids start thinking for themselves.

"Come on, Stacy," I said. "I'll read your part again and you tell me what the page said when Sly asked him to hop into bed." I repeated the paragraph slowly.

Thrice noble lord, let me entreat of you
To pardon me yet for a night or two,
Or if not so, until the sun be set.
For your physicians have expressly charged,
In peril to incur your former malade,
That I should yet absent me from your bed.

"What does that mean?" I asked.

"I don't know," Stacy said, staring at her book.

"Anybody else?" I glanced around the room, but nobody looked at me. Two minutes seems like forever in a silent classroom, but I forced myself to remain quiet. Finally, Phillip Rose ran his right hand over his red hair, then raised it tentatively into the air.

"They charged the bill to the doctor?" Phillip asked, without a shred of confidence. I couldn't believe that Phillip had actually answered a question in front of the class. Usually, he blushed and hung his head if I even looked at him. My first inclination was to hug him, or at least pat him on the back, but as I stepped near to his desk, Phillip shrank into his seat. I shoved my hands into my pockets so I wouldn't be tempted to scoop him up and squeeze him. My right hand met a dollar bill. Without thinking, I pulled the dollar from my pocket and handed it to Phillip.

"All right!" I almost yelled. "Here's a dollar for thinking!"

"Is that right?" Phillip asked, surprised.

"No," I said, "but that's not important."

Phillip was too shocked to respond, but Leroy Wyman wasn't. Leroy stood up and pointed at Phillip.

"How come he gets a dollar for telling the wrong answer?" Leroy demanded.

"Because sometimes it takes a lot of wrong answers before you get the right one," I said. "But if you're afraid to think, you'll never figure anything out."

After that, kids scrambled to interpret the story, hoping for a prize. When I asked for possible reasons for Kate's shrewish behavior, both of Leroy's hands shot into the air, waving wildly, before I finished the question.

"I know!" Leroy said. "She act like a bitch because

her parents are divorced. There ain't no mother in this story, because she probably run off with some other man and Kate probably looks just like her mother, so her father hates her and she has a attitude." Extremely proud of his psychological insight, Leroy sat down, beaming, and crossed his arms over his chest. "That's an A-one, prize-winning answer, Miss J., and you know it."

"That's a winner, all right," I agreed. I gave Leroy a candy bar from my spelling bee prize bag. I also gave candy bars to the other kids who offered their ideas on Kate's attitude. Leroy's candy bar lay untouched on his desk.

"How come Phil got a dollar for a wrong answer a while ago and we got these lame candy bars for good answers?" Leroy wanted to know.

"Because he was the bravest one," I said. "He answered first when everybody else was too afraid to say what they were thinking because they might have been wrong. And, besides, I don't have any more dollars in my pocket."

"You can give me that candy bar if you don't want it, Leroy," Raul Chacon said. Leroy quickly unwrapped the bar and shoved the whole thing in his mouth.

As we continued reading, every student who offered a valid suggestion—right or wrong—earned a prize. I hadn't been prepared to give prizes, so I gave them whatever I could find in my purse and desk, quarters, bookmarks, highlighting pens, neon colored pencils. I thought they might stop offering answers when the prizes dwindled to rubber covered paper clips, but they continued waving their hands and jumping out of their seats to offer ideas. When I ran out of rewards, I expected them to run out of ideas, but they didn't. By then, they were hooked on the challenge and intrigued by the story. The more we read, the better they got at translating the dialogue and understanding the story.

By the time we reached the end of the second act, the vote was unanimous to continue reading. The boys were delighted at the idea of Petruchio riding into town on his horse, partying with the local boys, and vowing to marry and tame the nastiest woman on earth in exchange for her money. Most of the girls were confident that Kate was more than equal to the challenge, and Jessi Alipate predicted that Kate would "whip Petruchio's butt."

One day, as we assigned parts for the kids to read, Jessi remarked, "I didn't know Shakespeare stories were so sexy. If I would of knew that, I might of read them before."

"Yeah," Detrick Davis agreed. "No wonder college kids like to read this stuff. They probably get some good ideas from it."

After we finished reading the play, we watched the film version starring Elizabeth Taylor and Richard Burton. In spite of the intense interest of both boys and girls in Ms. Taylor's impressive bosom, the majority of the kids preferred the written version to the video. The final assignment was a two-page essay comparing the two versions, with supporting arguments for the preferred version.

"I usually like movies a whole lot more than books," Leroy wrote,

> but I had better pictures in my own head this time. The movie was all right, but it didn't have as much action as the book and there was some seens in the movie that wasn't in the book and that ain't right. If somebody tells a story and you

make a movie out of it, you shouldn't make up
your own stuff and put it in the movie because
then it isn't the other guy's story anymore. Sha-
kespeer didn't say nothing about Kate and Petruchio rolling around in a big room full of cotton
which was the weerdest thing in the movie.

In her essay, Jessi tackled the question of who was
really tamed. She concluded with:

Well, if you ask me, it wasn't Kate who got tamed
in the end because she knew exactly what she was
doing. She didn't have to live with her rotten,
mean old father who liked her sister better, and
she got a good-looking husband with a fresh body,
and she got to live in a big castle with a bunch of
servants and Petruchio was really nice to her. He
said he was taming her by killing her with kindness but he used to be real nasty and macho and
all that stuff and he stopped being tough and
acted different when they got married. So, I think
Petruchio really was the one who got tamed, even
though Kate got tamed down a little bit.

When we finished the final essays, I thought the kids
would enjoy some "brain candy," so I distributed copies of a popular teen novel, *My Darling, My Ham-
burger*. My summer school students had enjoyed the
book, but the Academy kids hated it. After three chapters, they demanded a vote to see if anyone wanted to
continue. Nobody did.

"I'll have to check the book list to see what's in stock
in the library," I explained, as I collected the novels.

"Why don't we read some more of that Shakespeare
stuff," Leroy suggested.

"No!" a couple of kids shouted.

"Yes!" a lot of kids yelled. "Take a vote!"

Shakespeare won easily and the kids elected to read *The Merchant of Venice*. Most of the students were intrigued by the idea of a young man lending all of his money to his best friend just so the friend could impress a lady, but Curtis Jackson wasn't interested in the romantic aspect of the story; Curtis wanted to see Shylock cut a pound of flesh out of Antonio.

"I want to see him cut the dude," Curtis said. "That's pretty ruthless."

I didn't disillusion Curtis because I figured we'd be so close to the end of the story before he realized he wasn't going to see any blood that he'd be satisfied. Not that I expected Curtis to be awake at the end of the story. Curtis hated reading. He hated writing. He hated math. He hated history. The only thing Curtis liked was football, and he really liked football. His class attendance was perfect, but his performance was marginal; he did just enough work to maintain a C average and his position as quarterback on the varsity team. In English class, Curtis's regular position was slumped forward, chin in his hands, eyes glazed, eyelids half closed.

When we started reading *The Merchant of Venice*, Curtis was wide awake and attentive. He stayed that way throughout the entire play, in anticipation of the flesh cutting. When it became clear, during the dramatic courtroom scene, that Shylock wasn't going to make the cut, Curtis punched his desk.

"What a rip-off!" he yelled. "He's supposed to cut the guy. This is lame." In spite of his disappointment, Curtis remained involved in the play. When the judge ordered Shylock, a devout Jew, to denounce his religion and kiss the Christian cross, Curtis punched his desk again.

"That's cold!" Curtis said. "They didn't have to do that. The man already lost his daughter and his money and his land. They didn't have to take his religion, too. That's cold. That's real cold."

When the final essay assignments were turned in, I was shocked to find two full pages in Curtis's journal. In nearly two years, Curtis had never written more than three paragraphs and had never filled an entire page. His essay reiterated his belief that making Shylock kiss the cross was "too cold."

"I'm so proud of you, Curtis," I said, as I returned his journal. "You've never written such a good essay before."

"I never had anything to say before," Curtis said.

Shortly after we finished reading *The Merchant of Venice*, Mel Gibson starred in a movie version of *Hamlet* and the students asked if we could read the play and watch the movie later when it came out on video. They didn't have to twist my arm. I sent a request to the library for fifty copies of *Hamlet*. The next day, Charlie Myers called me on the phone.

"I hear you ordered *Hamlet*," Charlie said.

"Yes."

"That's a senior-level book, you know," Charlie said.

"Is that a problem?" I asked.

"Well, you ordered it for a junior class, didn't you?"

"Yes, but it's an Academy class," I explained. "I'll have the same kids next year, so they won't be repeating any of the work."

"But it's a senior-level book," Charlie repeated.

"Would you rather I waited and had the kids read it next year?" I asked. There was a good chance Charlie would be department head the following year and I didn't want him to start inspecting my curriculum and lesson plans. A lot of projects in my lessons were not on the standard curriculum.

"I think it would be a good idea to wait," Charlie said. "We wouldn't want those kids to get ahead of themselves."

"No, we certainly wouldn't want that to happen." I didn't remind Charlie that a few months earlier he had cautioned me against trying to teach Shakespeare to "those kids."

The class was disappointed to find out that they'd have to wait a few more months to read *Hamlet*. I consoled them by allowing them to read *Twelfth Night* in the meantime.

SIXTEEN

If I'm Not Dumb, Why Can't I Pass?

Halfway through the reading proficiency exam, Leroy Wyman threw his test booklet on the floor and ripped his answer sheet into little bits. He ducked out the door and was gone from sight before I could reach him. I knew I wouldn't see him the next day. Every time his class took a reading or writing proficiency exam, Leroy would bring a brand new pencil and carefully sharpen it until the point was perfect. Then he'd sit down and hum softly to himself, drumming his fingertips on his desktop until the test booklets were distributed. For a while, he'd struggle valiantly with the material, until he became aware that the other students were turning pages and moving on to the next section before he had even finished reading the first page. Then he'd close his test booklet and put his head down on the desk and refuse to open his eyes until the tests were collected. But he'd never destroyed his test before.

A gentle, soft-spoken boy, Leroy had been one of the first students to volunteer for the Academy program. During his interview, all of the teachers were impressed with his good manners, his enthusiasm, and his desire to succeed in school. Unlike most of the students, who were too cool to acknowledge their emotions publicly, Leroy hopped out of his chair and danced a little jig when we informed him that he'd been accepted into the Academy. He shook each teacher's hand warmly and beamed like a child who has been promised a trip to the circus. He was, in fact, very much like a child in his innocence and desire to be liked and to do well.

Two weeks into the school year, Don Woodford's math textbook disappeared. Don assumed he had misplaced the text until Leroy's homework, which had been barely adequate until then, suddenly became perfect, textbook perfect. Every single answer matched Don's answer key word for word. Don confronted Leroy and demanded that he return the text. Any other youngster would have denied having the book, but Leroy smiled and nodded and promptly returned the text the next day.

"Why did you steal Mr. Woodford's textbook?" I asked Leroy.

"Because I wanted to get a good grade," he said.

"But that's cheating," I said. "Cheating is dishonest."

"I didn't copy off anybody else," Leroy said. "I just looked in the book."

"That's still cheating," I explained. "You have to do the work yourself."

"Okay." Leroy nodded and smiled.

A few weeks later, a student named Ray Martin stormed into the classroom and grabbed Leroy by the shirt collar.

"I'm gonna kick your ass," Ray threatened.

"Not in my class, you aren't," I said. "What's your problem?" Ray loosened his hold on Leroy, but didn't let go.

"The little creep stole my gym bag and sold it to somebody else for five dollars."

"Did you take his bag, Leroy?" I asked. Leroy nodded.

"Why?"

"Because I saw it laying on the floor in here at lunch and nobody took it, so I did."

"But you can't take things that don't belong to you," I said. "That's stealing."

"I didn't steal it," Leroy said. "I just took it."

"Are you stupid or something?" Ray yelled.

"No!" Leroy screamed. "I'm not stupid!" His face contorted and his eyes filled with tears.

Ray dropped his hands and turned to me. "He's screwy."

"I'll get your bag back," I said softly.

"I already got it," Ray said. "I was just gonna kick his ass for stealing it, but I'm not gonna beat up on a nut." Leroy took off running. Ray shrugged his shoulders and left.

After that, I paid particular attention to Leroy's behavior and his work in class. His attendance was perfect and he did every single assignment, but his work in class was far better than anything he did at home, especially assignments that required reading. One day, I asked him to read aloud in class, to make sure that he could read, and he read willingly and quite well, yet when I asked him to answer simple questions about the material he had just read, he couldn't do it.

I sent a referral to the school psychologist's office, requesting that Leroy be tested for possible learning disabilities. Dr. Long interviewed Leroy and determined that testing was in order, but Leroy's mother refused to allow him to be tested.

195

"I thought he lived with his grandmother," I said, confused.

"He does," Dr. Long said, "but his mother still has legal authority and she flatly refused to allow any testing."

"Why?"

"She thinks the tests are for retarded students. I tried to explain that normal, intelligent children can have learning disabilities, but she wouldn't listen."

"Can't we test him anyway, without telling her?" I was willing to break the rules to help Leroy. Dr. Long shook her head.

"Sorry," she said. "Without parental permission, we can't do anything."

"But I don't think Leroy will ever pass the reading proficiency exam and if he doesn't, he can't graduate even if he has all the credits he needs."

"I understand," Dr. Long said, "and I sympathize with the boy, but we can't designate a child for the Resource Specialist Program without parental consent. It's not uncommon for people to fear the testing. They think people will blame their children's problems on them—accuse them of drinking or taking drugs while pregnant, or abusing their infants. And some people are just ashamed. They don't want anybody to know that their children aren't perfect."

Periodically, during the next year, I sent a testing request to Leroy's mother, but she returned them unsigned each time. And each time Leroy took the reading exam, he failed.

"When do we get our tests back?" he'd ask the day following each exam, and each day for the three weeks it took for the tests to be graded by the district office and returned to the teachers. By the time he reached his senior year, Leroy was completely discouraged. I wasn't surprised when he tore his answer sheet into shreds; I was only surprised that he hadn't done it before. He didn't come to class the day after he destroyed his test, so I called his home later, but his grandmother told me he was sleeping and she didn't want to disturb him. I asked if he'd been sick recently, but she said he was fine, so I didn't mention that he had been absent. I wanted to talk to him first.

"Please tell him that I called just to say hello," I said.

Leroy was the first person in class the following day. Slumped in his seat, he lowered his head and peeked at me out of the corner of one eye.

"I wasn't really sleeping," Leroy said, "but I knew it was you, so I pretended I was sleeping so my grandma wouldn't wake me up."

"Why didn't you want to talk to me?" I asked.

" 'Cause I knew you were gonna yell at me for messing up my test."

"I wasn't going to yell at you," I explained, "but I was concerned about you. Are you all right?"

"I'm okay," Leroy said, "but I hate that stupid test." He sat up straight and his back grew stiff. "I already took it three times and I flunked it every time. I know I'm not dumb. I can read. Look at this." He walked to my desk, picked up a short-story anthology, flipped it open and started reading aloud.

"Le Fanois turned around and saw a large woman with pale, puffy features and a complicated coiffure, on which was poised a hat laden with the remains of an entire aviary of exotic birds. She advanced toward them, her shoulders weighed down by a magnificent silver fox coat, her movements impeded by the folds of a lavishly embroidered dress, trailing in her wake a tall, rosy girl." He closed the book and crossed his arms. "See, didn't I read that?"

"Yes, you did," I said, "but what did it mean?"

"What do you mean, what did it mean?" Leroy asked.

"The passage that you read," I said slowly, "tell me, in your own words, what it said." Leroy's brow wrinkled in concentration.

"I don't know," he shrugged. "It was about a fat lady, but I can't remember it."

"Is that what happened to you on the reading test?" I asked gently. "Did you read the passages and then have trouble answering the questions afterward?" Leroy nodded.

"Yeah, but that test is stupid. It has a bunch of stuff from the yellow pages and newspaper ads and signs and stuff like that. Easy stuff. Anybody can read it. But I keep flunking the test. It makes me so mad. I'm not dumb. Do you think I'm dumb?"

"No, I don't think you're a bit dumb," I said.

"Then if I'm not dumb, why can't I pass that dumb test?" Leroy demanded. "Every time I take it, you tell me don't worry, I can take it again next year, but now I'm a senior and if I don't pass it I can't graduate. I know I get to take it every month this year, but it won't do any good." He slumped back down into his seat, his chin on his chest.

"Have you ever heard of dyslexia?" I asked. He shook his head.

"It means your eyes don't read letters or numbers correctly," I said. I wrote the words *bad* and *dab* on the chalkboard. "If somebody has dyslexia, his eyes might read *bad* and see *dab*. Or maybe the letters seem to move around. It doesn't mean the person isn't smart, it just means his or her brain isn't processing the information correctly. Like a short circuit." Suddenly, Leroy sat up, his eyes bright.

"That's like Cosby!" he said.

"Cosby?" I didn't have a student named Cosby.

" 'The Cosby Show,' " Leroy said. "One of the kids had that dyslexia thing and Cosby said it doesn't mean he's stupid."

"Exactly," I said. "And if you take a test and they find out you have dyslexia or a perceptual problem or some other learning disability, that would explain why you have trouble on that reading test. We have special classes where the teachers can help you read better. And you won't have to pass the test to graduate."

"For real?"

"For real," I said. For a minute, Leroy looked ecstatic, then he hung his head.

"But they probably won't test me after the way I hollered all over the office last year. Me and my mother, too."

"I'm sure they'll still test you if she signs the papers. Dr. Long won't be mad. She just wants to help you."

"She's gonna let me take the test!" Leroy announced the next day.

His tests showed that he did, indeed, have a perceptual problem that prevented him from processing written information correctly.

"I knew I wasn't retarded," he assured me. " 'Cause look at my transcript. I got a whole lot of Bs and I can do all my homework. Don't I do good in your class? I always get a hundred on the spelling tests."

He strutted around the classroom, explaining to whoever would listen that he had a learning disability just like the kid on "The Cosby Show." For once, I was thankful that a student had been watching TV at home instead of doing his homework.

*   *   *

I wish I could say that Leroy's happy ending was typical, but it isn't. Most of the time, students are more resistant than their parents when it comes to finding out why they have problems with math or reading or writing. They'd rather fail or take remedial classes or accept a barely passing grade than risk finding out that they have a learning disability; there is such a stigma attached to special education programs. Still, I continue to discuss the subject in all of my classes and, occasionally, a student steps bravely forward and requests the testing.

"If you're failing math or English," I tell the kids, "and people keep saying things like, 'You just aren't applying yourself; I know you could do this if you tried harder' or 'You used to get good grades, so you must not be trying,' then you might have a learning disability. If you know you are trying and people are telling you that you aren't, there might be a reason."

Another thing I discuss with my students is learning styles: auditory, visual, and kinesthetic. I give the same spelling test three ways—I spell each word three ways aloud and ask the students to select the correct spelling; I give them a worksheet with the words spelled on it and ask them to pick the correctly spelled words; and, finally, I dictate the words and ask the students to write them down. Students who do better on the first test are auditorially oriented; they process information best through hearing. Students who do better on the second test are visual; they learn by seeing. And the last group, the kinesthetic learners, need to learn by doing. The kinesthetic learners have the hardest time in school because many subjects don't lend themselves easily to active lessons.

To make sure that we have correctly determined the students' learning preference, we do another exercise.

Speaking quickly, I give detailed oral instructions to the class for folding a sheet of notebook paper into a specific shape, then see how many can follow the instructions without further help. Then, I demonstrate a similar, but different, set of instructions and ask them to follow my example. Finally, I walk the students through a third set of instructions, one instruction at a time, giving the next step only after they have performed the previous one. Usually, students have a distinct preference for one style or another. Once they know their learning styles, the problem is to help them learn to articulate their needs to teachers who do not teach in that particular style.

"What happens when you raise your hand and tell your math teacher that you don't get it?" I ask the kids.

"They tell you the same thing again," someone invariably answers.

"Exactly the same way?" I ask.

"Yeah," the student says, "except sometimes they might talk slower."

"Does that help you?"

"No."

"Then, if you know you are a visual learner," I ask, "what could you ask the math teacher to do if you don't understand?"

"Ask him to draw me a picture?"

"Exactly. Tell him you learn better if you can see things in pictures and ask if he can draw you an example of what he's talking about. And if you're a kinesthetic learner, ask him if he can help you do a few examples yourself on your own paper, because you learn by doing."

I type a brief description of the three learning styles and make copies to send to parents of children who have problems in class so they can help their kids with their homework. I also explain the testing program and emphasize that learning disabilities and intelligence are two distinctly different things. If a child is having problems, particularly in math or English, I urge them to consider having the child's vision tested to make sure it isn't a simple matter of not seeing correctly and, if that isn't the case, I ask them to allow us to test their child for some other problem.

Sometimes the parents respond positively, and when they do, the results in student performance are usually dramatic. One girl, Sharon, had been tested in the first grade and diagnosed as retarded. For years, Sharon had attended special education classes and was seventeen years old by the time she earned enough credits to be a sophomore. She applied for the Academy program and we accepted her because her attitude was so positive, her study skills and work habits were so good, and her parents were so supportive of her efforts.

After several class discussions about learning disabilities, Sharon brought a pair of eyeglasses with blue lenses in them. Her eye doctor had diagnosed her as suffering from both dyslexia and skotopic sensitivity, meaning that her eyes focused better if the background of the page was a specific color. Blue was Sharon's color. With the help of her colored lenses to focus the print and a cardboard guide to isolate one line of text at a time, Sharon was able to read well for the first time in her life.

At first, both Sharon and her parents had trouble adjusting to the idea that she wasn't retarded after all. They were so used to expecting her to fail that they didn't trust it when she began to succeed in school. But eventually they adjusted. A few weeks after she got the new glasses, Sharon wrote a note in her journal.

"I just finished reading *The Promise*. I read the

whole book. I never read a whole book before in my life. I feel real proud of myself. Now I'm going to read all the books I want to. It's fun to read. It's cool. Totally cool.''

SEVENTEEN

The Silent Student

Durrell Lewis was a "ghost," the invisible student who sits in the back of the class, never raises his hand, never causes trouble, never disrupts class, never talks, and usually disappears long before graduation, although no one notices. At the start of the school year, Durrell had quietly vegetated in the back of my classroom for a couple of weeks before I realized that he had not turned in a single assignment. I checked his private journal; it was blank. I remembered that the first time I gave an assignment, the autobiography, he had asked for extra time because he couldn't write in class. He never did turn in the autobiography. He simply turned in a blank journal each time I collected them from everyone. When I gave the notebook back to him to write the assignment, he'd always say, "I thought I did it."

Journal assignments and homework I could understand, but how could he have been present and still miss all the worksheets we did in class? I counted them when I collected them and I would have noticed if there had been any missing. I checked my files to make sure I hadn't misplaced any of Durrell's work, but I didn't have a single piece of paper with his handwriting on it, no evidence that he existed. I recalled a few times when I had reminded him that an assignment was overdue. Each time, he had nodded in agreement, but had never produced the work. When I asked him for it, he either said, "I forgot," "It's in my locker," or "I'll bring it tomorrow." I called Durrell at home and told him I was concerned because I had no assignments from him. He didn't respond. I thought he had hung up on me.

"Durrell?"

"Yes, Miss Johnson," he answered in a barely audible monotone.

"I'd like to talk to you about this," I said, in my most reasonable and gentle voice.

"Okay."

"Why haven't you turned in any assignments?"

"I don't know."

"Who knows then?"

"I don't know."

"Would you rather talk about it after class tomorrow?" I suggested.

"Okay."

"Are you always so talkative?" I asked. Durrell didn't respond.

"Durrell?"

"Yes, Miss Johnson."

"It was a joke," I said. "I was kidding."

"Oh."

My ear began to ache from pressing it against the receiver, so I gave up. Durrell wasn't hostile or rude. He wasn't defensive. He was nothing, and I didn't know how to deal with nothing. Our conversation the next day was even less dynamic. We sat in my office, me looking at Durrell, Durrell looking at the floor, his feet, the window, everywhere but my face.

"Do you want to be in this program, Durrell?"

"I don't have a choice." He stared at his shoes and spoke so softly that I found myself holding my breath as I listened.

"Yes, you do. It's completely voluntary."

"My mother wants me here."

"I don't care what your mother wants," I said. "What do you want?" Durrell shrugged.

"Nothing."

"Do you want to be here?" I asked again.

"I don't have a choice," Durrell repeated. I stood up and walked to his side. He stiffened, but still didn't look at me. I stopped about two feet in front of him and bent down so I had to look up into his face. He didn't turn away, but he didn't look at me, either.

"Would you please look at me for just one second?" I asked. "I don't feel as if I'm communicating with you." He glanced at me for a fraction of a second, then dropped his eyes. It wasn't long, but it was long enough to frighten me. His eyes were as empty as his journal.

"I'm trying to help you," I said. He didn't answer. Finally, I realized that he never responded to anything other than a direct question. "Do you believe that?"

"Yes," he whispered.

"I can't help you if you don't let me." He didn't answer, and even at such close quarters, I couldn't get a feel for whether he was receptive. I took a chance and lightly placed my hand on his forearm. When he failed to respond, I realized that I had expected him to move away or look at me or shrug my hand off or shudder or something. Anything. He did nothing. I was touching a warm mannequin. I dropped my hand.

"Do you want me to help you?"

"I don't know." Finally, I understood. He honestly didn't know because that would require thinking or feeling and he had no intention of doing either.

"Well, I'm going to try to help you until you tell me to stop. Okay?"

"Okay, Miss Johnson."

I told him I wanted him to do the first journal assignment, the autobiography, because it was the most important and carried the most points toward his grade. He nodded and started out the door.

"Durrell?" He stopped and turned halfway. "If you don't bring the journal tomorrow, or if you cut my class or don't come to school, I'll have to call your father." His head snapped around and he looked me full in the face for only a split second, but it was enough. Somebody was home after all, somebody who didn't want me to talk to his father.

The next day, Durrell took his usual seat in the back. He didn't look at me, but he did pull his journal out of his backpack and place it on his desktop. After class, he disappeared, leaving the journal behind. I hurried to pick it up, curious to see what he had written. It looked empty! I paged through it to see whether he had written in the middle—some kids simply opened their journals and wrote on whatever page had space—but every page in Durrell's book looked blank. That evening, I called his home. Durrell answered and I told him I was calling to talk to his father, since he had not done the assignment.

"I did it," he said, his voice one decibel above the usual whisper.

"You did not," I said. "I have your journal right here in my office and there's nothing in it."

"I did it," Durrell said.

"Then where is it?"

"In my journal."

"Look, Durrell," I said. "This is making me tired.

Your journal is blank. I checked all the pages."

"I did it, Miss Johnson," he said. "On the first page." Frustrated, I dropped the phone loudly on the desk and went to retrieve Durrell's journal. I opened it to the first page, and held it under the light of a small high-intensity lamp. I peered closer. There was writing on the page. It was so fine, written with such a light hand, that it was practically invisible. I picked up the phone.

"Durrell?"

"Yes, Miss Johnson."

"I apologize. It's very light, so I didn't see it, but it's there. I'll read it and talk to you about it tomorrow." No response, as usual. It was hard to remember to phrase everything as a question.

"Sweet dreams, Durrell," I said. Nothing. "Okay?"

"Okay." He hung up. I read his journal:

When I was little, I went to private schools because my mother wanted me to get a good education. She's a teacher. I got all A's and B's, but my cousin got all A's, so my mother always said I could do better and why couldn't I be like my cousin and get all A's. I tried, but I got a B sometimes and my mother never said anything about the A's, just the B's. And she said I have to be a good example for my brothers because I'm the oldest. I don't want to be an example. One day, we were at my grandma's house and my aunt was there and I was outside playing by the window and I heard them talking about me. They said why couldn't I be like my cousin. I hated my cousin so much, I went and got a branch off the tree that had thorns in it and I started hitting him with it. My father came out and lit some paper on fire and threw it at me to make me stop, so I stopped hitting him. But I still hate him. I'm not smart like my cousin and I can't get all A's, so I don't get anything. Whatever I do isn't good enough.

After reading his journal, I asked Durrell if he would object to a parent-teacher conference. He shrugged his shoulders, so I called his parents and arranged a meeting for the following afternoon. When Mr. and Mrs. Lewis arrived, we drew several student desks into a circle so that the Academy teachers and the Lewis family could all face each other. As soon as Durrell sat down, in the standard teenage slump, his father raised one bushy eyebrow and glared at his son. Durrell didn't look at his father, but he did push himself to an upright sitting position. That one glance was the only time that either of the Lewises looked at their son during the meeting.

"We don't know what to do with him anymore," Mrs. Lewis said. "We've tried everything."

"So have we," I said, "but we aren't making much progress. We've told Durrell that it's up to him. If he doesn't want to graduate from high school, he might as well drop out and get a job." Before I finished speaking, Mr. Lewis was on his feet, his eyes wide and angry.

"Are you telling my son to drop out of school?" he demanded.

"No," I said, quickly. "I don't think he should drop out. But I want him to understand that he's wasting his time if he continues to flunk all his classes. Eventually, he'll be pulled out of public school and placed in an alternative school. But he'll never graduate unless he decides that's what he wants to do. And if that isn't what he wants to do, maybe he should try to find a job now. That might convince him that graduating would be to his benefit.''

Mr. Lewis sat back down, eyeing me warily. "Well, my son isn't dropping out of school," he said. "I graduated from college and so did his mother, and he's going to college, too.''

Our meeting wasn't long because Mr. Lewis had to go to work, but it was long enough to see that Durrell was demonstrating control of his life in the only way he could.

"Do you think you're hurting your parents by flunking all your classes?" I asked Durrell the next day.

"No," he said.

"Then why do you do it?"

"I don't know."

"Are you trying to hurt yourself?"

"No."

"How about your father?" Durrell didn't answer and he didn't look at me, but I sensed an emotional response.

"Do you and your father get along?"

"I don't know."

"Durrell?"

"Not really."

"Why?"

"He hates me."

"Why?"

"I don't know."

"Then how do you know he hates you?"

"He picks on me."

"For what?"

"He says I'm too fat and he makes fun of me. He used to take karate lessons and I wanted to take kung fu but he made fun of me." Saying two complete sentences seemed to take too much out of Durrell. He was about five inches taller than I am, which would make him nearly six feet tall, but he suddenly seemed small and very young.

"Are you taking kung fu now?"

"Once in a while."

"Do you like it?"

"It's okay." I was excited. He actually liked something!

"Does your father object if you take kung fu?"

"No."

"Wonderful! I'll see you tomorrow."

One of the campus security aides, Randy Harris, taught kung fu on the weekends, so I asked him if he'd take Durrell into his class and try to give him an extra bit of encouragement. He agreed and Durrell became a regular in Randy's class. After about two months, there was a slight but noticeable difference in Durrell's attitude. He was still a ghost, and still didn't participate in class, but he turned in enough assignments in each class to fail. Flunking was a step in the right direction, since he usually earned No Credits for doing absolutely nothing. An F can become a D with a little extra effort.

By the end of the first semester, Durrell was straddling the line between D-minus and No Credit in every class; if he passed his exams, he'd pass his classes. The Academy staff was ecstatic. We all liked him and had treated him with a special, gentle kindness. Slowly, he was emerging from his silent shell and we tried not to appear to be watching him as closely as we were.

"It's scary when he just sits there like a zombie," Don Woodford commented at one of our Academy staff meetings. "Sometimes I wonder if he's suicidal." I'd had similar thoughts and they frightened me. The day before the English exam, Durrell came to school but cut my class, something he had never done before. I called him that night, planning to reprimand him gently, as usual, but when he answered in his usual dull monotone, I lost it. I was so worried about him that I became angry.

"You did something really dumb today, didn't you?" I said.

"I guess I'm just dumb," he said.

"Oh, no you aren't," I said, "but you do some really dumb things. So do I. But I'm not dumb enough to let you cut my class."

"Sorry, Miss Johnson," Durrell said, without a trace of regret in his voice.

"Sorry isn't good enough," I said. "Do you know what I'm going to do if you aren't in my class tomorrow and the next day and every day after that until the end of the year?"

"No."

Anybody else would have asked, "What?" but not Durrell. He remained silent. I couldn't even hear him breathing. It infuriated me. I was about to tell him that I wanted to talk to his father when, without warning, my mind changed itself and created a new threat.

"If you cut my class again and if you don't pass your exams, I'm going to come to your kung fu class and beat the shit out of you in front of all of your friends," I said, astounding myself. I couldn't beat up Durrell on my best day, and I started to apologize for cussing, but apparently he was one of the students who knew I'd been in the marines and believed that all ex–Marine Corps officers have lethal hands.

"Oh," he said softly, clearly surprised but, from the sound of his voice, completely convinced of my sincerity.

"Do you think I could do that, Durrell?"

"Yes, Miss Johnson."

"Do you think I would?"

"Yes, Miss Johnson."

"Damned straight I would. Good night, Durrell. Sweet dreams."

Durrell was in class the next day and he passed all his exams. A few weeks later, Randy Harris stopped by to report that Durrell had taken a second place trophy for performing a kata in a local kung fu competition. I congratulated Durrell in front of the class. He dropped his eyes and blushed when the kids applauded, but after class, the other kids managed to persuade him to demonstrate his form. Durrell stood up and slowly shuffled to the corner of the room, then moved into his fighting stance. The transformation was incredible. Suddenly, he was a graceful and powerful presence. When he finished, he actually left the room with a group of kids—the first time I had ever seen him interact with the other students.

A few weeks later, one of the biology teachers, Miss Barton stopped by the Academy office and interrupted our staff meeting to report that Durrell had been sent to the office, along with a group of other boys.

"What did he do?" Don Woodford asked.

"He was yelling rude comments back and forth with some other boys," Miss Barton said. "And I caught them writing graffiti on the side of the building."

"Durrell Lewis?" Don said. "Are you sure?"

"I'm absolutely positive," the teacher said.

"I can't believe it," Jean Warner said.

"Neither can I," I said, "but isn't it great?"

"Wonderful," Jean said. Don Woodford and Bud Bartkus nodded their agreement. Miss Barton stalked out of the room and shut the door firmly behind her, leaving the four of us sitting there, grinning like fools.

EIGHTEEN

I Have To and I Can't

urrell Lewis wasn't the only Academy student who responded to parental pressure by flunking. Control was a big issue with Academy kids—most of them felt helpless, always under someone else's control. Flunking was one of the few things that they could decide to do for themselves, and many of them chose to exercise that right.

In college, I had taken an experiential psychology class from a professor who had created a variety of programs designed to help people regain conscious control of their lives. Most of Dr. Brodeur's material was too sophisticated for teenagers, but his opening-day exercise, "I have to and I can't," had given me a new sense of power. I decided to try it on the Academy kids. On the chalkboard, in large letters, I wrote:

I HAVE TO   I CAN'T

As soon as the kids came to class, before they had a chance to start asking questions, I told them to take out their journals and copy the words on the board.

"Finish each sentence," I instructed them. "Don't

sit around and think about it. Just write down the first thing that comes to your mind when you say 'I have to.' " It didn't take long.

"Now cross off the word *have* and replace it with *choose*. Cross off the word *can't* and replace it with *don't want to (badly enough)*."

I could tell by their expressions that the kids were responding to the exercise exactly as I had responded. LaTisha resisted the loudest.

"That's crazy," LaTisha said, with a toss of her head. "I have to go to school. My mother makes me go."

"No, she doesn't," I argued.

"You never saw her mama!" Leroy yelled. "She's mean enough to make *you* go to school, Miss J." I shook my head.

"Nobody makes anybody go to school," I said. Disgusted, LaTisha crossed her arms and refused to discuss the subject. Detrick picked up where she had left off, since he had written the same sentence.

"My dad makes me go to school," Detrick said, "and you know it."

"Does he carry you in his arms and put you in the building?" I asked.

Detrick exhaled sharply. "No."

"Does he hold a gun to your head?"

"No," Detrick said.

"So what happens if you don't come to school?" I asked.

"I get grounded," Detrick said. "And I flunk my classes."

"Then you choose to come to school because you don't like the alternative—which is getting grounded or flunking. But you choose to come to school."

I could see lightbulbs over some heads, but some students still held out.

"You all know kids who don't come to school," I said. "Why don't they come? Because they choose not to. You could be like them. You could refuse to go to school, no matter what your parents or the school administration did to you. But you don't want to get yelled at, or grounded, or beaten up, or expelled, or put in juvenile hall—so you choose to go to school. It's a wise choice. You're a smart bunch of kids."

By this time, most of the kids were nodding, some were even grinning, although there were still a few holdouts. Before I could introduce the idea of "don't want to" versus "can't," Leroy tore the page out of his notebook and ripped it to shreds.

"This is the stupidest thing I ever did in school," he said. "Ain't nobody gonna tell me I don't want to get an A in math. I been trying to get an A in math my whole life and I never got one yet."

"Do you always flunk math class?" I asked.

"No," Leroy said. "But I always get a C or a B."

"Then, you can learn math, can't you?"

"I just told you I get a C or a B, so I guess I can learn it, can't I?" Leroy yelled, losing all patience.

"And is there no possible way in the entire universe that you could get an A in math, if you really really really tried?" Leroy sighed and looked to heaven for strength.

"Well, if I got a tutor and spent all night studying math and did every single homework and never was absent, I guess I might be able to get an A," he said.

"Well, then you could get an A if you wanted to badly enough."

"But who wants to do all that shit for an A?" Leroy yelled.

"I'm not saying you want to do it," I said, "but I'd like you to be honest enough to admit that you could do it, if you really wanted to, but you don't want to—so you aren't telling the truth when you say you can't."

"Give it up, Leroy," Raul interrupted. "She's got you, man. She got me, too." Raul had covered his journal with his forearm so no one could read his sentences. "Let's don't talk about this anymore today, okay? It's giving me a headache."

Several others looked as though they had headaches, or stomach aches. They weren't used to introspection and I didn't want to overdo it, so we read two short stories for the rest of the class period. The headaches disappeared as soon as we switched subjects, but the message remained. Since then, whenever anybody—including me—says "I can't" or "I have to" in class, somebody yells, "You don't really want to!" or "You choose to!" and sets the speaker straight. The kids still may not be happy with their lives, but at least they don't feel quite so powerless.

On the day we did the "have to" exercise, Raul stayed in his seat long after the bell rang dismissing the students for lunch period. Usually, he was the first one out the door. I asked him if he was all right.

"Yeah," Raul said, his voice tired. "I forgot my lunch money today and I don't want to smell all that food, even if it is just rotten school food, so I thought I'd just hang around in here and do my homework or something if that's okay with you."

"I was just on my way down to the deli to get some lunch," I lied. "Come on. It'll be my treat today and you can take me out when you're rich."

"That's okay," Raul said. "I can wait until dinner."

"Don't be silly," I said. "Besides, you deserve a reward for reading out loud today. Most of the kids are too lazy."

"They're not lazy, they're scared," Raul said. "They

217

think somebody's gonna laugh at them because they can't pronounce the words, but I don't care if they laugh at me. You told me it don't make you smart if you know a bunch of words, it just means you know a bunch of words. Right?''

"Right," I agreed. "Smart and educated are two different things. You're smart now and you're getting educated. Now let's get some lunch."

At the deli, Raul's eyes went directly to the barbecued chickens spinning on the metal spit, although he said he wanted the tuna sandwich special, which was the cheapest thing on the price list posted on the wall.

"I was in the mood for a little chicken," I said. "But I can't eat the whole thing. Would you help me out if I get one?"

"If you need my help, how can I say no?" Raul answered. He inhaled his sandwich while I ate a chicken leg, then polished off the rest of the carcass during the ride back to the campus. In spite of the cold weather, he wanted to put the top down on my ancient convertible so his friends would see him riding by. We lowered the top and I dug two pair of sunglasses out of the glove compartment. Raul found a rap song on the radio and turned the volume up.

"Gotta have shades and a big bass to be cool," he shouted above the rapper's voice. "We're cool now!" He settled back against the seat and hooked his elbow over the side of the door as he directed me to drive into the entrance where the Hispanic kids congregated at lunchtime. As we drove by, he lifted his index finger to acknowledge his "homeboys," but he was obviously too cool for words until I dropped him off at the entrance to the staff parking lot.

"Thanks, Miss Johnson," he said, as he stepped out

of the car and carefully folded the sunglasses he had been wearing. "That was the best lunch I ever had. Except for that one at the fancy French hotel."

He sauntered over to join his friends. I parked my car and stopped in the staff lounge for a cup of tea before heading back to my classroom. When I came out of the lounge and started up the walkway beside the building, I noticed Raul and Gusmaro standing among the kids at the top of the stairway. Several kids called greetings to me, so I was too busy waving to notice that both Raul and Gusmaro stood with their feet braced, fists clenched, facing another, much larger boy, until I was close enough to hear them.

"Go ahead and hit me," the boy taunted Gusmaro, who was almost as tall as the boy, but about forty pounds lighter. "Go ahead," the boy repeated, louder. He stepped forward until his flat face was only inches from Gusmaro's. Raul, meanwhile, began to remove his jacket as the other kids backed away from the trio on the stairs. Without thinking, I rushed forward and put my hand between Gusmaro and the other boy.

"Back up," I said. They ignored me, their eyes locked, chins jutted forward, nostrils flaring. "Back up!" I repeated, louder and with all the authority I could muster. It was enough, apparently, because both boys took one minuscule step back.

"If there's any fighting to do, I'll do it," I said. "You kids get to class, now! Go! All of you!" Raul, Gusmaro, and the third boy stood still, but the rest of the kids scattered. "Move!" I bellowed. Slowly, as though coming out of a trance the trio began to move. I walked quickly to the unfamiliar boy and put my hand on his arm. He froze and the look in his eye made me freeze, but I tried not to let him see the effect he had had.

"If you hit any of my kids," I said softly, through

clenched teeth, "I'll whup your butt. Hard. I swear it." His eyes went blank as he deliberately relaxed his body, which I interpreted as a sign that he did not intend to fight. "Get to class and behave yourself." He walked away without a word and I started down the sidewalk toward my room.

"Miss Johnson!" LaTisha Wilson hurried to catch up with me, a mass of tiny braids whirling around her head like fuzzy brown hummingbirds. "Those boys gonna fight," she gasped. "I heard them talking. They're gonna meet in the locker room sixth period and have it out. Emilio gonna kill that skinny little Raul. He have it coming. He got a mouth on him that don't stop. But that ain't gonna be no fair fight."

"What's Emilio's last name?" I asked.

"Lopez," she said. "You don't know him?"

"No," I said. "Should I?"

"Most people do. He got a pretty big reputation."

"For what?"

"Busting heads," LaTisha said. She sat down in her seat and dug a package of potato chips out of her purse. "Don't you tell nobody that I told you. I ain't a rat or nothing. I just don't like it when the boys don't fight fair. It ain't right, you know."

"I know," I said. I hurried to the phone to call Mr. Simms and let him know about the fight scheduled for the next class period so he could stop it. I explained the situation and asked him to call Security and make sure an adult was in the boys' locker room to head off Emilio. Mr. Simms assured me that he would handle the situation, so I turned my attention to teaching, satisfied that the boys' plan for a violent confrontation would be foiled. Fifteen minutes before the end of the period, the phone rang. It was Hal Gray.

"I just thought you might like to know that two of

your students are on their way home for a three-day vacation, transportation provided by the local police department."

I slammed the phone down and raced out of the room and across campus toward the main office. As I rounded the corner of the gym, I found myself in the midst of a crowd of boys leaving the locker room. From their remarks, it was obvious that they had all observed the fight. Quickly, I scanned the crowd until I found one of my kids, Detrick Davis. High on adrenaline, Detrick eagerly described the incident. All the kids had known there was going to be a fight, so they had hurried to the locker room to view the action. They climbed on top of the lockers and cheered as Emilio and Gusmaro squared off. Before either of the larger boys swung, Raul flew through the air and landed on Emilio's back, slugging with all his might. Emilio fell, hitting his head on the edge of one of the wooden benches in the center of the room, with Raul still clinging to his back. Emilio's head flew back, smacking Raul in the chin and splitting his lip. When the boys hit the floor, Raul was on the bottom and Emilio rolled over him and socked him in the eye. At that point, the campus security guards broke up the fight, took all three boys to the office, and called the police.

Gusmaro and Raul were climbing into the backseat of a black and white police car when I raced around the corner of the admin building. Gusmaro looked fine, but Raul's left eye was swollen nearly shut and blood trickled down his chin from the cut on his lower lip.

"Wait a minute!" I shouted. The boys and their police escort paused and looked at me. Gusmaro hurried into the backseat, but Raul stayed outside the car. I touched the side of his face as gently as I could, but he still winced.

"What happened?"

"The other guy looks worse," Raul said, with a lop-sided grin that looked so painful that I started to cry. Raul hung his head.

"I'm sorry, Miss J. I know you don't like fighting, but we had to do it or we couldn't walk around with our heads up no more. I know you would say we choosed to do it, but we had to. We got a reputation to protect. You probably wouldn't understand, but in our neighborhood, if you can't take care of yourself, you can't walk down the street." He raised his head and looked straight at me, so I knew he was serious. Eye contact was something Raul did not often permit. As I looked at him struggling to be a man, in spite of his youth and size, I realized that by intervening in the original argument—by trying to fight their battle for them—I had forced the boys to fight. Not only had a teacher protected them, but a woman at that. I had humiliated them and they had had to redeem their honor.

"It's my fault," I said. "I made you and Gusmaro look bad in front of that boy and all the other kids in school. I'm so stupid sometimes. I'm sorry."

"Don't worry, Miss J.," Raul said. "We know you didn't know what you was doing. You thought you was helping us. We told LaTisha we was gonna fight sixth period because we knew she'd tell you and we'd be done fighting by the time sixth period got there." The police officer stepped forward and put his hand on the door of the car.

"Excuse me, ma'am," he said, "but I have to take these two young men home now." I started to step aside, but changed my mind.

"One more thing, guys," I said. "I want your word of honor, both of you, that it ends here. Don't drag all your friends into this when you get home."

Raul leaned into the open door and grinned at Gusmaro. "I told you she was pretty smart!" he said. He stood up and extended his hand for me to shake.

"I wouldn't do this for nobody except you, Miss Johnson," he said. "But you helped me before and I already socked him good, so I can live with it." Raul climbed into the car and cheerfully waved at me. Gusmaro kept his head down. He had told me before that his father's disciplinary methods were much like my own father's had been: Both men believed that kids behave better if you beat some sense into them. I knew the fight with Emilio was mild compared to what he'd get at home.

"Gusmaro?" I reached in front of Raul and held my hand out to Gusmaro, who stared at it for a long time before he finally took it in his own sweaty hand and met my gaze for a brief second. His hand shook and there were tears in his eyes. My impulse was to jump into the backseat and hug him, but I stepped back and quickly shut the door so none of the curious kids gawking from the windows and peering around the corner of the building would see him crying. As soon as the police car pulled away from the curb, I went in search of Steve Simms.

"Sorry," he said. "We were set for sixth period, but they beat us to it."

"Did Emilio get suspended, too?"

"Emilio is in the detention center right now," Simms said. "He'll be there for the rest of this week."

"Are you kidding!" I nearly shrieked. "He starts a fight, my kids get kicked out of school for three days, and he gets a smack on his hand and gets to stay and do his schoolwork? What's going on here?"

"I'm sorry," Simms said. "Emilio may have taunted Raul, but Raul took the first punch, so he officially

223

started the fight." He stood up and started rearranging the stacks of paper on his desk. "I have an appointment in five minutes. You'll have to excuse me." He opened the door to his office and gestured me out.

I went straight to the detention center. Emilio was the only student in the room. He sat in the back row, at a cafeteria-style table with an attached bench. I sat down very close beside him, close enough to touch him if he moved the slightest bit. He glanced at me, closed his eyes, and turned his back, but not before I caught a glimpse of his face. His eyes were the same as I remembered them—ink dark and deadly angry—and an ugly red gash ran from his forehead across his right eye and down his cheek. Around the cut, the skin was bruised and discolored.

"That's a nasty cut," I said. He looked at me and his lip drew up into a sneer.

"Well, your little baby didn't hit me, if that's what you think," he said. "I wouldn't let no stupid Mexican hit me. I fell down. That's how I got this." He gestured toward his eye.

"Would you mind telling me what the fight was about in the first place?"

"You wouldn't care," he said, turning away again. I touched his arm and he immediately stiffened.

"Yes, I would," I said. "Please tell me." He didn't answer.

"How old are you?" I asked.

"Fifteen," he mumbled into the neck of his black nylon jacket.

"What grade are you in?"

"Tenth."

"Why aren't you in my program? I can see that you're intelligent. How are you doing in school?"

"Okay."

"Are you on track to graduate? How many credits do you have?"

"Forty."

"You should have sixty. What's the problem?"

"I don't have a problem."

"I think you do. I think you're a very angry young man and I think I can help you. Why don't you think about it?"

"I might."

"And I'd really like to know what happened. I'm not going to make any trouble for you. I just want to know what happened." I added, *"No voy a molestarte."* He turned slowly to face me, his eyes still guarded but no longer flashing fire.

"Victor stole my gym shorts."

"Victor?"

"Yeah," Emilio said. "And the teacher said I had to pay for them. So I told Victor he had to pay me and he said he wouldn't, so I told him I was going to punch him." Victor, another Academy student, was a grade behind the three boys and hadn't been anywhere near the group during either confrontation.

"If you have a problem with Victor, why were you fighting with Raul and Gusmaro?"

"They're all in the same posse," Emilio said. "They were trying to protect their little boyfriend."

"But how could Victor steal your gym shorts? You aren't in the same class, are you?"

Emilio drew an extra-length sigh and explained that Victor and Emilio were assigned the same gym locker and Emilio's shorts disappeared, so Emilio deduced that Victor had taken them. Victor, who maintained his innocence, said he didn't take the shorts, which were four sizes too big for him, and he had no intention of paying for them.

"How much money are we talking about here?" I asked.

"Seven dollars," Emilio said. For a second, he looked more sheepish than angry.

"For seven dollars, all three of you are in trouble with the principal and with your parents, you and Raul are bleeding, and Gusmaro is going to get the snot smacked out of him tonight. Was it worth it?" For a few long seconds, Emilio looked down at his large hands, which pressed against the Formica tabletop. Then he looked up at me.

"Yeah," he said. "It was worth it."

"Why?"

"Because it felt good when I hit him in the face. I got him good."

"You like to hit people?"

"Yeah," Emilio said, drawing out the word into two syllables. "I like to hit people."

"Why?" I probed. He shrugged and his face closed back up. "Do you feel mad a lot of times?" He nodded, but didn't speak. "Why do you feel mad?"

"I don't know," he said. "Things."

"Like what?"

"Lots of things."

"Like school?"

"Yeah," he agreed quickly.

"What about school makes you mad?"

"The teachers are always telling you what to do and stuff."

"That's their job," I said. "Why does that make you mad?"

"I don't know," he snapped. "It just does. Things make me mad."

"Things make me mad, too," I said. "Like when things aren't fair."

"Yeah," Emilio agreed. "Yeah. Lots of things isn't fair."

"Well, I can see why you might be mad about having to ride on a bus for half an hour to go to school in a neighborhood where people have a lot of money and there aren't any Hispanic people and—"

"I am not Mexican," Emilio interjected.

"Where are you from?" I asked. The transformation was amazing. Emilio drew himself up straight and thrust his chin into the air.

"I am Salvadoran."

"How long have you been in the United States?"

"Three years."

"And why did you move here?" Wrong question. Emilio shrank into his former defensive posture and shrugged.

"Where did you go to school before you came here?" I asked, moving back toward more neutral territory.

"I didn't," Emilio muttered, talking into his shirt collar again.

"Okay," I said. "I have to go teach a class. Come see me after school today if you want to talk about my program."

When Emilio swaggered into my room after school, I realized I hadn't expected him to come. I gave him a journal and told him to go home and write his autobiography. He returned it the next day, but insisted that I wait until he was out of sight before I read it. I opened the notebook, just to see how much he had written, but Emilio immediately slapped the book shut and pulled it from me.

"I won't give it to you if you're going to read it," he said.

"I have to read it," I said.

"I know, but not while I'm looking. It makes me feel stupid." He actually blushed as he walked to my desk and placed his notebook in my in-basket where it sat until two seconds after he stepped outside the door.

Emilio had come to the United States in the trunk of a car when he was twelve years-old. Before that, he had never been to school. He had worked all of his life in the fields, picking fruits and vegetables. There was a lot of fighting in his country, some military, some political. One by one, the adult males in his family—father, brothers, cousins, uncles—disappeared, some to jail, some to military service from which they did not return; some simply disappeared. Emilio was the only male left, so friends of his family smuggled him out of the country and arranged for his passage to Mexico, where he was stashed into the trunk of a car for the trip to San Diego. He was adopted by a Salvadoran couple and his new life began. He had nothing at all from his old life, no letters, no souvenirs, no family. Everything he had was gone, including his mother. He did not hear from her after he left El Salvador and believed she was dead. His new parents insisted that he go to school, an entirely new experience for him. Reading, writing, sitting at a desk all day, following a rigid schedule—these were unusual and unnecessary demands, in his opinion, but he tried to discipline himself. One thing he couldn't do was stop fighting, even though he got in trouble for it all the time. He thought he was good enough to be a professional boxer, and he certainly had the size and weight, but his adoptive mother objected; she was afraid he'd get brain damage. He tried to be a good son, he tried to stop fighting, but the boys wouldn't let him. He had a reputation. He was tough. He was the boy a kid had to tackle to prove himself. But he had a problem. His new parents had just received a letter from the school district: one more fight and Emilio was out of school, permanently. With nearly three years left to go, the odds didn't look good.

When Raul and Gusmaro returned to school, I called them aside before the first class to let them know that Emilio was now their classmate. Foolishly, I had expected them to be surprised; I had forgotten that the "homeboy hotline" carried news faster than UPI. Gusmaro assured me that it was okay for Emilio to be in their class, even if he wasn't Mexican, because he was a homeboy and a pretty good fighter.

"I thought you guys might think I was disloyal to you for letting him in the program while you were suspended," I admitted. Both boys shook their heads and Raul patted my hand.

"We know you have a big heart, Miss J.," Raul said. "It's okay."

I looked at Gusmaro and raised my eyebrows. He didn't talk as much as the other boys in his posse, but he was the unofficial leader of the group.

"I don't got no problem with him, if he don't got no problem with me," Gusmaro said. "I'm cool."

Unfortunately, the rest of the kids didn't share Gusmaro's attitude. When we walked into the classroom, Emilio and Kenny, a varsity football player known for his hot temper and hard fists, were squared off in the back of the room. Kenny was one solid hunk of brown velvet muscle. Emilio, his back to the corner, raised onto his toes and danced lightly back and forth, waiting for Kenny to make the first move. I made the first move instead. Grabbing both boys by their forearms, I stepped between them. Their hostility must have been contagious, because I found myself fighting the urge to hit them both.

"Stop it!" I shouted through clenched teeth. "Just

stop it right this second! I am so sick and tired of you kids fighting each other, fighting the world, fighting me when I'm trying to help you. You will not fight in this classroom. If you want to act like ignorant punks, you can get your asses out in the street and fight, because that's where you're going to end up." They stood staring at me, mouths open, shocked into silence. It was enough, but I couldn't stop. I looked at my hands holding two young arms, one light brown, one dark brown, and my own anger erupted.

"I know you kids are angry," I yelled, "because the world isn't fair. Well, get over it, because it's never going to be fair. The white boys have all the money and all the power and that's the way it is. And they aren't going to give it up—to you or to me. And you can't blame them for it because if you had it, you wouldn't give it to them, either. But fighting each other isn't going to fix anything. All it's going to do is let everybody go on insisting that black and Hispanic kids are ignorant and violent. That's perfect. It's easy. If you're ignorant and violent, people who don't like you can kick you out of school or put you in jail. And it's your own fault. Now sit down and shut up before I lose my temper!"

In slow motion and perfect silence, the entire class took their seats and stared at me, wide-eyed and slack-jawed.

"There are twenty people sitting in this room right now," I said. "If there were only twenty thousand dollars in the entire world, and each of you had one thousand dollars, and one-twentieth of the power, how many of you would give half of your money so that forty people could share the wealth? How many would give away half your power? Make the world more equal?" Naturally, nobody raised a hand.

"You're not selfish," I said. "You're human. So stop expecting other people not to be human. If you want some of that money, or some of that power, you have to work for it. You can go to school, or practice until you're the best at something, or start at the bottom and work your way up—but beating up on other people isn't going to get you anywhere except in jail or dead." Suddenly, I heard my own voice, doing its soapbox softshoe again. I felt foolish, as though I had been dancing around in front of the class in my underwear, and I felt tired, very tired. For the rest of the day, I taught my classes on autopilot, hanging on by my fingertips until I could go home and crawl into bed and forget about trying to rescue teenagers who seemed determined to self-destruct.

NINETEEN

Good Morning, Mr. Chacon

During the last quarter of the school year, the juniors started a study unit on employment. When I asked the class for a volunteer to show me how he or she handled a job search over the phone, Raul Chacon raised his hand. I held an imaginary phone to my right ear and motioned for Raul to do the same.

"Ring-a-ding-ding," I said. "Hello, Johnson's Department Store. May I help you?"

"Do you have any jobs?" Raul asked.

"What kind of job are you looking for, sir?"

"Anything. I just need a job," Raul said. I dropped my phone.

"Is that really what you say when you call up a company to find out about employment opportunities?" I asked. He nodded.

"Usually. Sometimes I say, 'Are you hiring?' " I looked around the room.

"Is that what the rest of you guys do, too?" Everyone nodded.

"Do you get many interviews?" I asked. They all stopped nodding and shook their heads.

For the remainder of that class period, we practiced telephone etiquette. The next day, the students wrote resumés and typed them in the computer lab. We discussed interviewing techniques and communications skills. We filled out actual job applications from a variety of major corporations and local companies. After a month of practice and preparation, the kids were ready for the big test: mock interviews with personnel managers from local companies.

Six managers agreed to come to the school and conduct brief interviews with the students to help them polish their skills. On the day of the mock interviews, the students were almost delirious with anticipation. They couldn't stop talking—until the personnel managers arrived. Then they couldn't start. Some of them fell apart completely; one girl hyperventilated and had to go to the nurse's office to lie down. Two boys refused, at the last minute, to participate. One of the boys who refused was Gusmaro.

"Come on"—I nudged Gusmaro with my elbow—"it's your turn."

"No way," Gusmaro insisted. "I ain't doing it."

"Why not?"

"I don't like rejection," he said.

"You aren't going to be rejected," I said. "This isn't a real interview. It's practice."

"Those look like real managers to me," Gusmaro said. "Look at them suits." He glanced quickly at the man seated at the desk of front of him. The man wore a three-piece suit, as did all of the interviewers, including the women.

"That's how people dress in offices," I told Gusmaro.

"Well, they look mean," he insisted. "I ain't doing it."

I didn't press Gusmaro because I thought he'd give in when he saw the other students breezing through their interviews, but I thought wrong. Many of the kids did breeze through, but not the Hispanic boys. With the exception of Julio Lopez, who received an Average rating from his interviewer, they bombed. Their rating sheets all said the same thing: no eye contact, hostile attitude, poor articulation, sloppy posture, unwilling to talk. Raul Chacon unwilling to talk? I had a hard time imagining it.

"What happened to you?" I asked Raul. "You were great when we practiced in class." Raul shrugged and looked at the floor.

"Did you look him in the eye and shake his hand the way we practiced?"

He shook his head.

"Why not?"

"I don't know," he mumbled. "I just couldn't talk to that guy."

"Why not?" I repeated.

"I couldn't," Raul said. "I don't know why, but I just couldn't do it, Miss J."

"Did he say something mean to you?"

"No," Raul said. "He was pretty nice."

"So why didn't you talk to him?"

"He's wearing that fancy suit," Raul said.

"That's just clothes," I said. "You know better than to judge a man by his clothes." Raul kept his eyes on the floor.

"Well, he kept staring at me," Raul said.

"How else is he going to see you if he doesn't look at you?" I asked. Raul shrugged again.

"He probably thinks I'm ugly. That's why he was staring at me."

"You aren't ugly!" I said. "Where did you ever get an idea like that?"

"From the magazines," Raul said. "And catalogs and stuff. I don't look like those white guys."

"Please look at me, Raul." He looked up. I put my hand under his chin.

"Have I ever lied to you?"

"No."

"And I'm not lying now. You are not ugly. You are beautiful. You are smart and you have a great sense of humor and you are very handsome. I'm going to arrange another interview for you and I want you to shake the man's hand and look him straight in the eye. Will you do that for me?" Raul drew a deep breath and exhaled. He shook his head and looked at the floor again.

"I can't." I knew he was telling the truth. He simply couldn't do it.

"Okay," I said. "Don't worry about it. We'll practice some more in class, all right?"

"Thanks, Miss J.," Raul said. He glanced at me. "I'm sorry I let you down."

"You didn't let me down," I said. "You just weren't ready."

Several weeks later, it was time for the real thing. As part of our program, we contact personnel managers of a number of local companies that hire students during the summer. Although the managers are supportive of our program and interested in hiring our students, the kids still have to arrange formal interviews and apply for available jobs in competition with the general public. One major department store called to invite student applicants for a job in the administrative office of a large warehouse. The warehouse was located on the East Side of the city and the personnel manager specifically requested applications from students who lived on the East Side.

By that time, some of the kids had already found jobs. Raul, Gusmaro, and the rest of their posse all worked together in the dining hall of a local university, busing tables and washing dishes.

"Here's your chance," I told them. "The lady who called wants a kid from the East Side for a good job. You'll get to use a computer just like the ones we have in our computer lab."

"How much does it pay?" Gusmaro asked. I checked my information sheet.

"Seven-fifty an hour. How much do you guys get at your jobs?"

"Six twenty-five," Gusmaro said.

"I only get six because I started later," Raul said.

Eight kids, including Gusmaro, Raul, and Julio, took applications for the job, but none of them applied. Every day for two weeks, they listed dozens of reasons why they hadn't gotten around to filing their applications. The personnel manager called to say that she had interviewed several students and couldn't wait any longer to hire someone. I collared Gusmaro and Raul after class and demanded an explanation. Julio came with them, but as usual, he stayed in the background, standing silently prepared if his friends needed him.

"They wouldn't of hired us, anyway," Gusmaro said.

"Why not?"

"Because we're Mexican."

"They specifically asked for a kid from the East Side," I said. "That means they expected you to be Hispanic or black."

"They probably didn't mean it," Gusmaro said.

"They just say that, but when you get there, they don't hire you."

"Why didn't you go find out?"

"I told you," he said. "I don't like rejection."

"What about you?" I asked Raul. He shrugged.

"You don't like the idea of doing anything on your own, either, do you?" I said. "You want to work at the same job with all your friends forever."

"I like working with my friends," Gusmaro said. "It's cool."

"But you can't advance in a career if you handcuff yourself to somebody else," I said. "You have to make your own way. Stand on your own."

Neither boy answered. They just looked at me. They knew that I knew their posse's motto: forever together.

"Well, if you're going to hold each other's hands," I said, "at least you could get a job where you don't have to wash dishes like a bunch of illegal aliens." It was a mean thing to say, but I was really feeling frustrated. They had worked so hard to make themselves eligible for good jobs, but they wouldn't apply for them.

Raul was waiting for me outside my room the next morning.

"I'm sorry I didn't apply for that job, Miss J.," he said. "I guess we were too afraid. I'll go to the next one, I promise."

"Promise?" I asked, holding out my hand. He took my hand in a firm grip and looked me straight in the eye.

"I promise," he said. "But can I ask you something?" I nodded.

He explained that he had been reading the vocational brochures from the career center and wanted to sign up for an after-school training program in his senior year, but he couldn't decide whether to choose landscaping, auto mechanics, construction, or automated office occupations.

"What kind of job do you want to have after you graduate?" I asked.

"A good one," he said.

"What's good?"

"Where I make a lot of money."

"You can make money at a lot of jobs, but it's better if you like the work you're doing," I explained.

"But how do you know what you like until you do it?"

"Good question," I said. "Taking different classes is one way to find out. But you can narrow it down by thinking of what you like and don't like."

"I don't get you," Raul said.

"Close your eyes," I said. "And imagine yourself getting up in the morning. You eat breakfast, get into your truck, and drive out to a big company where you check the sprinklers and all of the plants and trees. In the back of the building there is a new addition and you need to decide where to put the plants and bushes and sidewalks to make it look pretty. Most of the day you're outside, working with equipment and making sure your work crew does their job, but sometimes you work indoors in an office."

Raul opened his eyes and looked at me. "I could see myself doing that," he said. "It was all right."

We did the same thing for construction and auto repair. Both of those sounded "all right," too. But after I started to describe Raul's imaginary life as an office worker, he turned his face upward and smiled dreamily, although he kept his eyes shut.

"You adjust your tie and put on your jacket before entering the main lobby," I said. "You shift your briefcase to your left hand so you can open the big glass door. As you pass the receptionist, she says, 'Good morning, Mr. Chacon,' and you say hello. In your office, you turn on your computer terminal, check your in-basket, and hang your jacket on a hanger behind the door. You get your cup and go down to the lunchroom for a cup of coffee before starting your work.''

Raul's eyes flew open.

"Good morning, Mr. Chacon,'' he said, rolling the words out slowly, as though tasting them for flavor. He nodded. "That sounds pretty good, doesn't it?''

"It sounds wonderful,'' I agreed.

"And I liked it when I dressed up in that suit to eat lunch at that fancy hotel. I looked pretty good, didn't I?''

"Yes, you did.''

"Mr. Chacon,'' he repeated. "I like that.''

TWENTY

Maybe I Oughta Be a Teacher

"**D**on't spend your own money," Hal Gray cautioned when I told him I planned to buy a pair of glasses for Devon Jackson, but I ignored Hal's advice for a change. Devon was one of the smartest kids I'd ever had in class, but he squinted constantly, which gave his otherwise handsome face a belligerent look. When I asked him to read in class he refused, claiming that reading gave him headaches and "fuzzy eyes." I asked if he had had his vision checked recently and he nodded.

"My eyes don't see too good," Devon said, "so I can't take Driver's Ed. I guess I need glasses or something." He said he wasn't sure where his mother was living at the time, and his uncle, who was his guardian, couldn't afford to buy him glasses because he had four kids of his own to support and his insurance didn't cover Devon. I told Devon I'd see he got a pair of glasses, but when I checked with the school nurse, she said I'd have to fill out a form that went to the local Lion's Club. It would take a month or two to process the request, but they'd most certainly furnish a pair of glasses.

I didn't think Devon would last two more months in school. He had been suspended six times during his freshman year and had been called before the Academy staff to discuss his disruptive behavior several times during the first months of his sophomore year. I thought maybe if he had glasses, he'd settle down and read his textbooks instead of amusing himself by creating disturbances. So, I arranged to take him to an optometrist.

"There are government agencies and charities to handle that kind of thing," Hal insisted. "Use them."

"I already tried," I said, "but it takes so long and I'm afraid we'll lose Devon for good if I don't do something right now." Hal looked at me without speaking for a long time, then shrugged.

"I still don't think it's a good idea," he said, "but I never take advice myself."

"Thanks," I said.

"I'm on a roll today," Hal continued, "so here's one more piece of advice to ignore. Don't give so much of your heart. I know you have a big one, but you're chipping away at it pretty fast."

"I can't help it," I said. "I know it sounds melodramatic, but how can you just close up the food line and go home when there are still starving people waiting?"

"You teach them how to feed themselves," Hal said. He shook my hand, then abruptly pulled me to him in a fierce hug. Without another word, he was off, squeaking down the hall in his deck shoes, the same distinctive bounce in his step, as though he might break into dance at any given moment. I watched from the doorway until he turned the corner and disappeared from sight, but he never looked back.

Although I knew Hal was right, it didn't stop me

from buying glasses for Devon. His uncle drove him to the optometrist's office and filled me in on Devon's history while Devon was in the examining room. Devon's mother suffered a nervous breakdown shortly after he was born and wasn't emotionally strong enough to raise him herself. She worked part-time and couldn't afford to support him, even if she had had the desire.

"Devon's only been living with me since school started this year," the uncle explained. "The kid never had any structure in his life before he came to stay with us, but I told him if he wants to live at my house, he has to learn to follow rules. He has to do homework. He has to take care of chores at home. And he has to learn to act right. He's smart, but he's too smart for his own good sometimes."

Devon emerged from the examination room, grinning, the doctor's assistant right behind him. She patted him on the shoulder and said, "Devon is half-blind. He really needs glasses. I don't know how he even manages to recognize his friends at school."

"They have big bodies," Devon said.

Devon's prescription was heavy duty because, in addition to myopia, he suffered from astigmatism, too. The total bill came to two hundred fifty dollars. Devon's uncle looked horrified when he saw the amount, but it didn't faze Devon. He squared his shoulders and firmly shook my hand.

"Thanks, Miss Johnson," he said. "I really appreciate this. I hope I can show my appreciation."

"All I ask is that you graduate from high school," I said. "That will be my repayment."

"No sweat," Devon said. "I'm gonna ace every class now that I can see good."

I don't know whether Devon aced any of his classes,

because two weeks later, he was suspended from school for gambling. Shortly after he returned from suspension, he was dropped from the Academy for fighting. He and some of his friends formed a "blind posse." The posse would grab one of the other students, wrap a T-shirt around the kid's head, and beat him up. The last time I spoke to Devon, I asked him about the beatings.

"It wasn't as bad as they're making it out to be," Devon said. "We took turns. We only took one punch apiece." I noticed he wasn't wearing his glasses and I asked him where they were.

"They got broke," he said, "but they're getting fixed." A few days later, Jack Whittier, Devon's science teacher, stopped me in the hallway to ask if I knew what had happened to him. I explained about the suspensions. Jack shook his head.

"He said you bought him some glasses," Jack said. "That was generous of you."

"Well, he said his family couldn't afford them, and he needed them. Imagine going to school for years without being able to see clearly. No wonder he acts out in school." Jack started to say something, then changed his mind.

"What were you going to say?" I urged him. "That I'm a sucker?"

"I'm hardly the person to make that accusation," Jack said with a sheepish grin. "I bought the kid a pair of glasses last year."

I felt like a first-class ass.

I didn't waste much time feeling sorry for myself, though, because when I got to the office, there was a letter in my mailbox from Shamica Stanton, thanking me for helping her make it to college where she had just received three A's and a B on her midterm grade report. I was pleased, but not surprised.

When she was a sophomore at Parkmont, Shamica's mother had contacted me to ask if Shamica could enroll in the Academy, although she had not signed up at the beginning of the school year. Shamica had been lukewarm about the idea, but she was obviously bright and well behaved, so we had accepted her. She was a loner and always selected a seat in the farthest corner of the room, where she quietly took notes and rolled her eyes impatiently when her fellow students interrupted class by poking each other in the back or throwing paper wads at the wastebasket. By the end of her sophomore year, Shamica had moved to the head of the class academically and showed a real aptitude for computers. Although she restricted her journal writing to impersonal subjects, she impressed me as a girl with a promising future.

Then, without warning, Shamica disappeared; she didn't show up for her junior year of high school. I called her several times, but the phone rang unanswered. I stopped by her house one night after school, but the house was dark and there was no car in the driveway. I left a note on the front door asking Shamica to contact me, but I hadn't heard from her. I checked with the office to see whether she had notified them of a new address, but they had no information. Finally, I reached her.

"Are you all right?" I asked.

"I'm fine," she answered.

"Where have you been?" She didn't answer my question.

"My mother wants me to transfer to Clearview High," Shamica said. "Can I do that?"

"Why would you want to transfer?" I asked. "You were doing so well here. I was looking forward to seeing you this year. I miss your shining face."

There was a long pause before she answered, "I miss you, too." Then she stopped and didn't say anything else.

"If you really want me to, I'll check to see if you can transfer," I said, "but I don't want you to. I want you to be in my class."

"I want to be in your class," Shamica said. Her voice trembled. "But my mother thinks I should transfer."

"Why?" There was another long pause before she answered.

"I'm going to have a baby."

"Well, lots of women have babies," I said brightly, to cover my dismay. "It shouldn't affect your brain. You can still go to school."

"Well, they told me not to come."

"Who?"

"The people at the office. I called them and they told me not to come."

"Stay right where you are," I said. "I'll call you back in a few minutes." When I hung up, I asked Marge Wilson, the head of the guidance office, if pregnant girls were allowed to go to school.

"We prefer that they go to SAMP," Marge said.

"SAMP?"

"School-Aged Mothers Program. It's state funded. They teach the kids things like nutrition and child care. Then they come back to regular school after they have their babies."

"Do they really come back?" I asked.

"Sometimes," she said, but her voice held no conviction.

"But do they have to go to SAMP? Can't they go to regular classes if they want to?" Marge pursed her lips and her eyes darted to the principal's office next door.

"You'd better talk to one of the administrators," she said.

"I just want to know what a student's legal rights are," I said. Marge drew in a long breath. I knew she was a sympathetic and caring woman, but she also had a job she liked and wanted to keep, so I backed off and went in search of an administrator. Phil Horner was on the way out of his office, but he stopped long enough to listen to my question.

"I wish I could help you," Dr. Horner said, glancing at his watch, "but that's one I can't answer. Try Chet." Mr. Norton was out and his secretary didn't know when he'd be back, so I knocked on Steve Simms's door and stuck my head inside before he could escape out the rear entrance.

"Got a minute?" I asked. He checked the clock.

"That's about all I have," he said, shuffling the ever present piles of papers on his desk. "I have a parent conference in ten minutes."

"Good," I said, taking a seat in front of his desk. "This won't take a minute. I just need a yes or no answer."

"Shoot," Steve said, still shuffling.

"Can a pregnant girl come to school if she wants to?" Steve stopped shuffling and stared into space.

"We prefer that they attend SAMP or some alternative program—" Steve began.

"But is she *allowed* to come to school?" I interrupted.

"There are a number of disadvantages to having pregnant girls in the classroom," Steve said. "It distracts the other students and—"

"This is a yes or no question," I reminded Steve. He glanced at me, then at the clock, then through the glass wall at his secretary's desk, where a pair of anxious parents stood staring at him. I crossed my arms and sat back in my chair. "No one else seems to know the answer and I want to know now. If you open that door, I'm going to start screaming and yelling. Those parents will really be impressed."

Steve sighed. "I don't know why I ever recommended you for this program," he said. "You're a pain in the neck most of the time."

"Yes or no?" I repeated.

"Yes," he said. "Pregnant girls can attend school here if they want to. They still have a right to the same education as any other kid. Satisfied?"

"Yes," I said. I hopped to my feet and opened the door to motion the parents in. "It has been a distinct pleasure talking to you, as always, Mr. Simms," I said. "Thank you very much."

Back at the guidance office, I told Marge Wilson what Mr. Simms had said.

"Well, they try to discourage the girls," Marge confided, "because it makes the administrators nervous to have them around. It's like they think it's contagious or something."

"Do you know who told Shamica Stanton not to come back to school?" I asked.

Marge shook her head. "I don't know, but I think that's the unofficial word. One of the counselors must have talked to her. We're supposed to refer them to SAMP."

"What happens if they don't want to go to SAMP and learn how to put diapers on a baby? What if they have mothers who can teach them that? What if they want to learn algebra and biology while they're pregnant, so they can get a good job or go to college after their babies are born? Shamica wants to go to school."

Marge shut the door to her office and returned to her

desk. She sat down and leaned forward, speaking quickly and quietly.

"Then she'd better hurry up and get here," Marge said. "If Shamica's absent thirty school days, the district will drop her from the rolls and then she won't be allowed to come back, even if she wants to."

I called Shamica back and told her to come to school the next day, if she ever intended to go to Parkmont again. When she and her mother arrived, I explained her options and they both agreed that Shamica would benefit more from attending regular classes.

"I'm very supportive of my daughter," Mrs. Stanton told me, "although I think she's too young to be a mother. I want her to have the best education, but they told me when I called that she should go to an alternative school."

Shamica returned to class and quickly made up the missed work from the first few weeks. At the end of the first quarter in early November, she had earned four A's and two B's on her report card. Although she didn't discuss the baby, and she wore loose clothing that hid her blossoming belly, a few of the kids figured out what was happening. They asked a question or two, then shrugged it off as nothing extraordinary. Shamica was due during Christmas break and planned to extend her vacation for a month before returning to finish the year.

Shamica didn't return to finish her junior year at Parkmont; she went to SAMP. When I learned that she didn't plan to come back, I was crestfallen, certain that she'd given up. I couldn't imagine being fifteen and trying to raise a newborn baby while attending classes full-time, but Shamica surprised me. On the last day of school, she showed up in my classroom with a beautiful baby boy and a transcript listing seventy credits for the year. I was amazed. Sixty credits are considered a full-time load for high school students.

"Are you still saving my seat for next year?" Shamica asked with a shy smile. My impulse was to grab her and hug her, but she was such a private, dignified girl that I was afraid it would offend her, so I didn't.

"You can have any seat in the house," I said.

"I'm sorry I didn't come back to finish this year in your class," Shamica said, "but I was kind of busy and it was easier to stay at SAMP."

"That's okay," I said. "I'm so proud of you." I bent down to touch her baby's shining black ringlets. "I don't think I could have left this little sweetie to go to school either."

"Oh, they had day care at SAMP, so he went to school with me," Shamica explained. "But it was kind of hard leaving him to go to work every day."

"Work?"

"I got a job at Target."

I was dumbstruck with admiration, but Shamica apparently misinterpreted my silence as skepticism. She shrugged.

"It isn't anything great," she said. "I'm just a cashier. I'm saving my money to go to community college after high school."

I couldn't resist. I hugged her.

Remembering Shamica's success and determination often kept me going during the following year when the other kids did their best to wear me down. I thought if a teenage girl could handle a full academic load, a baby, and a job, I could certainly handle teaching four classes per day. Maybe my energy was fading, but it seemed as though the kids intentionally created as much stress as possible. Just before Thanksgiving vacation, two of my best students—a boy and a girl—got into a fistfight during class. In the middle of a grammar exercise, the girl hauled off and whacked the boy across the ear so hard she knocked him off his seat. While he was on the floor, she kicked him in the ribs and said, "I'll kill you, you little motherfucker."

He scrambled to his feet and grabbed her by the neck, spinning her around into a half nelson. She writhed and screamed, but he wouldn't let go. One of the other girls took a slug at him and caught the corner of his jaw. He released his hold with one hand to swing at the second girl. I stepped into the middle, thinking they'd be intimidated by having a teacher intervene, but I thought wrong. Neither of them stopped swinging and they both hit me. I screamed at the top of my lungs, "STOP!" They paused momentarily and I took advantage of the lull. "Sit down right now or I'll have you both expelled."

The boy and the second girl smoothed their clothing and their hair and sat down, but the girl who had started the fight remained on her feet, her fists clenched at her sides.

"I don't want to sit down!" she bellowed. "He hit me and I'm gonna kill him."

"You hit him first," I pointed out.

"Well, he had it coming," she huffed, "and he had no business hitting me."

"I'm gonna hit you again," he retorted, jumping out of his seat. "I'm gonna kick your ass."

"Sit down immediately!" I yelled. "I'm going to lose my temper in a minute and I'm going to kick both your asses." Shocked, he sat back down. She still refused to sit.

"If you can't control yourself, then you'll have to go

to the office," I said. Without a word, she stalked to the door, walked outside, and slammed the door so hard that the glass shattered from top to bottom. Fortunately, the glass was embedded with wire, so most of it remained in the door.

After school, I stayed to type up referral forms and a maintenance request for the window glass. When I finished the official paperwork, I sat at my desk, where one hundred student journals were stacked, waiting to be read. I knew that if I didn't read them immediately, I'd be sorry. The next day would bring new homework assignments, worksheets, and quizzes to be graded, so I started reading.

When I closed the last journal, I remembered that I had promised to call Rosemary Martinelli's father. Rosemary and her twin brother, Roman, were nice-looking, bright, and energetic. They were also bad-tempered, hostile, and violent. When the pair first entered the Academy, the teachers focused on Roman as having the greater potential for problems, but Rosie was the one who drove us to distraction. When she didn't cut class, she was tardy. On the few days she wasn't tardy, she refused to participate in the classroom exercises. We had spent hours in counseling with her and I called her parents at least twice a week to discuss possible solutions to her behavioral problems. Both the Martinellis supported our efforts to help the twins, but neither of them seemed able to control their children. Rosie had been suspended twice for fighting during the three months since school started and was facing an expulsion for the latest fight. She had smacked another girl across the head so hard that she broke the girl's eardrum, just because the girl looked at her the wrong way.

"I'm sorry, Mr. Martinelli," I said, after explaining

the circumstances, "but surely you understand that we can't keep Rosie in our program if she consistently defies the rules. Our program is designed to help students who want to succeed, not those who continue the behavior that has prevented them from being successful in the past."

"She didn't tell me she broke the girl's eardrum," Mr. Martinelli said. "She just told us she got in a little scrape." He blew his breath out in a long sigh and I heard a whack, as though he had slapped his hand flat on a tabletop. "I tell you, I wish I lived out in the country where the neighbors couldn't hear me. I could solve this problem in a minute, if you know what I mean."

"Yes, I think I do," I said, glad that he didn't live in the country.

"But the cops already told me I can't hit my kids," Mr. Martinelli continued. "If I even raise my hand, Rosie starts yelling, 'Child abuse! Child abuse!' How can you expect to correct them if you can't smack 'em when they need it?"

"It's difficult, I know, Mr. Martinelli," I said. "But it's quite late and I have to go now. I just wanted you to know that we will be dropping Rosemary from the program at the end of this semester."

"Well, thanks for letting me know," Mr. Martinelli said. "By the way, Rosie tells me there's no school this Friday. Is that right, or is that another one of her little fiction stories?"

"She's right. There's no school for the students. It's an in-service day for the teachers and staff. We have a series of meetings and workshops to attend, as well as lesson planning for the next quarter."

"Hell, you teachers got it made." Mr. Martinelli snorted, and I could envision him hitching up his pants by his belt buckle. "You don't work a full year, you don't work a full day, and you haven't worked a full week yet this year. Christ, maybe I oughta be a teacher."

I wanted to say, "Maybe you ought to shove your phone. It's ten P.M. and I'm still at work, calling you to discuss your obnoxious children who cause more problems and take more of my time than any other ten students combined. Maybe if you worked a little harder at being a parent, I'd be able to do my job."

I didn't say any of that. What I said was, "Maybe you ought to try being a teacher, Mr. Martinelli. I highly recommend it. It's the most wonderful job in the world."

TWENTY-ONE

To Be or Not to Be

My conversation with Mr. Martinelli pushed me over the edge. I was already depressed and felt like giving up; trying to hold the kids together was tearing me apart. After I hung up the phone, I started stuffing papers into my briefcase, muttering to myself.

"Oh, yes, this is a great job. Astronomical pay. Luxurious working conditions. No stress. No overtime. Tons of prestige in the community. Lots of respect."

I yanked open the middle drawer of my desk and shuffled through the rubber bands, paper clips, hall passes, referral forms, and attendance reports until I found a tattered copy of my professional resumé. I slapped it down on the top of the foot-high stack of papers in my in-basket.

"Time to get a real job." When I reached over to turn off the high-intensity lamp attached to the far side of my desk, my sleeve knocked something to the floor. I crouched down and reached under the desk. As soon as I touched it, I knew what it was. Isabella's bear.

Isabella Carrillo, one of my Spanish students, had tiptoed up to my desk one day and placed a carefully wrapped package in my in-basket. Inside the box was a little white ceramic teddy bear holding a red plastic rose. A little red heart was painted on the bear's chest and a note was tucked under his feet.

"*Maestra,*" Isabella had written,

I just want to give to you this small gift to thank you for give to me everything. Every since I been in your class, you help me learn so much. You sing the songs in español to make me smile when I'm am feeling sad for my home. I work hard so go to college and return my country and be a pediatrician and help the little sick children. You tell me to come to these hard class and you help me to get the good grades. You are so beautiful. I love you with my heart full.

Isabella's grandfather had broken tradition by sending a female to the United States to be educated, so Isabella was fiercely determined to succeed in school and return to Nicaragua as a doctor. A small, thin girl, Isabella was extremely shy but quick to grasp new concepts and meticulous in her study habits. During class, she often asked questions, but always in Spanish, although I could tell she understood everything I said in English. Whenever I asked her to speak English, she would shake her head and shrug her shoulders.

One morning, before the first bell, Isabella asked me if she and her friend, Maria Hernandez, could borrow some books from the bookcase in the back of the classroom. I nodded without looking up from the papers I was grading. Later, during the first break, I noticed both girls had their heads bent over their desks. Isabella's hair was twisted into a tight braid, but Maria's waist-length hair created a shimmering ebony curtain over the front of her desk almost to the floor.

"What are you reading?" I asked Isabella. She smiled and held up a copy of *The Adventures of Tom Sawyer*. Maria sat up and tossed her hair over her shoulders. She held an identical copy on her desk.

"Can you understand this?" I asked. Both girls were in the advanced NEP reading group and I had tried to transfer them to a higher class, but both tested at below first grade level on the standardized reading exam and the admin office had vetoed the move. Isabella looked at Maria.

"We understand—" Maria paused to look up a word in her dictionary, "most of the words. This people talk different. Very—" she paused again to page through her dictionary. After a minute, she looked at Isabella.

"Como se dice divertido en ingles?" she asked. Isabella flipped a few pages, then whispered "funny" to Maria.

"Do you want to go to college, too?" I asked Maria. She nodded emphatically and flashed me a brilliant smile.

"I will be a nurse," she said proudly. "Do you think so?"

"Oh, I definitely think so," I said, "and I also think you two girls are going to be in the Academy next semester. In my regular English class where everybody speaks English." Isabella's eyes grew large and round.

"No, *Maestra*," she said.

"Yes, *Estudiante*," I said. "You are never going to make it through college if you don't speak English well and you are never going to speak English well until you start doing it. It's settled. I'll make the arrangements and contact your guardian, Isabella, and your parents, Maria."

Giddy with excitement, Maria giggled until her

cheeks were flushed bright red and her eyes were wet with tears. She fanned her face with a sheet of paper and placed one chubby hand on her chest.

"What if we cannot do the work?"

"You can do the work," I assured her. "And I will be there to help you. *No te preocupes.* Okay?" I smiled at Maria until she nodded, then looked at Isabella.

"Okay," Isabella said softly. She cleared her throat and leaned forward and, in perfect English, said, "I will not worry."

I contacted Isabella's guardian and Maria's parents before putting in the paperwork to transfer the two girls, because I knew there would be resistance from the office. Earlier in the year, I had tried, but they wouldn't let me move the girls up to a higher level English class for non-native speakers. With parental support on my side, I convinced the principal to let me have the girls for one semester. Nineteen weeks.

The first few weeks were heart-wrenching for all three of us. Isabella and Maria were clearly lost most of the time, although the other Hispanic students worked hard to help them. The first time I assigned a one-page essay in class, Maria became so frustrated that she burst into tears at the end of the twenty-minute writing period when everyone else turned in a full page and she hadn't even completed the first sentence.

"I cannot write English, *Maestra,*" she wailed. "I try very hard, but I cannot." Isabella said nothing, but shook her head to indicate that she could not write, either.

"Take it home and fill a page," I said. "If you have to write it in Spanish first and then translate it to English, do that. But I want a page tomorrow."

They both stood there, staring at me in disbelief. I had never spoken harshly to them before. When I looked at their tender little faces and their big brown eyes, I was tempted to shorten the assignment to half a page. But I loved them too much to make it easy on them. If they were going to quit, I wanted them to quit before they had spent too much time to make up the work, but neither of them quit. They wrote their pages. The grammar was atrocious. The spelling was creative. The sentence structure was abysmal. But they wrote their pages.

At the end of the semester, Mr. Norton approved my request to retain the girls for the following year. They worked hard over the summer and took classes in summer school to further develop their English speaking and writing skills. At the end of the first semester of their junior year, Mr. Norton called me to his office.

"I just wanted you to know that I received a complaint about Isabella's and Maria's grades," Chet said.

"But they both have A's in my class," I protested. Chet nodded.

"That's just it," he said. "Their grades are in the top five percent of the junior class. Someone at the district wanted to know why students with such high grades were in a program for at-risk students."

"You mean they're complaining because the girls' grades are too high?" I asked, incredulous.

"You got it."

It was wonderful, helping little buds develop into full-blooming flowers. Too wonderful to give up. Gently, I placed Isabella's bear back on my desk, stuffed my resumé back inside the middle drawer, and turned out the light.

In the spring, I pulled my resumé back out when Raul Chacon disappeared. I couldn't believe it. Raul had earned the highest grade in class on the last math exam before the semester final and the rest of his grades were dynamite. He was rarely absent from school, so I was afraid something terrible had happened to him. I called him and he assured me that he'd be back the next day, but he wasn't; he wasn't in school on the day of the math final, either. When he didn't arrive for the English final, I told the teacher next door to scream if anyone left my classroom, and ran to find a phone to call off campus. Raul was at home, but said he couldn't talk. I told him if he didn't talk to me, I'd come to his house and camp on his doorstep until he did. He promised to call me that night.

"I'm sorry I couldn't talk today, Miss J.," Raul said. "But my father was listening and he had a few beers, so he might have punched me if I said anything about him. He's real busy working right now and he needs me to help him."

"Help him do what?" I asked.

"Landscaping and gardening."

"You mean he's making you miss your final exams to mow lawns for him?" I nearly screamed. "That's illegal. I told you to tell him that a few months ago. Did you tell him?"

"I told him," Raul said, "but he makes me work and then writes me an excuse for being sick. He said if I tell anybody at the school that I wasn't sick, he'll beat me and make me quit school and work full-time."

Raul explained that his father had only completed third grade and didn't understand why Raul, who was almost eighteen, wanted to spend another year in school when he could be working full-time.

"I'm sorry I missed my exams," Raul said. "I guess I probably flunked everything, huh? If I did, then my dad won't let me come back next year."

I called Raul's teachers and made arrangements for

him to take his exams in the evening. He passed, but his grades were much lower than they would have been had he been allowed to attend school during review week and exams. I was afraid he'd be discouraged by his low grades and give up. I was almost afraid to ask him if he'd be back for his senior year. When I asked him, he grinned and winked at me.

"Are you worried I'll quit and you won't get your hundred dollars that I owe you?" Raul asked.

"Of course not!" I snapped. "I don't care about the hundred dollars! I care about you."

"Jeez, I was only kidding," Raul said. "You're too nervous. You need to take a tranquilizing pill or something, Miss J. I promise I'll be back in the fall."

I didn't promise that I would be. Sometimes I felt that teaching Academy kids was like pouring water into the top of a bucket with a tiny hole in the bottom. The bucket looked full for a long time, even while it was leaking, and if I walked away for a while, it would be empty when I returned.

I felt sick at heart and completely out of energy as we entered the final week of the school year. I tried to project a positive attitude so the kids wouldn't notice my lagging spirits, and I convinced most of them, but there is always one kid in every class who looks right through me and puts his hand directly on my heart.

Unable to think of an inspirational topic for journal writing, I told the kids to make the final essay a free write—they could write whatever was on their minds. One of the Spanish boys, Bryant Majernik from Argentina, wrote:

"I don't know what is in my brain. I can't see anything, is like a white wall. But I feel something, is something strong and deep. That is that I want to tell you, and thank you for all. For gave me your time and taught me all that I know in English. Thank you."

I taped Bryant's note up over my desk and once again shoved my resumé back into the drawer.

TWENTY-TWO

All Aboard for Alcatraz

"**A**re you sure you want to go visit a prison during your summer vacation?" I asked. Gusmaro and Raul nodded.

"It'll be cool," Gusmaro said. "We know a lot of people who are in jail."

Relieved that the entire class survived the first year of school intact, I had asked the kids if they wanted to go on some minifield trips during the summer. They chose the places—an amusement park, a concert, and a trip to Alcatraz Island.

Ten boys signed up for the Alcatraz trip, which was the first one on our summer list. We met at the train station at 8:00 A.M., chugged into San Francisco, and walked three miles to Chinatown.

On the train and later in the city, people kept looking at us and at first I thought they simply found us interesting. But as we were crossing the street to enter a large department store, I realized that we were quite a sight: one medium-size white woman, surrounded by a gang of ten large Hispanic and black teenage boys. All of the boys were wearing black nylon jackets with Raiders logos, the unofficial uniform of the East Side. The bystanders probably thought I was either a clever cover or had been kidnapped by a vicious street gang.

As we passed the open markets in Chinatown, where bins of colorful souvenirs lined the sidewalks in front of the stores, I had to remind the boys several times that they had to pay for anything they took from the stores. They fingered the fans and poked each other with the bamboo back scratchers, but none of them could bring themselves to spend any of their hard-earned dollars. Since it was a sunny day, I had announced that we would walk across the city toward Pier 39. Emilio, the macho boxer, stopped after about eight blocks and refused to walk any more.

"This is too far, man," Emilio said. "I'm getting on a bus or something." He crossed his arms and leaned against the side of a nearby building. Raul and Gusmaro immediately joined him. Before the others had a chance to defect, I grabbed two of them and linked my arms through theirs and kept walking.

"The truly ruthless guys will walk," I called over my shoulder. "See you wussies later." Delighted, Raul sprinted to catch up.

"Eei! She called you pussies!" Raul screamed, then clapped his hand over his mouth. He gave me a sidelong glance. "I know you didn't say pussy, Miss J.," he confided, "because you're a teacher and a lady, but I said it for you."

"Thank you, Raul," I said. "That was very chivalrous of you."

"I don't know what that means, but I hope it's good."

. Emilio and Gusmaro lagged behind long enough to prove that they were independent, but they were careful to keep us in sight. At the pier, we boarded a ferry for Alcatraz. Raul disappeared for a few minutes, then reappeared with a napkin-wrapped pastry in each hand. He sat down beside me and extended one of the napkins. Gusmaro sat down on my other side and stared straight ahead. Raul nudged me with his elbow and extended one of the napkins.

"Would you like one of these little pies, Miss J.?" Raul asked.

"He stole them things," Gusmaro said, just loud enough for me to hear. "Ask him."

"Raul, did you pay for that pastry?" I asked. Raul stuffed half a pastry into his mouth and pointed to his bulging cheeks to indicate that he couldn't talk at the moment. I grabbed the collar of his jacket and pulled his face close to mine.

"I can't answer that question, Miss J.," Raul said, little bits of crust spurting from his mouth.

"Why not?" He swallowed hard.

"Because I promised I'd never lie to you."

I sighed. Raul hung his head and mumbled, "It was only a dollar."

"Only a dollar!" I said. "Is it worth getting arrested for a dollar?"

"I won't get arrested," Raul said. "I been stealing for years and nobody ever caught me yet."

"That was before," I said. "I'm talking about now. I thought you had a job."

"I do."

"Don't they pay you? Don't you have any money?"

"My father takes most of it," Raul said. "But I got money in my pocket."

"Then why didn't you pay for that pastry?" I nearly screamed.

Raul shrugged. "I guess I could of but it didn't make no sense when I could have just took it like I did."

When we reached Alcatraz, the boys grew unusually

quiet. At one point, the tour offered the chance to step inside a solitary confinement cell. The boys took turns, most staying inside only for a few brief seconds, then racing outside, their brown faces a shade paler than they had been when they entered. Most of them had friends or family members in prison, and a few of them had spent time in juvenile hall themselves. Spending those few seconds in a cell had more of an effect than all the lectures they'd heard from counselors, teachers, and police officers. On the ride back to the pier, the boys were subdued, but they made a remarkable recovery as soon as they stepped off the boat. They raced to North Beach, downed a remarkable number of pepperoni pizzas, then headed back to the train station. As we passed FAO Schwarz, the toy store, Gusmaro recognized the name. He wanted to know if they had a piano on the floor like the one Tom Hanks danced across in the movie *Big*. We went to investigate.

When we entered the store, the boys emitted a collective gasp, overwhelmed by the sheer volume of toys. Emilio checked the price on a life-size stuffed horse standing in the window. He held the price tag for several seconds, frowning at the number written on it, then dropped it and put both hands behind his back, looking guilty.

"Two thousand bucks!" he said. "It probably costs a dollar just to read the tag. That's crazy." He backed away from the horse, shaking his head. We spent nearly an hour investigating the treasures, and I bought a few small ones as surprise souvenirs. I planned to pass them out during the train ride home. As we were leaving the store, I handed my shopping bag to Gusmaro to hold while I stopped at the restroom. When I came out of the restroom, Emilio and Raúl were standing in the doorway, looking stricken. As I approached them, I noticed the other boys huddled outside on the corner.

"They got Gusmaro," Emilio said.

"Who got him?" I asked.

"The cops," Raul said. "They put handcuffs on him and everything."

"Are you kidding?" I couldn't imagine what could have happened during the three minutes I'd been inside the restroom. "What did he do?"

"Shoplifted," Raul said, hanging his head. Emilio looked at the floor and nodded.

"Gusmaro?" I didn't believe it. Of all the students, I trusted Gusmaro the most. It wasn't in him to steal. I knew it. But the police didn't. Outside, a very large police officer stood next to his patrol car, watching the boys.

"Excuse me, officer," I said. "I'm a teacher at Parkmont High School and I understand one of my students was arrested for shoplifting a few minutes ago. Could I please talk to him? I'm sure there was some mistake."

The officer shook his head. "No mistake, lady. We got it on videotape. One of these other boys was involved, but his back was to the camera and we can't make an ID, but we got the kid with the bag."

"Could I talk to him? Please?"

"You'll have to speak to the arresting officer," he said, nodding his head toward the second story of the building. "She's upstairs filing the report right now. Excuse me." He adjusted his cap and walked down the street toward where a crowd was gathering around an old man, dressed in rags, brandishing a Bible and screeching at the top of his lungs.

As soon as he was out of earshot, I gathered the boys and backed them up against the building.

"Talk fast," I ordered. "I want to know what happened. The truth. I can't help you if you don't tell me."

266

They all stared at me except Emilio, who had grown intensely interested in the tops of his shoes.

"I'm waiting," I said. "Waiting makes me crabby."

Raul spoke up. "We was just standing around waiting for you and somebody put one of those dancing Coke cans in your bag. I think it was a joke. Then we walked outside and they grabbed Gusmaro and dragged him upstairs. They're probably beating him up. Police always beat up Mexicans." He glanced nervously at the windows above us.

"I doubt if they're beating him up," I said. "Did Gusmaro put the can in the bag?" Raul shrugged. So did the other boys.

"Come on," I said. "Somebody must have seen it." They all shook their heads, their faces closed tightly.

For nearly an hour we waited outside, huddled on the sidewalk, straining to hear any sound from inside the building. Finally, I couldn't stand it another minute. I started pounding on the unmarked door that the policeman had indicated earlier. After several minutes, a wimpy little guy with pasty skin and giant glasses came to the door. He was the chief of security for the store. I explained who I was and that I wanted to see Gusmaro. He said I'd have to wait until all the paperwork was completed and Gusmaro was brought outside for transfer to juvenile hall. He shut the door in my face and scuttled back up the stairs before I could argue. The boys, who had overheard the interchange, started fidgeting. I could feel the tension and I knew by the look on Emilio's face that he knew more than he was saying. I called him aside. He insisted that he didn't know anything, but refused to look at me.

One by one, I drew the boys aside and questioned them. Most of them insisted that they hadn't seen anything, but Raul obviously had. He had vowed never to lie to me, but he maintained his right to claim ignorance. The only way I could get information from him was to ask direct questions, which he could not refuse to answer.

"Gusmaro didn't steal that stupid can, did he?" I asked. Raul shook his head.

"Who did?" I pressed. Raul shrugged and inspected his fingernails.

"Was it Andre? Jerome? Leroy?" At each name, Raul shook his head.

"How about Emilio?" I asked. Raul didn't shrug. He froze, like a deer in a spotlight. "Did Emilio put the can in the bag?" Raul bit his lip.

"I know you don't want to be a rat," I said, "but you have never lied to me and I trust you. So does Gusmaro. He's your friend and he's upstairs getting sent to jail. Did Emilio put the can in the bag?" Raul nodded.

"Why?" I said. Raul jiggled nervously back and forth from one foot to the other. I wanted to grab him and shake him, but I knew if I pushed too hard, I'd scare him. "Raul, come on. If Gusmaro didn't do it, why doesn't he say something? He doesn't owe Emilio anything."

Raul spoke so softly that I barely heard his reply. "Gusmaro didn't want to do it, but Emilio put the can in the bag and he said don't worry because it was your bag. He said, 'It's Miss Johnson's bag. If they don't catch her, then we'll get to keep it. If they catch her, she can talk her way out of it.'"

I was stunned. Emilio had set me up and then, when that plan fell through, he let Gusmaro take the blame. He stood silently by, prepared to let Gusmaro go to jail.

"Why didn't Gusmaro say something?" I asked Raul again.

"Gusmaro didn't want Emilio to think he was a

chicken or something, but he said he wasn't going to let you get in trouble, so he walked outside with your bag so you wouldn't get arrested."

"And he got arrested instead!" If Emilio had been standing closer, I'd have socked him in the mouth. In the short time I had known him, he had been responsible twice for getting Gusmaro in trouble with the police. First, the fight in the locker room, for which Emilio got a smack on the hand, and Gusmaro got a police escort home for three days' suspension from school. And now Gusmaro was upstairs, taking the rap for Emilio to protect me. Gusmaro was willing to go to jail to protect me. I waited a few minutes until I felt sure that I wouldn't grab him, then approached Emilio.

"The policeman told me you were the one who put the can in the bag," I said.

"No he didn't," Emilio said. "Raul ratted."

"He did not," I lied. "They have you on videotape. The policeman said they were going to take you upstairs after they get done talking to Gusmaro."

"They are?" Emilio's eyes grew wide with fear.

"Yes," I said. "And I suggest that you tell them the truth, since they already know it. And maybe I'll be able to get you out of this mess. But if you lie to me, I won't even try to help you. And I won't have you in my class at school. I don't like liars."

"It was only a joke," Emilio said.

"I'm not laughing," I said. Armed with the truth, I went in search of the tall policeman. When I explained the situation and described our program at school and that I was trying to help the boys learn how to cope as responsible adults, he softened a little. He put in a radio call to the arresting officer, who appeared in the doorway a few seconds later. When I saw her, I said a silent prayer. She had coal black hair, an intelligent expression, and, best of all, Rodriguez on her name tag. She listened patiently to my story, then sighed and passed her hand over her forehead.

"Listen," she said, "I can relate one hundred percent. I was born in Puerto Rico and I moved here when I was a kid. I couldn't speak English and I was poor and I stole food from stores because I was hungry. But these kids aren't hungry and I already started the process. We have to follow it through."

"What will happen to Gusmaro?" I was afraid to hear the answer.

"We took his statement and his photograph. Now he goes to juvenile hall to be fingerprinted and booked. We'll call his parents and fine them two hundred fifty dollars, since he's a minor. As soon as they pay the fine, they can come and take him home."

"Trust me," I said, "his parents don't have the money. And he didn't do anything wrong." Ms. Rodriguez raised one eyebrow.

"Okay," I corrected myself. "He could have protested. He could have stood up to Emilio and taken the can out of the bag. He isn't that strong, but he isn't a criminal, either. He's a boy and he's scared. Please don't call his parents. They'll be humiliated and they'll never forgive him. Let me pay the fine."

Officer Rodriguez stared me straight in the eye for several seconds, then marched over to Emilio's side.

"Please come with me," she said. "You, too," she nodded to me. Emilio and I followed her upstairs. It was only one flight, but beads of sweat lined Emilio's forehead when we reached the small room at the top of the stairs where Gusmaro sat, looking very small and young, in a stiff wooden chair. The sweat was the only sign of Emilio's fright. He squared his shoulders, stuck out his chin, and adopted a belligerent attitude.

"You're only hassling us because we're Hispanic," Emilio said, after Officer Rodriguez explained the charges. Her eyes registered surprise for a split second, then grew bold and businesslike. She looked at Gusmaro and then at me.

"Would you please step outside for a moment?" she asked. Gusmaro was out of his chair like a shot. As Ms. Rodriguez closed the door behind us, she turned to Emilio and said, "Sit." The rest of her words were muffled by the door, but the sound wasn't, and I wasn't surprised to see a different Emilio when the door opened silently ten minutes later. He sat in the stiff-backed chair, looking at his folded hands, tears glistening in his eyes and on his cheeks. He made no effort to wipe them away, but sat unmoving while Officer Rodriguez explained that the store manager was willing to make an exception to policy because the boys were enrolled in a special school program. The fine of two hundred fifty dollars would be waived for both boys, and they would be released into my custody, instead of their parents'. But they had both been photographed. Their photos would be posted in FAO Schwarz and if they ever entered the store again, at any time in their lives, they would be arrested on the spot for trespassing, and charges would be pressed at that time, including the fine.

None of the boys talked on the train ride home. They sat, staring out the windows, their faces glum, expecting the worst. I let them expect. They thought I planned to call their parents, but I had no such intention. I figured they had been sufficiently scared. Although only Gusmaro and Emilio had had to face the police, the others had stood on the sidewalk outside the store for nearly three hours, contemplating the consequences of breaking the law.

At one point, Raul clambered down from his seat on the second deck and hopped into the seat next to me.

"Pretty exciting, huh, Miss J.?" he said, with a wicked grin.

"Too exciting for my taste," I said. "But I guess now you know what I meant when I said it isn't worth it to steal. They did all that for a little can that only costs twenty dollars. Imagine what they'd do if you stole something really valuable."

Raul nodded thoughtfully. "Yeah, I guess if I steal something, I should steal something big, huh?" I drew a sharp breath, but before I could scream, he touched my arm. "Relax, I was just kidding."

"Ha, ha," I said dully.

"I do have one question," Raul said. "If they're going to fingerprint you and take you to jail and fine you and all that stuff, don't you think they could at least let you keep what you stole?"

"It doesn't work that way," I said.

"Yeah," said Raul. "Most things don't work that way, if you think about it." He went back to join the others, who were staring out the window, wondering what I was going to do. I was glad they were sweating it out; I wanted them to sweat just as hard as I had sweated while I was trying to get the police to release them in my custody—and as hard as I did at night trying to create lesson plans that would inspire them to do their homework. I wanted them to spend at least one sleepless night worrying about me to make up for the many nights I'd spent worrying about them.

When we reached the local train depot, the boys roused themselves and slunk down the steps to the platform, where they huddled in the shadows, avoiding the bright streetlights surrounding the parking lot. They looked very young and vulnerable and scared.

272

Some of them even looked as if they might cry, although I knew they'd die before they'd break down in front of me.

"Thanks for taking us on the trip, Miss Johnson," Gusmaro said, his eyes on the ground. The other boys echoed his thanks.

"You're welcome," I said. "It was a memorable experience."

"I don't think I'm gonna steal nothing no more," Raul said. "I didn't like the looks of that jail."

"Yeah," Gusmaro agreed, and the rest of the guys nodded. Relieved and thankful that the arrest had ended up creating a positive change, I hugged each one of the boys and bade them good night. They headed for the bus stop en masse, but Raul broke away from them and came running back.

"You know you're wrecking my posse, Miss J.," he said, his face grim. I took a deep breath and prepared to launch into a lecture about responsibility, but Raul interrupted me.

"We used to be ruthless. Then we stopped cutting classes, then we started doing our own homework instead of copying it off the geniuses, and now we ain't even gonna steal no more. We're a bunch of pussies." He grinned and wriggled his eyebrows at me. "Don't you feel bad for wrecking us?"

"Not a bit."

"I don't feel bad, neither," Raul said. "And if any of the other guys feel bad, I'll sock them until they stop. Okay?"

"Good idea."

"I got a lot of good ideas," Raul said. Without warning, he hugged me again and said, "Good-bye, Miss J. Have a nice summer. Maybe I'll call you up once or twice so you won't forget me before next year."

"I'd like that very much."

"*Hasta la vista.*"

TWENTY-THREE

See Gusmaro Run

"**G**usmaro came to see me this morning," Don Woodford said when I stopped by the staff room to check my mailbox several days before the new school year started. "He says you signed him up for my geometry class and he doesn't want to take it."

"When did you see him?" I asked, surprised. On my way to the admin building a few minutes earlier, I had passed by the gym. Gusmaro and Julio were among the crowd of boys lounging on the steps outside the locker room. When I stopped to say hello, several kids had asked me about their class schedules, but Gusmaro hadn't said a word. Don looked at his watch.

"About an hour ago," he said.

"I just spoke to him," I said, "and he didn't mention it."

"Well, I think he should take the class," Don said. "He's fully capable. He earned a B in algebra one and he didn't put a lot of effort into it. I told him he'd have to talk to you if he wanted out."

I walked back to the gym. The boys were gone, but as I crossed the parking lot, I heard someone shout,

"Run, Gusmaro!" It was Raul Chacon's voice coming from the bleachers on the football field. Raul and Julio were perched on the railing above the top row of seats, cheering on the football players who were practicing on the field.

"Hey, Miss J.!" Raul yelled when he saw me. He hopped to his feet and took my hand. "I'm a senior now. I made it. Can you believe that?"

"I never doubted it for a minute," I said. "I'm going to dance at your graduation." I looked around, but didn't see Gusmaro. "Didn't I just hear you yelling at Gusmaro?"

"Yeah," Raul said, his eyes on the football field.

"Where is he?"

"Out there," Raul said, pointing with his chin toward the players who were lined up in four rows, running fifty-yard sprints. Raul raised his right hand in a fist and yelled, "All right!" The coach blew his whistle to signal a break and the players whipped their helmets off their heads. Gusmaro's long black hair fell from his helmet and he drew his forearm across his forehead to wipe the sweat off his brow. He had been one of the first players across the finish line.

"What's he doing?" I said, stupidly.

"He's playing football," Raul answered.

"Gusmaro is on the football team?" I asked, incredulous.

"He's just trying out," Raul explained. "He's doing pretty good, though. He might make second string."

I was flabbergasted. Gusmaro was halfway to the gym before I recovered. I ran to intercept him before he entered the locker room.

"Hey, Miss J.," he said softly, still slightly out of breath.

"You look pretty good out there," I said.

"Yeah."

"Risking rejection, I see," I said.

"Sometimes you gotta put it on the line," Gusmaro said with a sheepish grin.

"Mr. Woodford tells me you don't want to take geometry," I said. "You don't have to take it, if you really don't want to. It isn't required to graduate. But if you're going to college, it would be a good idea to take it." Time and again, I had tried to convince Gusmaro to consider college, but he said he didn't like homework and he didn't think he was college material. His reading scores were off the high school charts and he easily earned an A in English each semester. Still, he insisted that he didn't have the brains to earn a four-year degree.

"I guess I can take geometry," Gusmaro said. "But you signed me up for another algebra class, too."

"That's to make up credit for the class you flunked when you were a freshman and were too ruthless to go to school."

"Yeah," Gusmaro said. "I know."

"So you want to keep geometry?"

"I guess so," Gusmaro said. "I'm thinking about going to college."

I could have kissed him. Instead, I patted him on his shoulder pad and wished him luck. I met Raul and Julio again, crossing the parking lot to their car. Raul stopped to say he'd see me in a week.

"You're not going to try out for the team?" I asked Raul. He grinned. He had grown only two inches since his freshman year and still weighed under a hundred pounds.

"Nah," he said. "I can't be messing around with those jocks. I'm signed up for computer class after school. I'm going to get a job in an office this year."

"I'm happy to hear that," I said. "See you next week."

"You can count on it," he said. Julio tapped the horn lightly and pointed to his watch. Raul climbed into the car and rolled down the window. "I didn't forget about your hundred dollars, neither, you know." As they drove away, he stuck his head out of the window and cupped his hands around his mouth to yell, "Don't worry. I'm gonna pay you back, Miss J."

"You already did, Mr. Chacon," I said as he and Julio drove through the school gate and out of sight.